Build Your DREAM HOME For LESS

R. DODGE WOODSON

BETTERWAY BOOKS

CINCINNATI, OHIO

Disclaimer

Every precaution has been taken in preparing *Build Your Dream Home For Less* to make your home construction project as safe and successful as possible. However, neither the publisher nor the author assumes any responsibility for any damages incurred in conjunction with the use of this manual.

Library of Congress Cataloging-in-Publication Data

Woodson, R. Dodge (Roger Dodge)
    Build your dream home for less / by R. Dodge Woodson.
        p.   cm.
    Includes index.
    ISBN 1-55870-383-7 (alk. paper)
    1. House construction. 2. Contracting out. I. Title.
TH4812.W66   1995
690'.837—dc20   95-9087
                                                           CIP

Edited by Adam Blake
Content edited by Mike Malone
Production edited by Marilyn Daiker
Cover design by Stephanie Redman
Interior designed by Angela Lennert

METRIC CONVERSION CHART

TO CONVERT	TO	MULTIPLY BY
Inches	Centimeters	2.54
Centimeters	Inches	0.4
Feet	Centimeters	30.5
Centimeters	Feet	0.03
Yards	Meters	0.9
Meters	Yards	1.1
Sq. Inches	Sq. Centimeters	6.45
Sq. Centimeters	Sq. Inches	0.16
Sq. Feet	Sq. Meters	0.09
Sq. Meters	Sq. Feet	10.8
Sq. Yards	Sq. Meters	0.8
Sq. Meters	Sq. Yards	1.2
Pounds	Kilograms	0.45
Kilograms	Pounds	2.2
Ounces	Grams	28.4
Grams	Ounces	0.04

ACKNOWLEDGMENTS

I would like to thank Dawn Gearld-Hall for her assistance in the production of this book. Her efforts are much appreciated.

A special thanks is due to my parents, Maralou and Woody. They have always been there for me, and I love them both.

DEDICATION

This book is dedicated to my fabulous family, Kimberley, Afton, and Adam.

Table of Contents

Introduction

Is building your own home a possibility, or is it just a dream? Most people never know the thrill of building their own home, but you can. Did you know that it is possible to build your own home without investing any of your own money in the deal? Well, it is. I've done it before, and I'm doing it right now. You see, I'm in the process of building a new home for myself, and when the dust settles, I'll have no cash investment in the house. How can I build a house that is worth $185,000 without a cash down payment? I can do it by being my own general contractor. This is nothing new to me. I've built as many as sixty single-family homes per year as a professional contractor.

Are you wondering if you—someone who has never built a house—can follow in my no-money-down footsteps? I'd be surprised if you weren't. You have the potential to do the same thing I'm doing. It is more difficult for amateurs to arrange prime financing for the construction of a home, but you should be able to do it.

If you act as your own general contractor, there is potential for you to save about 20 percent of the total value of your home. On a $150,000 house, this savings amounts to $30,000. When you consider that you can have a house built in less than six months on a part-time basis, it is easy to see that the reward is worth your efforts. If you perform some of the work yourself—and most people can—the savings can escalate to 35 percent or more. If you build a $150,000 house and do some of the work yourself, you may be building in equity of $52,500. For a $200,000 house, your equity could climb to $70,000. This is not nickel-and-dime money, especially when you consider that you can keep your regular job while you're making it. Think about it. You might get your dream home and a year's income in equity just by devoting an hour or two a day and some weekends to building your new home, even if you never pick up a hammer.

If you have average organizational skills, you can be your own general contractor. It's helpful, but not necessary, to have skills in the construction trades. As long as you can find, contract and coordinate good people, you can shave a huge amount of money off the cost of your dream home. If you have trade skills, you can extend your equity by a considerable amount. In either case, building a new house could be your ticket to getting a great home and a nice nest egg of equity.

Can anyone build their own home, act as a general contractor, and save a lot money? Just about anyone can act as their own general contractor and save a minimum of 10 percent on the cost of their home. In most cases, the savings will be between 15 and 20 percent. Everything you need to know to cash in on this opportunity is in this book.

I've worked in construction for over twenty years. I'm licensed as a general contractor, a master plumber and a designated real estate broker. I've built as many as sixty homes a year. My combined knowledge as a broker, builder and tradesperson is substantial. I'm going to share this knowledge with you. By following my advice, you can avoid the many mistakes that I've made over the years. This book could be worth tens of thousands of dollars to you.

Take a few moments to scan the table of contents. You will see that there are thirty chapters. They are laid out in a logical order that mirrors the progression of your job. Each chapter contains professional information. You will see what to do, when to do it, and whether or not you should roll up your sleeves and dive into the hands-on work yourself. Not only this, but you will be advised on the feasibility of various materials, procedures and potential resale values.

This book is written to help you build your own home as a general contractor. While some people will want to take an active part in the building process, others will feel most comfortable in an administrative capacity. Either way, there is a lot of money to be saved by getting involved in the construction of your own home. Even if you can't drive a nail, you can be your own general contractor.

I could go on and on about the virtues and benefits of this book, but the best way for you to learn how valuable the following pages are is to turn to them and start reading. There is no doubt in my mind that everyone, even seasoned builders, will find this book to be priceless in the construction of a new home.

THE FIRST FOUNDATION

DEVELOPMENT AND GENERAL CONTRACTING

An enormous amount of work has gone into any house long before the excavators pull up to the site with their bulldozers and backhoes. The legal, financial, architectural, and topographical/geological parts of the project have been thoroughly examined and accounted for by the developer and the general contractor. In this case I am talking about *you*. As the developer and general contractor of your own house, you perform the most important (and best paid) roles in home building.

CHAPTER 1

ACTING AS YOUR OWN DEVELOPER AND GENERAL CONTRACTOR

Acting as your own developer and general contractor can save you 20 percent, or more, on the cost of your custom-built home. This chapter shows you what is involved in making the commitment to be your own developer and general contractor. Additionally, see what financial benefits are available from being involved in the construction of your home and how to obtain them. As a bonus, you learn how doing the simplest forms of work can save you thousands of extra dollars. If you have any desire to own a new home, this chapter is the cornerstone to your success and savings.

If you're planning to build a new home, acting as your own developer and general contractor can save you a lot of money. Even if you have no construction skills, you can still be your own general contractor. Both jobs require organizational abilities and the ability to manage people, but direct knowledge of the various trades is not a requirement. How much money can you save? Typically between 10 and 20 percent of the appraised value of your new home. The exact amount varies with economic conditions, the value of the house being built, and other considerations. We will dig deeper into the financial rewards of being your own developer and contractor later in this chapter.

Building your own dream home is an experience you will not likely forget. There will be many fond memories and a few experiences you may wish not to recollect. Frustration will at times take control of you. Building a house is not easy, even when you do none of the physical work yourself. The roles of developer and general contractor are critical ones. If you are your own developer, then *you* must ensure that the project is legally, financially, and functionally sound. If you are your own general contractor, *you* must keep the job running on budget and on schedule. The smallest slip in either of these responsibilities can create a chain reaction that is tough to deal with. Even with all the possible pitfalls, being responsible for the construction of your own home is a fulfilling and rewarding experience.

Moving into a house that you created will give you a sense of pride and accomplishment. By planning and contracting your own home, you will see to it that the house is built exactly as you wish it to be. In addition to the mental and emotional rewards, you will also be pleased with the equity you build as your house is constructed. Building your own home is well worth the effort.

CAN I DO IT?

As you contemplate building your own home, you may ask yourself this question: Can I do it? The answer is yes. Can you do it alone? Probably not, but you don't have to. There are plenty of professionals and skilled tradespeople available to work for you as consultants and subcontractors. You also have this book as your hip-pocket consultant to being a developer and general contractor. What more could you need?

I don't mean to simplify the responsibility of building your own house. The job is not simple at all. In principal, developing and general contracting involve little more than a few phone calls and meetings. The details of the work are far more complex. The path towards building a new home can be full of unexpected surprises and financial dangers. If you take the job lightly, you are likely to regret it. However, if you read this book, follow the instructions you are given, and mix in a little common sense, you can do it. Let's take some time now to look at what it takes to get this project off the ground.

- Money
- Land
- A Design
- Legal Approval
- Material Prices
- Subcontractors
- Production Schedule
- Management

HOW MUCH MONEY

How much money do I need and can I save money by acting as my own developer and general contractor? These questions are the first to arise when people contemplate the construction of a new home. You can calculate how much money you'll need by reading this book. There is no clear-cut answer to the amount of money that can be saved. The factors that influence the costs of construction are many. A rule-of-thumb figure is a savings somewhere between 10 and 20 percent of the appraised value of the home, but this figure is not carved in stone. Much of the savings will depend on how well you do your job.

FINANCING

Financing is usually a logical place to start when dreaming of building your own home. This is where developers start, because making money building houses is their business. For most people, borrowing the money for their home is a necessity, so they must find a lender who will provide them with a construction loan which can be difficult. Acting as your own developer and general contractor can complicate this matter further. Many banks have grown wary of offering construction financing to individuals without a track record in construction. This is not to say that you can't secure your own financing, but don't expect to walk out of the first bank you come to with construction financing.

NO DOWN PAYMENT

Is it possible to realize your dream with no down payment? The days of no-money-down deals are slowly disappearing, but it is still possible to build your own home, as a general contractor, without investing any of your own money in the long-term financing. In most cases you will be required to have cash on deposit in an amount equal to a down payment, but if you do your job well as a general contractor, you may not have to use your money. We are going to talk much more about financing in the next chapter, but I'd like to take a few moments now to tell you a little about your ability to own your own home without spending your nest egg.

Lending policies are as varied as the lenders who make the loans. There are some traditional procedures that are usually followed, but unconventional loans are also made. I'm not talking about loans from questionable loan companies; I'm talking about clean deals made at commercial banks. You don't have to get far into creative financing to arrange circumstances that will allow you to build your home without using your own cash as a down payment.

While very few banks will let you "cash out" when building a house, many of them will not require a hard-money down payment. In the old days, I could build a house for myself, spend 80 percent on the construction costs, finance 95 percent, and walk away from the closing table with 15 percent of the home's value in my pocket as payment for services rendered as a general contractor. Those days are almost gone. It is, however, still possible to use sweat equity as a general contractor as a down payment. I'm doing it right now. In my case, I'm borrowing 80 percent of my home's value and leaving my 20 percent profit as a builder in the deal as equity. My only out-of-pocket expenses are closing costs, construction interest, and a few miscellaneous expenses that were incurred during the early stages of planning the job.

Lenders will probably require you to have cash equal to a down payment, but they probably won't require you to use it if you are successful in building equity as a general contractor. This means a lot. In my case, I could have gotten a permanent loan with a down payment of less than 20 percent, but I would have been parting with my own money. By doing the deal myself, my house payments will be less, I'll have more equity in the home, and I'll have the lion's share of my cash. What more could you ask for? I'll tell you more about how to do this in the next chapter.

IT TAKES LAND

To build a house, you need land. If you were buying a pre-existing house, it would come with land, but building a house will require you to find and acquire a suitable building lot. You might work with real estate brokers, or you might find your own land. Either way, there are many potential hazards in buying undeveloped land. If you are going to take full responsibility for your home-building project, you must be prepared to work through the maze of real estate acquisition, which we will cover a little later on.

YOU NEED A DESIGN

The design stage of building your own home is wonderful. This is where you are able to let your imagination run wild. While you may not be able to afford all of your creative ideas, it's still fun to work them out on paper. Once you have a design you like, you must obtain blueprints. If you go to an architect and have the plans drawn to your specifications, expect to spend a sizable chunk of change. You might find it more feasible to buy a set of stock plans and have them altered to meet your personal preferences. In any event, you will be required to provide blueprints to your lender and your subcontractors.

BUILDING CODES MUST BE SATISFIED

Building codes vary from state to state. They can even vary from city to city. The codes are usually extensive in their content and often confusing. If you will be hiring licensed professionals to perform the hands-on work for your home, most of the code-related burden will rest on their shoulders. You should, however, have a working knowledge of the code requirements.

KNOW THE COST OF MATERIALS

You will need the prices for labor and material to build a working budget. This is something you will need before you can obtain your construction financing, and it is one of your major responsibilities as a developer and general contractor. If you make many mistakes in your cost estimates, your dream home can evolve into a nightmare. You must dedicate enough time and energy to this phase of your work to ensure that mistakes are kept to a minimum.

SELECT SUBCONTRACTORS

Every general contractor needs subcontractors. You may very well do some of the physical work required to build your home, but it is highly unlikely that you will do all of the work. For every phase of construction that you will not perform personally, you will need a subcontractor. Picking the right subs is another key role of a general contractor.

PRODUCTION SCHEDULE

A production schedule will also be needed before you start to build your house. Usually the developer and the general contractor put their heads together to determine a realistic and workable time frame for the whole project. Because *you* will be wearing both hats, you won't need to deal with the conflicting interests that sometimes arise between these two positions.

The schedule can be of great importance. For example, not all construction loans are issued for the same periods of time. Some loans are good for four months, some for six months, and some for a full year. Since you are new to the home-building business, it would be very risky to accept a construction loan with a short time period. A six-month loan is a minimum, and a one-year loan would be a safer alternative. The production schedule will also be very important in coordinating your building project.

MANAGEMENT

As the developer, you are the person ultimately responsible for *everything*. You are at the highest level of construction management. The job does not stop at securing buildable land, lining up financing, and telling the general contractor, "Go!"; your job as developer is to constantly manage the payment of material bills, interest, taxes, insurance, draws, and change order invoices. In addition, you must ensure that all contractors are properly insured, licensed, and paid accurately with the proper lien waivers in effect. Inattention to detail can spell complete disaster. What if you've already paid off the plumber and then find out that the plumbing supply house has affixed a lien against your home because the plumber did not pay for the material and took off for parts unknown? Or what if the roofer's helper, who fell two stories, institutes a claim against you after finding out that the roofer's insurance had lapsed two days before he began the job? These possibilities may seem scary, and they should, but developers who do their job well can easily avoid being hurt by others' lack of responsibility. How? Never pay off a job until you have releases from *everyone* who worked on or supplied material for your job, and never allow any contractor or subcontractor to so much as pick up a tool at your job site without certificates of insurance that you've checked out. Remember, *you* are the boss!

As a general contractor, you are responsible for getting the work done. While you might think all you have to do is call a plumber and issue a work date, the reality of the situation will prove different. Subcontractors can be a very independent bunch. Having a start date settled with your electrical contractor doesn't guarantee that workers will show up then. You must allow time to perform on-site inspections to ensure that work is done on schedule and in the manner specified. While daily visits to your job site are not mandatory, they do keep the job running more smoothly. In fact, a visit every morning and every afternoon is often in order, and even then things can go astray.

FLEXIBILITY

Acting as your own general contractor will require you to wear many hats. One moment you are a cost estimator, and the next minute you are a quality-control inspector. We've talked about the key roles that you will play in the construction of your home, but there are many other duties that will crop up. You will have to meet with the power company to determine how electrical service will be provided to your home. Landscaping will be needed, and you may find it necessary to do some last minute shopping to keep your crews running on schedule.

If you have time in your normal schedule that can be devoted to being your own contractor, you can save a lot of money and enjoy many aspects of the job. However, if your time is at a premium and you can't dedicate some portion of it to your home each day, you should give serious consideration to hiring a general contractor. Being your own contractor is not a full-time job by any means, but there are certain time requirements that must be met or the job will suffer.

AN EXAMPLE

Our first example of cost savings as a developer and general contractor is of building a home with an appraised value of $150,000. You are not going to do any hands-on work, but you will be in charge of the project. We will further assume that economic conditions are average and stable.

In this example, you build the house in six months. Professional builders can build a house like this in as little as 60 days, with an average building time of three to four months. Since you are not an established contractor, we will give you two extra months to work with. The length of the building time is relevant to the cost savings because of construction interest. Interest on a construction loan is computed on a daily basis, so the longer it takes to complete the house, the more you must pay in interest fees. Let's stop right here and see an example of why the rule-of-thumb numbers don't always hold true.

The cost of construction interest goes up as more money is borrowed. You only pay interest on the amount of money advanced for construction. Your first month of construction will not amount to much in terms of interest, but as you get further along in the construction, the interest fees will rise considerably. By the time drywall is hung, your monthly construction interest may be upwards of $400.

If one contractor can shave two months off the building time for a home, an extra $800 can be counted as profit. The contractor who spends $800 for two additional months of construction time cannot recover the money paid out in interest. If you took six extra months to complete your home, you might lose $2,400 to construction interest. As you can see, something as simple as this can have a significant impact on the percentage of profit or cost savings experienced in building a home.

Now, back to our original scenario. As a general contractor, it is up to you to shop for the best prices in both labor and material. If you do this job extremely well, your savings can be substantial. Do it poorly, and your percentage of profit as a general contractor will sink. Let me give you a quick example of how this works.

The house that I'm building now is fairly big, about 2,800 square feet. The house has a unique design that is complicated and contains a lot more wood than a conventional home. There are seven different roof lines on the house. My point is this, a large amount of building materials are going into this home, so the cost of those materials is very important.

When I solicited quotes for material prices, suppliers were reluctant to hold their quotes for more than 30 days, some of them would only guarantee their prices for seven days. As you know, a house isn't going to be built in seven days, so their price quotes were useless. The market for building materials has been very volatile lately, and the fear of cost increases is one that cannot be taken lightly. I needed some way to assure myself protection from runaway material prices.

When the material bids came in on my house, there were differences of thousands of dollars. The value of my house will be about $185,000. So let's assume that I'm shooting for a savings of 20 percent by being my own general contractor. In terms of dollars, 20 percent is $37,000. The spread on material prices was nearly $4,000. This is more than 10 percent of my anticipated savings. If I had not shopped aggressively, my savings on the house would have been $4,000 less than what they

will be now. At $33,000, my savings would be 18 percent. This drop would have been due to only one factor, material prices. If the same type of thing happened with subcontractors, my profit might have been cut in half. See how easy it is to have your 20 percent profit dwindle?

What I did was negotiate a deal where I paid $700 more for my materials than what the lowest bid was. Why would I pay more than I had to? It's simple really, I got what I wanted, a guarantee from the supplier to hold the prices for the entire length of my construction period. I gambled that prices would go up by more than $700 during the time it took to build the house. By giving up $700 in the beginning, I protected myself from the possibility of spending thousands of extra dollars at the end of the project.

The main point of these examples is to show you how difficult it is to put a firm price on what you will save as a general contractor. It is possible to save more than 20 percent, but it is also possible to save next to nothing. It all depends on how well you prepare yourself for the task. This book is going to give you all the information needed to make you a formidable general contractor. If you study it and use it properly, this book can be your ticket to a huge equity gain in your new house.

PUTTING YOUR FINGERS IN THE PIE

Putting your fingers in the pie, so to speak, is another way to build more equity in your home. If you are able to do some of the hands-on work yourself, your savings increase. Instead of saving 20 percent on the cost of your house, you might save 30 percent, or even more. Let me give you a few examples from my most recent activities.

I'm a licensed general contractor, a licensed master plumber, and a licensed real estate broker. I've been in the construction business over twenty years, and I've built, sold, and plumbed a lot of houses. Not everyone has the extensive background that I do in building and real estate, but everyone can bring something to the table to save themselves money. Even if it is only cleaning up the job site, money can be saved. Let me tell you how much I've saved so far by doing some of the work on my own house. We've already talked about my savings as a developer and project manager, so we'll concentrate on the skilled labor I've done.

I did my own plumbing in the house. My wife, who has been instrumental in our building business for the last fourteen years, solicited bids for all phases of the construction, even the ones I planned to do. We wanted to see just how much money we would be saving, and I wanted some hard facts to give you in this book. The plumbing bids we got averaged $7,300. At the time we got the bids, we were having the job priced with just two bathrooms. We have since added a whirlpool and a third complete bathroom that wasn't on those bids. On the original plan, my cost savings were in excess of $4,000. If you factor in the plumbing additions, my savings would exceed $5,000.

I've done most of the hands-on work at my house just as any other homeowner would have to do it, at night and on weekends. I have also done it all alone, since Kimberley, my wife, was due to have a baby in less than two weeks. My brother-in-law helped me for two days, and my carpenters have provided a second set of hands from time to time, but basically, I've done it all myself. The time spent on the plumbing, so far, is less than 32 hours. By the time I install the well pump and set fixtures, my total time will be about 48 hours. I will also save an additional $1,250 by buying and installing my own well pump. My total plumbing savings will amount to more than $6,000 for less than 50 hours of work. Think about this. That's a lot of money for the time invested, and that's $6,000 I won't be paying interest on for the next 30 years.

Now, onto the heating. The heating bids were around $8,300. My material costs for the same equipment were about $3,000. The time spent to install the heating system will total less than 40 hours. Here is another $5,000 saved for a week's work.

The electrical bids for the house were upwards of $5,000, excluding light fixtures. I'm not an electrician, and I'd never wired a complete house before in my life. I hired a master electrician as a consultant and had him do the service entrance and panel box. These two parts of the job involved high voltage and I was afraid to do it myself. My total cost for the master electrician was a mere $200. The materials to wire the house cost less than $2,000, and I upgraded the wiring beyond the specs given out in bid packages. This job took me about 40 hours, and I will still have to hang fixtures and install switches and outlets. I expect my total time will be somewhere in the neighborhood of 60 hours, but I saved about $3,000.

I could go on with other examples, but I'm sure you're getting the point by now. By doing physical work on the house, my cash savings are extremely good. As we move into later chapters, I will discuss with you the potential savings and the feasibility of doing various phases of the building process yourself. While you might not be able to install your own plumbing or heating, there will certainly be some jobs that you can handle.

GET SERIOUS

Now that we've covered the basics of what is involved in being a general contractor, it's time to get serious. The following chapters are provided in the order in which most houses are built. Each chapter goes into great detail on what you will need to know. There will be some information that may not apply to your home. I recommend that you either take notes as you go along or highlight areas of the text that pertain to your situation. Remember, the amount of money you save is related directly to your ability to perform. These chapters are going to give you the knowledge to get the job done, but it is up to you to absorb and use the advice properly. Now, let's see about getting your dream home built for less.

CHAPTER 2
FINDING FINANCING FOR CONSTRUCTION AND BEYOND

Financing can be a problem for anyone, but it can be especially tough for people wanting to build their own homes. This chapter shows you—step by step—how to find financing for your land acquisition, construction, and long-term mortgage. You will find formulas that show you the house payment you can qualify for and information on how different types of loans can allow you more house for the same monthly payment. Not only discover how much lenders may allow you to borrow, but find proven ways to get your loans quickly and easily. There are even tips on how to use combination loans to reduce the costs of your financing.

Finding financing for construction can take some time, and a lot of effort. If you're like most people, you need a supportive lender to make your dream home a reality. Few people can afford to pay cash for their homes, and a lot of people want the tax advantages of having a home loan. Financing doesn't have to be the starting point for building a new house, but it often is. Since financing is so important in the process of building a new house, this whole chapter is dedicated to financing, both for construction and beyond.

WHICH COMES FIRST?

Which comes first, construction financing or permanent financing? Logically, you might assume that construction financing would come first. It can, but it seldom does. Unless you are a professional builder, it is unlikely that you will be able to obtain construction financing without first having a permanent loan approved. Permanent loans, or take-out loans as they are often called, are a wise requirement for construction lenders. Not only is having long-term financing in place prior to construction good for construction lenders, it's smart for home builders as well.

Even if you are able to get a construction loan prior to establishing a permanent loan, you are taking a big chance. Suppose you near the end of your construction loan and haven't been ap-

proved for a permanent loan, what will you do? The construction lender will expect payment in full for the balance owed on the construction loan when its term expires. Unless you have a lot of cash, you could lose your new house to foreclosure. There is no doubt in my mind, you should have your permanent loan in place before you do any substantial construction.

LAND ACQUISITION

Land acquisition is one of the preliminary steps in building a house. How you buy the land can vary a great deal. Perhaps you can pay cash for the land and use the land's value as your down payment on a permanent loan for the house. This will work if you have enough money to pay for the property, but what will you do if you don't have that much money? Getting a land loan from a traditional lender normally requires a heavy down payment. It is not unusual for lenders to require down payments ranging from 30 to 50 percent of the land's value. If you're buying a $30,000 lot, this can mean spending $15,000 of your cash just to get started. One alternative option is to seek owner financing on the land.

OWNER FINANCING

When land is financed by the seller, terms are usually very favorable for the buyer in terms of little out-of-pocket cash. The interest rates are sometimes steep, but most land sellers will accept a very small down payment. A 10 percent down payment is common, 20 percent down payments are sometimes requested, and it is not at all uncommon to buy undeveloped land with owner financing where no down payment is required. However, there is risk in this type of financing.

CONTINGENCIES

Suppose you buy land with owner financing and then find that you cannot get approved for a home loan? You now have a mortgage payment for land that you can't build on. This, of course, is not desirable. Is there a way to get around this problem? Yes. You could put a contract on the land making it contingent on construction financing. This reserves the land for you while you arrange financing for the building. There are other creative ways to aquire the land, but a contingency contract is the safest way. We'll talk more about contracts and how you can use them to your advantage in the next chapter. For now, let's assume that you have your lot under contract and are ready to secure financing for the rest of the project.

PUTTING YOUR PROPOSAL TOGETHER

Putting together a proposal for your lender is a critical step in getting your dream home. How you present yourself to the lender can determine whether you get the loan you want. Lenders see a lot of loan requests, and they don't hesitate to turn them away if they suspect any risk. You've got to remove the lender's objections before they arise. A solid loan proposal can truly make all the difference in the world. What do I mean by a solid loan proposal? Well, let's talk about it.

THE BASIC COMPONENTS

The basic components of a loan package are the same for all lenders. Loan applications request information that you may not know off the top of your head. Items like bank account numbers, credit card numbers, even social security numbers can elude you when completing the paperwork. To avoid confusion during your loan application, you have to be prepared and organized. Remem-

ber, you want to impress your lender with the fact that you are a good manager. If you expect the lender to take you seriously as a general contractor, you've got to send out the right signals.

Start your package with the basics. List all your bank accounts and credit cards. Write down the account numbers of all installment loans, such as car payments, and include the number of payments remaining. Loans with only a few remaining payments, six or less, may not count against you, but you should take all the information with you to your loan application. If you receive or pay child support or alimony, bring documentation of the payments. A copy of a divorce decree might be required if you have been divorced. If you're self-employed, bring copies of your tax returns for the last two years. Copies of the stubs from your paychecks and copies of your bank statements for the last three months can be beneficial. You will need to know your social security number, as well as your current address and any other mailing addresses for the last couple of years. Credit references will also be required. All of this is the basic information needed for any loan application, but it is not the only information you will need.

When you are applying for a loan to build a new house, you will also need these items.

- Deed or land contract (This may be a purchase agreement or an option to purchase.)
- Blueprints
- Work specifications
- Estimate of construction costs
- A "when-done" appraisal of the structure
- Comprehensive feasibility study of the entire project
- Schedule

Land Ownership or Control

You need to demonstrate to the lender that you do indeed have a parcel of land for your home. You should be able to demonstrate that you have control over the property and that it will pass muster with zoning, building, and legal persons. The more information you can supply about your land the better. Has it passed soil tests? Has zoning looked at it? Are there any restrictive deed covenants or easements?

Blueprints

You will need a set of blueprints. A complete breakdown of specifications for everything to be installed inside and outside of the home will be needed. An approval stamp from your local building department will also go a long way towards impressing a lender.

Specifications

In addition to your blueprints you should have a list of specifications that covers the quality of work to be done and specific materials and fixtures to be used. More on this in chapter six.

Estimate

You could pay a professional estimator to do this for you, or, based upon your research into material costs and discussions with subcontractors, appraisers, and real estate agents, you could provide your own estimate. Be careful—don't try to low- or highball a lender. They may have a pretty good idea of construction costs from years of experience evaluating loan applications.

Appraisal

Before it's all over you are going to pay for an appraisal. Your appraiser can read your blueprints and specifications and come up with an opinion on the "when-done" value of your home. Lenders put great stock in their professional appraiser's reports, and they usually have a list of approved appraisers that they will share with you. More on appraisers later in this chapter.

Feasibility Report

A comprehensive feasibility study of the project should include every cost associated with the building of your home. What are the pre-development costs? Blueprint costs, appraiser fees, lawyer fees for land contract preparation, land acquisition, and anything else you can think of that you will have spent before you get to the bank.

How much will it cost to hold the property before it is done? Be sure to include taxes, insur-ance, and interest on the construction loan. In order to figure the construction loan interest, call your lender ahead of time and ask them for the formula they use, or for one that is commonly used in your area. Many lenders use a formula something like this: two-thirds of the loan amount times the interest rate divided by 360 (days in a banker's year) times 180 (6 months).

This formula assumes that the average outstanding balance on the loan is going to be two-thirds of the loan amount and that the construction period is going to last 6 months (180 days).

In your feasibility report be sure to leave in a percentage for contingencies—the unforeseen, and the calamitous. Most lenders will respect a 10 percent contingency on the construction and holding costs. This will protect you against shortfalls and will demonstrate to your lender a sound, conservative approach to your home-building project.

Production Schedule

All schedules get upset and derailed, but builders know and expect this, and produce production schedules anyway. Why? How else can you see what went wrong without an expectation? This may well be the only house you ever build, but to your lender it will demonstrate more thoroughness than, "Oh, I guess I'll be done by November—or at least by December, I guess."

FACE TO FACE

Put yourself on the other side of the loan officer's desk. If someone walked in off the street and simply told you they were going to build their own house, what would you think? Would you give them the loan? I doubt it. You have to convince the lender that you have the ability to be your own general contractor. To help in this matter, you should prepare an essay of your experience, background, and qualifications for being your own general contractor. Dig through your background and pry out every nugget that can be used to show your potential.

What can you do to build an image as a general contractor? Look at what you do and what you've done. If you are a supervisor at work, that fact indicates that you have management ability. Use this information to build your case. If you've done remodeling projects around your home, put it on your resume. If you happen to be an accountant, you can use that as experience for your ability to budget the construction cost. Anything you can produce to impress your lender will help.

DON'T GO HAT IN HAND

Remember, the lender makes loans. That's how they make money. Go to your lender with a win-win proposition on how you can both profit from your idea. You are entering into a partnership with the lender that is sound, respectable, and good for everybody. Even though the lender will probably outline a pre-packaged loan for you, you can still negotiate terms and conditions to some extent. If some part of the loan proposal doesn't look good to you, bring up the issue with the lender so that everyone has a chance to ensure that the loan will be as successful as possible.

WHAT'S RIGHT FOR YOU?

What's right for you? Well, that's a question only you can answer. While I can't tell you what you want, I can tell you, based on my experience, what makes a good deal under average conditions.

In my opinion, the ideal financing package will start with a liberal, cooperative lender. It will involve a construction loan that will roll over into a permanent loan. This will reduce the closing costs you have to pay. The down payment will be made with equity built from being the general contractor. A term of at least six months will be provided for the construction loan. A draw disbursement schedule will allow you ready access to payments on at least a monthly basis. This will allow you to save money on material costs by taking advantage of discounts offered for prompt payment. Interest rates, of course, will be competitive, and the loans will not have any hooks hidden in them. You can tailor your loan package to your personal needs, but these items make for a more productive and successful building experience.

QUALIFYING

Qualifying for your loan is something you can do without any cost. Any normal lender will be happy to meet with you and qualify you without any fee. If you want to pre-qualify yourself, I can give you the ratios that are normally used in this process.

There are two sets of ratios that are normally used by lenders. Conservative lenders use a 25/33 ratio. More liberal lenders use a ratio of 28/36.

The first number is the percentage of your income that can be used for monthly payments. The second number is the percentage of your income that can be tied up in total debts, including car or other loans and the potential house payment. If you apply for a government loan, like a VA loan or an FHA loan, the ratios are different and these loans have other requirements as well. If you qualify under the standard ratios, you will almost certainly qualify for VA and FHA loans if you can also meet their other requirements. The qualifying procedure for these government loans is often confusing even to real estate professionals, and would fill a book on its own.

Let's discuss loan ratios. As mentioned before, the lower number of the ratio is the percentage of your income that can be used for your house payment. House payments include principal, interest, taxes, and insurance (PITI). So, let's say your household income is $50,000 gross (before taxes are taken out). Using the 28/36 ratio, you would multiply $50,000 by 28 percent to get $14,000. Divided by 12, this allows you a house payment of $1,166.67 a month. This is the first of three steps in qualifying yourself. Next you have to use the other number in the ratio.

The second number, 36, is the percentage of your income that can be used for your house payment (PITI) and your installment debt. Let's say that you have two car payments, one of which is $175 a month and the other $195 a month. In addition to the cars, you have credit card debts with monthly payments of $50. This is all of your monthly debt. Payments for insurance and such don't count against you when qualifying for a loan. Your total monthly debt in this example is

$420. Now, we take the $50,000 income and multiply it by 36 percent. We get $18,000, or $1,500 a month. You deduct the $420 of installment debt, which gives you $1,080.

The final step in calculating the amount you can qualify to borrow is to compare the two numbers. If you recall, your first number was $1,166.67. Your second number is $1,080. You must use the lower of the two numbers to determine your house payment. In this case, you qualify for a house payment (PITI) of $1,080. If you paid off your credit cards, you could qualify for a payment of $1,130, but in no case would you qualify for more than $1,166.67. Any lender or real estate broker should be glad to help you qualify yourself.

If you want to be ultra-conservative, you can use the 25/33 ratio instead of the example we used. The procedure is the same. To estimate your PITI payment, you will need to know the mill rate for property taxes and you'll have to have an idea of what your homeowner's insurance is going to cost you. Before you can determine either of these, you must know the value of your home. If you call an insurance company and tell them you want homeowner's insurance on a $100,000 house, the company can give you a close estimate on what your premium will be. Your local tax assessor can do likewise on the anticipated taxes. But how will you know what your house is worth? Well, that is a dandy question.

When you make a loan application, you will ultimately pay an appraisal fee. This fee is for the purpose of establishing the value of your new home. Most people wait until this point to find out what their new home's anticipated value will be. I never do. I always consult with a licensed appraiser prior to making a loan application. By spending fifty to a hundred bucks, I can have a strong ballpark figure to work with in my projections. If you want to pay for a full-blown appraisal up front, the cost will be a few hundred dollars. If you do this, make sure the appraiser you engage is on the approved list of any lenders you may seek money from. If the appraiser is on their list, you won't have to pay for the same appraisal twice, provided that you go to the bank within a

reasonable time since the appraisal was made. Most lenders will not accept an appraisal over six months old.

THE APPRAISAL PROCESS

The appraisal process for real estate doesn't work the way some people think it does. You don't get a dollar-for-dollar return on your investment. Sometimes you are assigned more value than what you paid for, and other times you get an appraisal that is lower than what you have spent. If you learn to master the manipulation of appraisal techniques, you can maximize your equity gain. If you don't, you can lose your shirt.

The subject of appraisal practices could easily fill an entire book. We, of course, have only a small section that can be devoted to it. Without going into great detail, I will give you a broad view of what goes on during the appraisal process. You can combine this information with your personal research to make the most out of all of your home investments.

THE COST APPROACH

The cost approach is the appraisal method that most people would love to see be the last word in the value of their homes. It, however, is only one of three methods normally used to compute the value of a house. When appraisers use the cost approach, they figure the actual cost of labor and materials. This typically benefits the builder. If the specified carpet costs $20 a yard, a value of $20 a yard is assigned to it. Unfortunately, the cost approach is not the final word in terms of appraised value.

THE REPLACEMENT COST

The replacement cost approach is another method used in appraising real estate. There is no need for us to go into this method, since the cost approach and the replacement cost approach will be the same for new construction.

MARKET COMPARISON

Another appraisal step involves market comparison. This is when the home you are building is compared to other homes in the area that have been sold and closed within the last six months, or so. The direct market comparison approach is the one that shoots down your expensive carpet. Since this is the only major part of an appraisal that may have an adverse affect on your home's value, it is the one we will concentrate on.

Appraisers will often start with the cost approach when placing a value on your home. The amount arrived at will be tempered with the use of a direct market comparison. It may be altered with other factors as well. If you build a house that does not conform to local standards, your value will drop. A decision to build a house that is functionally obsolete will also result in lost value. An example of this could be building a four-bedroom home that has only one bathroom.

When appraisers look at market comparisons, they are looking at the prices of homes, as similar to yours as possible, that have been sold and closed recently. They are also comparing the quality of construction and the materials used in the home. This is where you begin to lose by going overboard on expensive carpet. If every house that has sold in your neighborhood over the last six months was equipped with $18-a-yard carpet, there is no way you are going to get full value for $30-a-yard carpet. You might get $20 or even $22, but you won't recover the full cost on your appraisal. This means you must build your home in compliance with surrounding homes, or be prepared to pay the difference out of your pocket.

I'm not trying to tell you that your dream home has to be a carbon copy of all the homes around you, but there are certain guidelines that you should work from. If many of the homes in your area have tiled floors in their bathrooms, you can assume it is safe to install tile in your bathroom. If everybody else has vinyl floors in their bathrooms, you could be going out on a limb to put tile in yours. Do you see what I mean?

Hardwood floors are another good example of how you can spend a lot of money that you will have trouble recovering. While it may be safe to put hardwood flooring in your dining room or formal living room, it would probably be a financial flop to put it throughout your home. It may seem that you are helpless in making these deci-sions, but you are not. You can call licensed appraisers and consult with them before you make a buying decision. For a reasonable hourly fee, most appraisers will be happy to advise you on the values of various options you may choose to exercise when it comes to designing your home.

Any appraiser can give you an estimated value of your proposed home from a set of blueprints. This type of estimate is not expensive, and it will usually be fairly accurate. The only way to get a rock-solid number is to pay for a complete appraisal, but I would just seek an opinion of value in the early stages. This is cheap, fast, easy, and effective. It also shows your lender that you are thinking ahead. You can find real estate appraisers listed in the advertising section of your phone directory, and most of them will provide you with an hourly consulting fee.

THE MORTGAGE MAZE

When you enter the mortgage maze, be prepared to become confused, frustrated, and possibly even frightened. Seeing a truth-in-lending statement that details what your house will cost you after making 30 years of principal and interest payments is enough to scare anyone. The business of loaning money is a big one, and the options available to borrowers are vast. Sifting through the many loan programs available will take time and patience. Jumping quickly on one of the first loans to come along can create a mistake that you may regret for the rest of your life.

As a builder and broker, I've dealt extensively with financing and lenders. I've seen many professional real estate brokers who couldn't make sense out of the multitude of loan packages available, and I've seen a lot of people make serious mistakes when matching a mortgage to their needs. I must admit, I've made a few of these mistakes myself. Let me tell you about the first time I used an adjustable-rate mortgage (ARM).

When I built my second house, I financed it with an ARM. This particular ARM was set up with negative amortization. Being young and new to what I was doing, I didn't know what negative amortization was, and I failed to ask anyone. When the loan officer showed me the different loans available and the payments each created, I selected the loan with the lowest monthly payment. This seemed logical at the time. Well, I found out the hard way what negative amortization is and why I shouldn't have chosen it.

Kimberley and I lived in the house for a while and then decided to build a new home. We wanted more land and a bigger house. When we called the bank to get the payoff amount on our existing house, so we could budget for the new house, we were astounded to find that after paying mortgage payments every month, we now owed more money on the house than what we had borrowed originally. That's right, we owed more than what we had borrowed, even though we had been making monthly payments. How can this be? I'll tell you.

Negative amortization keeps house payments low, but it can increase the amount of principal owed on the loan. In our case, it did just that. Even though our payments remained steady, rising interest rates resulted in our loan amount increasing. This was not a pleasant surprise. Since we couldn't sell the house at that time for a suitable profit, we rented it out and built our new house anyway. We were fortunate. For some people, the increased loan amount could have been disastrous. Take some advice from a seasoned pro who's been burned, don't take a loan that is set up with negative amortization.

THE LENDERS

The lenders who offer home loans are as diverse as the types of loans available. There are the most apparent lenders, such as commercial banks, and then there are the not-so-well-known sources of money, such as mortgage brokers. In between, there are savings and loans, credit unions, mortgage bankers, private investors, and so forth. Each source of money has its advantages and disadvantages. For most people, a commercial bank will be the best place to seek both permanent and construction financing. Many mortgage companies offer attractive permanent financing, but are unable to provide construction loans. Since a lot of construction lenders don't want to loan money for construction unless they are providing the permanent financing, you must do some research before making a commitment.

I had a customer a few years back who had been approved for his permanent loan by a local mortgage company. When he tried to get his construction loan, he couldn't. The local banks and savings and loans (S&Ls) wouldn't provide the construction financing because they were not in control of the permanent loan. In this case, my company arranged the financing and all went well. If this man had been working as his own general contractor, he would have lost all the money he paid to the mortgage company in loan fees, because he would have had to start all over with a lender that offered both permanent and construction financing. Before you commit to any lender, make sure you can get both your short-term and long-term money.

PICKING THE RIGHT ONE

There are so many lenders available, picking the right one is often a mystery in itself. A logical place to start is with the bank where you currently do business. Don't be surprised if your regular bank isn't cooperative. This may sound strange, but it happens frequently. Not all banks are alike, and not all of them want to make construction loans. My own situation is a good example.

For years I've done business with a particular bank. It is a large, well-known bank, and it has been good to me. I've gotten loans for vehicles from the bank, and many of my clients and customers have gotten loans from this bank. As a builder and broker, I often help people arrange financing, and this bank has made a lot of loans for people I've worked with. You can imagine my surprise when I went to my bank for a personal home loan and construction loan only to strike out. I put all of my cards on the table, and walked out with nothing. It was not my credit rating, it was the method in which I wanted to arrange my financing. You see, the bank wanted me to put a cash down payment into the house based on my cost to build it. Standard procedure is to make the down payment based on appraised value. My bank wouldn't do it. I started shopping.

The next bank I went to wanted a 30 percent

down payment on the appraised value, due to the construction loan. The next few banks gave me similar grief. I was starting to get depressed. Then I found an S&L that wanted my business. They set the loan up with my down payment based on appraised value. This gave me the opportunity to arrange the financing with no money down. So you see, even a professional can have trouble setting up financing. I'm not trying to scare you, but I want you to understand that getting the best financing is not necessarily easy. Getting a loan is not so tough, but getting the right loan is more difficult.

To find the best lender for your needs, you are going to have to do some comprehensive research. Start with phone calls. You can learn a lot without ever leaving your house or apartment. There are some key questions to ask. I'll even list them for you.

- Do you make construction loans?
- Do you have a rate sheet you can send me?
- What down payment is required on a permanent loan?
- What is required to obtain a construction loan?
- Do you prohibit borrowers from being their own general contractors?
- What should I bring with me to make a loan application?
- How many points will I have to pay for my long-term and short-term loan?
- Will two closings be required, or can my construction loan roll over into my permanent loan?
- How long does the loan-approval process take?
- What is the term on your construction loans?
- Can I use my equity, from being my own general contractor, as my down payment?
- Is land acquisition part of your construction loans?
- In what fashion do you offer draw disbursements?
- What else can you tell me about your loan programs?

This list could obviously go on, but the questions above are the basic ones. You can modify the list to meet your own needs. The key is to make sure you keep good notes and compare the details you discover. Be careful to compare the details on an apples-to-apples basis. Look out for one-year ARMs, negative amortization, and construction loans with short terms, excessive points, and origination fees. Take your time and compare everything carefully.

THE LOANS
LOAN FEES

Loan fees and closing costs can add up quickly, especially if you are paying them on both your construction loan and your take-out loan. This is an expense you must budget into the overall cost of your home. There are usually origination fees, loan application fees, legal fees, survey costs, appraisal fees, pre-paid interest fees, and a host of other expenses. It has been my experience that closing costs generally amount to something between 3 and 5 percent of the home's value. In other words, the closing costs for a $100,000 house would run between $3,000 and $5,000 dollars. This is not chump change, so don't leave it out of your budget. Most of these expenses will not be incurred until you close on your loan, but you must be prepared for them.

FIXED-RATE LOANS

Fixed-rate loans are traditional loans. These loans provide a borrower with stable payments for the life of the loan. The principal and interest is paid regularly every month with common terms being 15, 20, and 30 years. If you are a conservative individual, this type of loan will suit your personality best.

ADJUSTABLE-RATE LOANS

Adjustable-rate loans got a bad rap when they first came out. Part of the reason for this was negative amortization. ARMs were dreaded because a lot of people lost their homes when interest rates rose and payments rose with them. A lot of this has changed with today's ARMs.

Modern ARMs typically, but not always, have interest rate caps. Caps are limits on how far a loan's interest rate can increase or decrease in a given time. A standard ARM will have caps of two and six. This means the rate can't move more than two points, in either direction, in a single year and not more than six points over the life of the loan. This gives more security to borrowers than the early ARMs, without any caps, did. However, there is still risk. If you get an ARM today at a rate of 7.5 percent, you could be making payments at an interest rate of 13.5 percent in six years. Unless you have a healthy, growing income, you might lose your house if this happened. There is, however, a safer alternative.

CONVERTIBLE ARMS

Convertible ARMs are structured like regular ARMs, but they offer a very desirable advantage. Normally, you can convert the loan to a fixed-rate loan at any time after the first year. In other words, if you have lived in your house for a year and see a trend in rising interest rates, you can pay a modest conversion fee and create a fixed-rate loan. If you borrowed at 7.5 percent today, your worst case scenario would be 9.5 percent for the fixed-rate loan.

Keep in mind that not all loans that seem the same are the same. Some convertible ARMs have large conversion fees, but most don't. Most ARMs have caps of two and six, but not all do. You have to stay on your toes when you are shopping for money.

PORTFOLIO LOANS

Portfolio loans are loans that lenders don't sell on the secondary mortgage market. These loans are similar in structure to other types of loans, but the qualifying criteria can be more lenient. If you have a tarnished credit history, finding a lender who keeps its loans in house is your best bet. Since the loans are not sold, the lender can bend the rules a bit, and this can be to your advantage, especially if you have a credit hurdle to overcome. Not all lenders make portfolio loans, but several do, and they are worth finding if you are running into trouble with loan approval.

THE MOST BANG FOR YOUR BUCK

How can you get the most bang for your buck? Well, in terms of financing, the interest rate is the key concern. If you can get a 30-year, fixed-rate mortgage at 9 percent interest or a convertible ARM at 7 percent interest, you will qualify for a more expensive house with the ARM. Some conservative lenders will qualify you at a higher rate than the starting rate of an ARM, but others will work with the lower interest rate. Let me show you what the difference amounts to.

Assume that you are qualified for a principal and interest payment of $1,000. You are going to get a 30-year mortgage. The fixed rate is 9 percent, the adjustable rate is 7 percent. With the fixed rate mortgage, you could borrow about $124,000. With the ARM, the loan amount could be as high as $150,000. The big difference is in the interest rate and monthly payment. If you want to stretch your borrowing power, an adjustable-rate mortgage is the way to go. Should you want to play the game conservatively, a fixed-rate mortgage is better.

I could write an entire book on financing your home, but the emphasis of this book is on building a home. Since space constraints are in effect, we must end our financing lesson and move on. Fortunately, you already know more than most people do about financing, and you can learn the rest as you investigate various lenders. At this time, we're going to move on to the next chapter and teach you what you need to know to buy your building lot with minimal risk.

CHAPTER 3
LOT SELECTION AND ACQUISITION

Before you can begin to build your home, you must have land to work with. This chapter zeros in on the methods used by professional builders in lot selection and acquisition. You learn about perk tests, easements, land contracts, subordination, covenants, deed restrictions, zoning, and other aspects of land acquisition that could ruin your otherwise perfect deal. If you want to protect yourself and make a prudent land purchase, you must read this valuable chapter.

Lot selection and acquisition is a big part of building a new home. The cost of a building lot is sizable, and proper selection and acquisition methods are essential. It is easy for any average person to make major mistakes when buying raw land and building lots. The mistakes can prove disastrous. Even if you are working with a real estate broker, risks are still present. Your odds improve if you are working with a "buyer's broker," but unless you possess more than a common knowledge of real estate, you are involved in a big-stakes gamble. Even top professionals fall into traps when buying land, so you must take this phase of your building project very seriously.

WHAT TO LOOK FOR

If you have been thinking about buying land for some time, you probably already know what to look for. You know if you want an in-town lot, a five-acre parcel in the country, or a farm. There is no point in my going into all of the facets of personal preferences, since this is an area that only you can answer. I can, however, point out some key elements to look for from a builder's point of view.

BASEMENTS

Not all houses have basements and not all people want basements. If you do want a basement, you

should put this on your list of things to look for when shopping for a building lot. If you want a walk-out basement, you should seek land with sloping topography at the house site. This will save money on excavation and provide a more attractive walk-out basement that is not as likely to leak. If you're after a buried basement, you should check to see if digging a hole for the basement is feasible. There may be bedrock under the surface that will be cost-prohibitive. Blasting bedrock gets expensive. You can test for this with an auger, a drive rod (a metal rod with a thin diameter that can be driven into the ground), or with a backhoe.

LOW GROUND

Low ground can give you trouble with insects and moisture. If the lot you select does not offer natural drainage, you are likely to have problems in the future. This can be overcome with drainage piping and fill dirt, but the work will be expensive. Avoid lots that collect water.

UNEVEN TOPOGRAPHY

Uneven topography at a house site will result in additional foundation costs. Unless you are seeking a daylight basement, stay away from ground that has extreme fluctuations in its topography.

ACCESS

Access to your land can be a problem. Your attorney should check to confirm how you have legal access to the property. From a builder's perspective, you should pay attention to the number of trees that must be cut, the length of the driveway, and other access aspects that will affect your building costs.

UTILITIES

Utilities are a big issue. Does your prospective building lot have service from municipal water and sewer services? How much will the city charge you to tap into the services? Is a septic system or well going to be required? Will the power company have to set numerous extra poles to get electricity to you? Investigate all angles of utilities and their costs before committing to a parcel of land.

STUMPS

The disposal of tree stumps can get expensive. If you will be clearing trees from your house site, this is an expense you must keep in mind. When you look at land, consider all aspects of what must be done with it in order to build your home.

LAND AND LEGALITIES
GET A GOOD REAL ESTATE ATTORNEY

My best advice to you is to get a good real estate attorney. I stress the fact of the attorney being an expert on real estate, because not all lawyers work with the same type of law. An attorney that might represent you in a divorce is not necessarily a good choice when it comes to a real estate transaction.

EASEMENTS

Many parcels of land are affected by easements. This does not taint the land beyond use and consideration. For example, utility companies often have easements along the front edge of property. These easements are common and rarely are cause for concern. There are, however, other types of easements that are not so easy to accept. For example, someone might have an easement to use a path through your property to get to theirs. There are many types of easements, and you should investigate the possibility of easements on any land you are thinking of purchasing. This job is best left to your attorney.

COVENANTS AND RESTRICTIONS

Like easements, covenants and restrictions have become common in real estate. Some are sensible, and some are so restrictive that they can make the land undesirable. Covenants and restrictions are usually placed on property by the developer. The intent is usually to maintain a certain quality within the subdivision. For example, a developer may make it illegal for property owners within a subdivision to keep livestock, such as hogs or cows. This may not bother you, but do you want some developer telling you what colors you may paint your house? Well, they sometimes do. They may also say that no commercial vehicle may be parked in your driveway on a regular basis. If you're a plumber who has a company truck, you may not be able to keep it at home. Recreational vehicles are also prohibited at times. The list of possibilities is nearly endless. Have your attorney obtain a copy of any covenants and restrictions for you to review before making a firm commitment in the purchase of property.

ZONING

Zoning is similar to covenants and restrictions in the fact that it tells you what you can and can't do. Zoning regulations are made by municipalities. An example of a zoning law could be one where your house must not be closer than twenty feet to the property boundaries on the sides of your lot. A more important one might be that only single-family residences are allowed to be built. If you were planning a house with an in-law apartment over the garage, you might not be able to have it. Have your attorney provide you with all local zoning regulations that pertain to your property.

SOIL EVALUATIONS

If you are buying rural land where a septic system must be installed, you have to be concerned with soil evaluations. These tests are often called perk tests. Satisfactory results from these tests should be in your hand before making a final commitment to purchase a piece of land. It is all right to put land under contract prior to the testing, so long as your contract has an escape clause contingent on satisfactory soil evaluations.

When I was building in Virginia, the soil evaluations were done by local county extension offices. A representative would come out, auger a few test holes and evaluate the soil, usually right on site. In Maine, private engineering firms are hired to perform the soil tests. This costs more, but provides the same results.

When a perk test is done, the septic system is rated for the maximum number of bedrooms a house may have. If you are planning to build a four-bedroom home and get a perk test that is only good for three bedrooms, you've got a problem. It would seem logical that the test would regulate the number of bathrooms, rather than bedrooms, but bedrooms are used because they give an indication of the number of people using the septic facility. With this being the case, you need your contingency clause to state something to the effect of this: This contract may be voided by the purchaser, and all earnest-money deposits returned to the purchaser, if a satisfactory site is not located for the installation of a normal septic system capable of supporting a four-bedroom house. Now, I'm not a lawyer and I'm not saying you should use my words in your contract. Consult a local attorney and have the professional word your contract for you. The key is to protect yourself with satisfactory placement of the septic system, satisfactory capability of the system, the fact that the system will be of a standard design (not some high-tech, high-cost system), and that your contract is voidable, by you, if these conditions are not met, with any deposit money being returned to you.

FLOOD ZONES

Real estate is sometimes located in flood zones and plains. When this is the case, you may not be able to build on it. If you are allowed to build, insuring the home can be extremely expensive. I had to back out of a contract once because the building site was affected by flood regulations. This problem is not common, but it does exist for some properties.

AN EXAMPLE

I've already told you that I'm in the process of building a new home for myself, but I haven't told you the rough experience I had acquiring my land. Keep in mind my years of experience and professional training in building and real estate as you read this story.

My land consists of seven acres with 800 feet of river frontage. The parcel is located in rural Maine, and no other houses are visible from the land. When I first saw the property advertised, I almost didn't go to look at it, because the price seemed cheap. The river frontage convinced me to at least take a look. Well, I fell in love with the land. It has the river, a pond, white birches, pines, hemlocks, hardwoods, and good topography. The man who was selling the land was something of a developer, and I suspected he was rather cagey.

I entered into a contingency contract to buy the land. Part of my contingencies were tied to site inspections by code officers and environmental regulators and so forth. If anything turned up from these inspections that didn't suit me, the contract was void, and my deposit of $100 was to be returned. Notice that I gained control of the land with only $100. I've done this many times with land, houses, and even larger commercial properties.

The first group I called to investigate the land was the Department of Environmental Protection. This agency is tough and stops a lot of subdivisions and building when they are believed to have too much impact on the environment. Since the river is in my backyard, I thought there was cause for concern. To my surprise, the land was issued a clean bill of health from this agency.

The next inspector of the land was the local code enforcement officer. He walked the land and assured me that he would issue a building permit without any problem, subject to a satisfactory septic design. While these inspections were being done, I was working shoulder to shoulder with my attorney at the county courthouse. We were investigating previous land transfers, subdivision laws, any possibility of liens or judgments, and so forth.

After exhaustive work, I was convinced the land was safe to buy and a great deal at the asking price. I bought the land. Since the land was purchased in winter, I didn't apply for a building permit for a few months. When I did, I got a serious surprise. I was told I couldn't have a building permit. The same code officer who had assured me a permit would be issued was now telling me he would not do so.

To make a long story short, I got my permit, but not before going to planning board meetings and through a board of appeals meeting. I had covered every base, and was still tagged out. If I had been a person with only an average knowledge of real estate and law, I doubt that I would have gotten my permit. Fortunately, I knew what buttons to push and when to push them.

Why was my permit denied? Well, Maine has some very tight laws on subdivision. All state laws had been followed in the dividing of several hundred acres, of which my parcel originated. The catch was that the town where the land is located had rules that were different from the state requirements, and the developer appeared to have violated the town's requirements, thus creating an illegal lot. With enough work on my wife's

part, and mine, we were able to prove the town wrong. It turned out that their own town tax map was drawn incorrectly and numbered improperly. My lot, which the tax map showed as lot 4, is really lot 5. The title work I had done with my attorney proved me to be right and the town to be wrong.

The story you've just read is true. Fortunately, problems like mine don't occur often, but this example proves that even real estate professionals can get mired in the muck. While it is unlikely that you will run into anything as horrible as I did, there are plenty of potential pitfalls waiting for you when dealing with raw land.

We've touched on many of the most common problems you might encounter in buying land, but there are others. Since this is a building book and not a real estate book, we don't have the space to go into every possible problem. If you get a good lawyer, you should be all right.

Now that you know the basics of land selection and acquisition, you can turn your attention to the design stage of your project. It is best if you have at least a rough sketch of your house before you buy a lot. Some houses simply won't fit on some lots. Also, the design of your home can affect the type of lot you should buy. With this in mind, let's turn to the next chapter and explore house designs and blueprints.

CHAPTER 4

HOUSE DESIGNS AND BLUEPRINTS

Settling on a house design is fun, but it is also an important step in your building process. Everyone gets excited when they are planning the construction of their new home, but this is no time to let your emotions take control. Think your needs and desires through thoroughly to assure your satisfaction with the finished product. This chapter shows you how to design your dream home in a way that is both affordable and attractive. Once you have your design sketched out, you need blueprints. You could pay an architect 10 percent of the anticipated appraised value of your new home to draw your blueprints, or you could have them drawn for free. This chapter describes all of your blueprint options and their pros and cons.

House designs and blueprints are needed before you get very far into your building activities. Designing your own home is fun. You can sit down with a pad of paper and pencil to draw your dream. It doesn't matter if you're not a great artist, you can get by with just drawing straight lines. An architect or draftsman will take your sketch and turn it into a set of working plans. Your job is to have fun and to design a home that provides everything you want, within reason.

Your first few drawings can be done without concern for accuracy. You are creating ideas, not scaled drawings. However, as you get more serious about your design, keeping your sketch to scale is important. This can be done with graph paper and a ruler. Again, your work doesn't have to be perfect, the professional you engage to create working plans will smooth out the rough edges.

When you begin to draw your plans to scale, you must pick a scale and be consistent. Most blueprints are drawn to a scale where one quarter of an inch on paper is equal to one foot in real life. You don't have to use a ¼" scale, but it is an easy unit of measurement to work with. The only downside is that you will need large sheets of paper to work with. A scale of ⅛" to the foot will allow you to work with smaller paper. You can pick any scale you are comfortable with, but you must pick a scale and stay consistent.

Why is drawing your plan to scale so important? If you don't put your drawing to scale, you may be unpleasantly surprised with the realities of what you have drawn. I worked with a couple once who had drawn what they perceived to be the perfect kitchen. The layout was very nice, but there was a big problem. The couple had not made the drawing to scale. When I converted their sketch to a scaled drawing, the room was not big enough to accommodate all that the couple had drawn into their sketch. It's easy to make a refrigerator fit on paper in an unscaled drawing, but making it fit on the job site is quite another matter. If your work is not to scale, you cannot be sure your features will fit.

START WITH TOTAL SQUARE FOOTAGE

When you begin to design your home, you should start with total square footage. A real estate appraiser can give you a ballpark figure of what a cost per square foot will be. This cost will be different in various regions of the country. For an example, an average house in Maine will appraise for about $60 per square foot, plus $10,000 for site work. In other words, a house with 1,000 square feet would be worth about $70,000, plus the value of the land it is built on. This type of estimating has limits to its accuracy, but the process usually works pretty well. If you start with this type of approach, you don't waste your time looking at a design that is way out of your price range. Let me give you a quick example.

Let's use the appraisal figures I've just given you in this example. We will further assume that you have run qualifying ratios and found that you can afford a house with a total appraised value of $125,000. The building lot you have your eye on costs $25,000. As a rule of thumb, builders try to keep their land costs to no more than 20 percent of the total appraised value of the finished product. This leaves you with $100,000 to spend on your new home. Based on the appraisal figures, $10,000 of that will be needed for site work. This leaves $90,000 for the primary house construction. If you divide $90,000 by $60 per square foot, you find that you can afford a house with approximately 1,500 square feet. Now you have a starting point.

A house with 1,500 square feet isn't tiny, but it's no mansion. There are some limitations on design related to size. A ranch style house with 1,500 square feet will be easy to design. However, a two-story design in this size will present some challenges. To get decent room sizes on both levels, it will be difficult to fit everything in with only 1,500 square feet. A cape-cod style might be a good choice if you want living space on two levels but cannot flesh out a good two-story on your budget. Can you see how size pertains to style?

Over the years, I've kept track of my building costs to determine the most cost-effective styles of houses to build. If you're after the lowest price you can get, in terms of house payments, a ranch will usually give you the most bang for your buck. A cape cod is also a cost-effective style to build. You can even leave the upstairs unfinished until you are stronger financially. Straight-up two-stories cost the least per square foot to build, but their increased size runs the total price up. Most starter homes are either ranches or cape cods. Contemporary designs are expensive. Roofs that are anything other than traditional A-roofs add to the cost. There are many ways that you can control overall costs in the way that you design your plans.

By starting with square footage in your design process, you can come up with a basic box to represent the size of your house. From there, you can divide the box into rooms. Referring to plans books will help you get an idea of what size a particular type of room should be. For example, a typical bathroom will contain about 40 square feet. Few bedrooms will have less than 100 square feet. As you begin to compile a list like this, you can total up the square footage and see if it will fit into your box. Don't overlook the square footage consumed in closets and hallways.

After you have listed each room you want in the house and assigned it an estimated square footage, you can begin to put your puzzle pieces together. Don't be surprised if you spend several days working on the layout of your house. The chances are good that you will change the sketch even after you first think it is finished. This is okay. It is better to make your changes while they can still be made with an eraser. Once your changes involve trade labor and tools, the cost will be considerably more.

GETTING IDEAS

Getting ideas for how your new home should be constructed is enjoyable. You can look through magazines and find all kinds of ideas. Purchasing books of home plans is another way to get visual stimulation on the subject of design. In fact, these plans books are ideal for generating a dream home. While you may not find the perfect house in a set of stock plans, you can borrow features from several plans to combine into one set of plans for your house. This is the way most of my customers decide on what they want built.

If you are able to find a set of plans in a plans book that you like, you are lucky. These plans are relatively inexpensive. For example, I bought a set of stock plans for my house and modified them. The basic blueprints, for seven sets, cost about $400. For this price, I couldn't afford to draft the plans myself and have them printed. The stock price was low enough to make it a waste of my time to draw my own plans on the computer.

It is difficult to find a set of stock plans that offers everything you want in a house. However, it is not difficult for carpenters and other trades to work from plans that have been modified slightly. These simple modifications don't require the expensive services of an architect. You can just write on the plans to delete this window, relocate that window, or to add a window here. Interior, non-bearing partition walls can be moved without structural problems, and all sorts of other changes can be made by you. As long as your workers understand the changes you've made, there shouldn't be any problem.

Structural changes are a different matter. You may have to hire an engineer or architect to work with you on these changes. For example, my plans showed a garage with an attic above it. I wanted to put an office over the garage. This change involved structural aspects that had to be engineered. In my case, the change only meant beefing up the girder and ceiling joists in the garage. It also called for a set of stairs to be built. With my experience, my carpenters and I did the engineering ourselves. Most people would have had to hire someone to make these changes. Knowing what size girder and joists are required for a specific live load on a floor is not common knowledge.

If you can't find a set of stock plans that will not have to undergo major structural changes, you will be better off to create your own plans. You'll do this by drawing your sketch, to scale, and then hiring a professional to convert the drawing into a set of working plans. This doesn't have to be expensive.

When Kimberley and I were building in Virginia, Kimberley designed most of the houses we built. She would generate a scaled drawing and then the drawing would go to a drafting firm. The drafting firm would create all the information needed for a set of working blueprints. Usually the cost for their services was several hundred dollars, but it never exceeded $1,000.

Another way to obtain affordable plans is to find a material supplier who will draw the plans for you. Many lumber companies will provide you with working plans free of charge, so long as you buy all of your building materials from them. There can be a hook in this free deal. If the material prices are substantially higher than they would be at a competitive supplier, your free plans are no bargain. Before you agree to buy all of your materials from one place, make sure their prices are competitive.

Getting ideas for a new home is not normally any problem for prospective home builders. The trouble usually arises when the ideas must be sorted through and culled. Invariably, people want more than they can afford. This is when you must separate your needs from your desires.

NEEDS AND DESIRES

Knowing the difference between needs and desires is important in the designing of a house. There are certain features that you must have. These are needs. Then there are those goodies that you would like to have, but do not necessarily have to have. These are desires. Unless money is of no concern to you, there will come a time in the designing of your house when you must sort through your ideas and put them into the category of either a need or a desire. Then you will assign priority ratings to them in order to tighten up your house plans.

I don't think it is necessary to spend a lot of time on this subject, since it is pretty easy to understand, but let's look at a few examples of needs and desires. A kitchen is a need. A bathroom is a need, and so is a bedroom. Windows, doors, electrical wiring, heat, plumbing, and so forth are needs. A whirlpool tub is a desire. Skylights are desires. Walk-in closets are desires.

There is nothing wrong with putting some desires into your home plan, but you must keep your financial obligations in mind when doing so. You may have always wanted a sun room, but can you afford it? A sun room is a desire, not a need. If you go through your list of ideas in this way, you will find it easy to pinpoint your needs and desires. You may not be pleased with some of the items you must label as desires, but if you're working on a budget, you may have to face the fact that you can't have it all.

FINISHING TOUCHES

Putting finishing touches on your design will consume more of your time. This is when your plan has been finished for a day or two, and you've thought of a few items you simply must change. One such example might be adding a foyer or a deck. Keep your sketch to yourself until you are sure you are happy with it. Once you give it to a professional to have it made into blueprints, changes will be costly. It is a good idea to let your sketch season for awhile after it's finished. Just set it aside and let it cure. If you haven't made any changes to it in a week or so, it is probably ready to be turned into blueprints.

THE NEXT STEP

The next step after having your sketch turned into blueprints is the review process. People make mistakes, and they may make some in the preparation of your blueprints. While you probably won't have the knowledge to catch technical errors, you can check the overall accuracy of the blueprints. Go over them carefully, room by room, to see if the finished product matches your sketch. Allow for some minor changes in dimensions, but make sure all of your closets, doors, windows, and other components are essentially the way you planned them.

After you are satisfied with your plans, call in your carpenters and have them study the plans for flaws. It's a good idea to have each trade review the plans for potential problems before you begin the building process. Your plumber might discover a beam blocking the drain of a toilet. The electrician might tell you that there is a better place to install the panel box. Your heating contractor might point out that the chimney is drawn in the wrong location. There are a multitude of potential problems that can be headed off with preliminary planning and a review of the plans. You may even get some cost-saving suggestions from your tradespeople.

Once all the bugs are worked out of your plans, it will be necessary to have copies made. Plan on having at least five sets of plans made up. Seven to ten sets of plans can make your job a little easier as a general contractor. Copies of blueprints are not cheap, but they aren't so expensive that you should cut corners on who has good plans and specifications to follow. It is not necessary to have a set of plans for each trade, because they won't all be using the plans at the same time. While you might get by with five sets, I think ten—or more—sets are likely to be needed.

Code officers will want a set of plans. In many cases each type of inspector will want a set. Depending upon where you live, this can eat up a half dozen sets of plans. For example, you might have to provide a set to the building inspector, the electrical inspector, the plumbing inspector, the heating inspector, the appraiser, and the lender. There's six sets gone, and you haven't given any to your subcontractors yet. It would not be unusual to need twelve sets of plans. We don't have many code officers in my part of Maine, so I'm getting by nicely with seven sets of plans. I have, on occasion, used as many as fifteen sets during the course of building houses in Virginia.

This concludes our discussion on designing and planning your home. We are now ready to move on to the next chapter and discuss code enforcement issues.

CHAPTER 5

CODE ENFORCEMENT ISSUES

Code enforcement issues cannot be ignored. Your failure to request a required inspection could cost you plenty of time and money. For instance, if you hang your drywall before getting your mechanical rough-ins inspected, you may have to cut your new walls open to expose the pipes, ducts, and wiring for appropriate inspections. This chapter tells you, in chronological order, what permits and inspections you are likely to need and when you should call for the inspections.

Code enforcement issues can play a significant role in the construction of your new home. Building codes exist in most, if not all, locations. They are more strict in some areas than in others, and not all locations have the same rule book. There are three major codes in use. One of them covers most of the western states, another covers the southern states, and a third covers the northeast. What is more confusing is that every jurisdiction has a right to interpret the codes in their own way. This can make for some difficulty in abiding by the code book. To be safe, talk with the local code officers who will be involved with your project.

WHO'S RESPONSIBLE?

As a general contractor, you will not be responsible for obtaining all of the permits. Being the homeowner, it is possible for you to obtain all of the permits, in most jurisdictions; but normally, licensed trades provide their own permits. Examples would include plumbing, heating, and electrical trades. You will be responsible for getting your own building permit, and your own septic permit, if you will be having a septic system installed. But remember, *you* are the developer and the general contractor. More importantly, *you* are the owner, and are the one who has the most to lose if permits are missed, fudged, or improperly handled. Don't leave it all up to your contractors.

As I've said, not all locations operate under the same guidelines when it comes to code issues. Generally, the permits that will be required to build a house are:

- Building Permit
- Plumbing Permit
- Heating Permit
- Electrical Permit
- Septic Permit (when a septic system is required)

To obtain a building permit, you normally have to supply two sets of blueprints and specifications to the local code enforcement office. Authorities will look over your plans and either approve or reject your proposed work. Once the plans are approved, one set remains in the code office, and one set is given back to you. These plans will be stamped and marked as approved plans. It is your responsibility to keep this set of approved plans on the job at all times, so that an inspector will always have access to it in the field.

In addition to your approved plans, you will be issued a permit. This permit must be posted in a conspicuous place, where it can be seen easily from the street. It's a good idea to wrap the permit in plastic to keep damp weather from deteriorating it. I've always used a ladder to mount my permits high on a tree or post to deter vandalism of the permit.

If you are issued a septic permit, you may

keep it in your files. It is not normally required to be posted. Other permits, however, like plumbing, heating, and electrical permits, must also be posted so that they are visible from the road. These permits must be acquired by the person who will be doing the work. In other words, if you pull your own plumbing permit, you must do the work. You cannot allow your brother-in-law to do the work for you. If you will be hiring a licensed master plumber to do the job, it is the plumber's responsibility to provide the permit.

There is another permit that you may be required to get. It is a driveway permit. Where these permits are required, an inspector will come out and look at where you want to have your driveway enter the main road. If the location is safe, you will be told what size culvert pipe is needed and given a permit. If the location is close to a curve or dip in the road, you may be required to choose another location. This is a permit that many people fail to think about, so make a note to ask if a driveway permit is required for your house. It would be a shame to install a driveway and then to have to tear it out.

INSPECTIONS

Along with permits come inspections. The types and number of inspections you will be required to comply with will depend on the rules in your locality. Some areas are very lax, and others are quite strict. I've worked at both ends of the spectrum. I'll tell you first how laid back the inspections where I'm building my new house are, and then I'll tell you how tight they are in Virginia.

The only permits I was required to obtain for my new house were a septic permit, a building permit, and a plumbing permit. The only inspections required by the town were a septic inspection and a plumbing inspection. The town was not concerned with doing a building inspection or any other type of inspection, except those related to plumbing. Amazing, huh?

Virginia presented quite a different set of circumstances for inspections. This state required driveway permits and inspections. The code officers in Virginia inspected the footings for a house before concrete could be poured. Then they in-

spected the foundation when it was done. A framing inspection was done before insulation could be installed. The insulation work was inspected, as was plumbing, heating, electrical, and gas work. When the house was completed, a final inspection of the house and all of its mechanical work was required. As you can see, Maine and Virginia are as different as hot and cold when it comes to inspection procedures.

Since you will be your own general contractor, but probably will not do all of your own mechanical work, there will be very little involvement for you with code officers. You may, however, have to coordinate and request the inspections. Someone has to. If you fail to get a phase of work inspected, the results can be bad, very bad. For example, if you forgot to get the plumbing inspection and drywalled your house, the plumbing inspector could force you to remove any drywall necessary for a complete plumbing inspection. Imagine how this would make you feel. Would an inspector actually do that? I don't know, but I wouldn't be willing to take the gamble.

Because it will be your responsibility to see that all inspections are performed at the proper time and are passed, let's spend a few moments discussing this subject. Keep in mind that the code requirements in your area may be a bit different that those that we discuss. I don't believe, however, that the local requirements in your area will be any more strict than the ones we will discuss. For simplicity, I will talk to you about inspections in the order in which they normally occur.

SOIL TEST

A soil test will be required if you will be installing a septic system. This is not a typical building inspection, but it is a requirement for building a house with a septic system. This test should be done and approved before you buy a piece of land. The test will be done either by a representative of a county extension office or a private engineer who you engage and pay.

DRIVEWAY PERMIT

A driveway permit may be required in your area. Check with your local code enforcement office and possibly your local department of transportation. If this permit is required, one of these offices will be able to provide information to you.

FOOTING INSPECTION

Most places require that a footing inspection be performed before any concrete is poured. Once the trench is dug and prepared for concrete, you should contact the local code enforcement office for an inspection request. Standard procedure gives the code office a 24-hour period of time to respond to your request. Allow for this when co-ordinating your concrete. It is not normally required that someone be present to meet an inspector, but I've always found that inspections go better if someone is there to talk with the inspector. By being on the job, you are also able to collect the approval form and know that it is safe to pour concrete.

While we are on the subject of inspections, I want to mention something that can apply to builders working with houses that are financed with government loans, such as Veteran Administration (VA) loans. With this type of loan it is common practice to have to get two inspections for each phase of work. A VA inspector will inspect the job and so will a local code enforcement officer. The penalties and costs of missing a required inspection can be very expensive, so make sure you comply with all inspection requirements.

FOUNDATION INSPECTION

After the footings are poured and a foundation is installed, the foundation may have to be inspected. This is not always the case, but you should verify if a foundation inspection is mandatory.

PLUMBING INSPECTIONS

Plumbing inspections are done at two points during construction. The first inspection will be done when all the rough plumbing is installed. By rough plumbing, I'm talking about pipes that will be concealed in either concrete floors or walls. A second inspection will be required when the job is finished and all plumbing is operational. If you are installing a septic system, you will also have to have it inspected prior to covering it up. The rough plumbing must be inspected while it can still be seen.

HEATING INSPECTIONS

Heating inspections are also a two-part inspection. The first is done at rough-in, just as is the case with plumbing. A second inspection will be done when the job is complete and the heating system is up and running. If you are installing a chimney for any reason, you may also have to have it inspected.

ELECTRICAL INSPECTIONS

Basic electrical inspections work on the same principal as plumbing and heating inspections. One is done at the rough-in stage, before insulation or drywall is installed, and a second one is performed at the end of the job. In addition to these inspections, there are two others that you may have to have. One is if you will be setting up a temporary electric service to use while building your home. In this case, a temporary electrical service is installed and an inspector comes out to check it prior to power being brought to it. Another inspection can involve the main entry service for your home. Once the meter hub and weather head are installed, they must be inspected and approved before power is brought to them.

INSULATION INSPECTIONS

Insulation inspections, when required, are done after the insulation is installed and before drywall is hung. These inspections are often done at the same time a framing inspection is performed.

FRAMING INSPECTION

A framing inspection is done when the shell of the home is complete, all mechanical rough-ins are done, and insulation is installed. Once you pass this inspection, you are free to hang drywall. This is the last inspection you will normally have until your home is complete.

FINAL INSPECTIONS

After your house is finished, final inspections will be needed. These will include plumbing, heating, electrical, and building inspections. Your house must be completely finished, including the grading around the outside of your home.

CERTIFICATE OF OCCUPANCY

After you have passed all of your inspections, you will be issued a certificate of occupancy. This is your permission to move into the home. People are generally not allowed to take up residence in a new home until the certificate of occupancy has been issued.

STAY ON TOP OF YOUR INSPECTIONS

It is your responsibility to stay on top of your inspections. Even though your subcontractors are responsible for coordinating their own inspections, it is your job, as the general contractor, to make sure they do. If insulation or drywall is installed before a rough-in inspection has been approved, you may have to absorb the cost incurred to remove the coverings. Don't take this risk. Require each subcontractor to provide a copy of their inspection approval before you pay them and before you conceal their work. Now that we are done talking about code issues, let's move on to the next chapter and see how you can save some money.

CHAPTER 6

WORKING WITH MATERIAL SUPPLIERS

Taking bids and selecting subcontractors play a significant role in the overall cost of your new home. Money is not the only issue to consider in this phase of your work as a general contractor. You must also weigh the value of workmanship, dependability, and experience provided by your subcontractors. This chapter shows you how to solicit bids for all types of labor and teaches you how to evaluate what you are getting for your money.

Prepare your material list before you take bids from contractors. While complete familiarity with your list may not be necessary when you are examining contractor bids, it won't harm you, and you will be better prepared to talk with the people who are going to supply your materials. Although your material list may change after a subcontractor finds an error in it or makes a valuable suggestion, you will need to have a material list for subcontractors to make good bids. However, your material supplier won't need the subcontractor information to price your take-off.

Working with material suppliers is somewhat easier than working with subcontractors. For one thing, you are dealing only with materials, not materials and labor. There are, however, plenty of problems that can pop up when working with suppliers. Some are quite serious, and others are merely annoying. Since your building materials account for a very large portion of your overall job expense, their selection and acquisition becomes of paramount importance.

Buying building materials would seem to be a straightforward deal, but this is rarely the case. Some material suppliers are not ashamed to play games with your mind and your money. And this is not all. There are plenty of honest mistakes

made. These mistakes, if not caught by you, can cost you thousands of dollars.

BID PACKAGES

The bid packages you use for material suppliers will be a little different from those used for subcontractors. There will be no need to give suppliers a set of blueprints. You will, however, have to provide a detailed list of specifications. One thing that you will need for suppliers that you will not need for subcontractors is an accurate take-off. A take-off is two things: a list of items needed to complete a particular job, and a list of specifications covering items you have decided must be supplied *exactly* as you want them. For example, a take-off for the roofing material needed for your house might include shingles, roofing paper, nails or staples, ridge vents, drip edge, and any other materials associated with your particular roof. Additionally, you may specify an exact brand and color of shingle and a particular brand name product used to prevent ice intrusion underneath your shingles. If you don't list some items precisely, you could be in for a surprise when the supplier delivers your material.

Suppliers will often figure a list of materials for you from a set of plans, but I've found this to be an undesirable way to arrive at a list of needs and their prices. You will fare better if you give each supplier an identical material list to price.

PREPARING A TAKE-OFF

Preparing a take-off is a job that you probably do not possess the skills to accomplish accurately enough to assure a solid working budget. Unless you are experienced in estimating materials, you need to find some professional help for this part of your building process. Where can you get help? There are many potential sources for advice and assistance.

The company or individual who draws your working plans is an ideal source for an accurate take-off. Whoever draws your plans is best qualified to figure the materials needed to execute them. This might be an architect or a drafting firm, but either should be willing, for a fee, to provide you with a list of needed building materials.

BUYING YOUR MATERIAL LIST

If you feel overwhelmed by the list of materials, then you have several options for having it done. You may have to pay, but for many people the small cost of a professionally prepared material list is well worth the expenditure.

. . . From the Blueprint Company

If you buy a set of stock blueprints from a plans book, you will probably notice that a material list is offered for an additional cost. While the material lists are not usually expensive, they also are not always right on the money. Depending upon where you are building, the code requirements or standard building practices may differ from those shown on the blueprints and material lists. Skilled tradespeople can compensate for such changes, but the material list becomes useless. For example, most homes in Virginia are built with exterior walls of 2×4 studs. In Maine, almost all exterior walls are framed with 2×6 lumber. The plans I bought for my house showed 2×4 exterior walls. I simply noted on the plans to change the exterior walls to 2×6 studs. This was simple enough, but it would make the material list confusing, if not obsolete, in terms of 2×4 lumber (used for inte-

rior walls) and 2×6 lumber (used in exterior walls).

If you purchase stock blueprints and a material list to go with them, have your tradespeople look them over to make sure the plans and take-off are in compliance with your local code requirements. The professionals may even be willing to make adjustments to the material list for you, if any are needed.

. . . From a Management Firm

There are companies who specialize in construction management. These companies can be hired to do as much, or as little, as you request of them in the construction of your home. If you have a set of plans and need a take-off, perhaps you can locate one of these companies to do the estimating for you. The company will likely have computerized estimating equipment that can do the job quickly and accurately.

. . . From Your Supplier

The suppliers you deal with will probably be willing to make a take-off for you. They do this free of charge in hopes of winning your business. Not all suppliers will spend the time to make take-offs for customers, but many will. One problem with this approach is that the material list made may not be accurate. If the estimator is in a hurry, mistakes are likely. Since the service is not being paid for, it may not be taken as seriously as it would be by someone being paid to do the job. This is not to say that a supplier can't or won't do a good job. Really, no matter who does the take-off, you can never be sure it's right, unless you know enough to do it yourself and check it over.

While we are discussing the possibility of having suppliers do take-offs, there is one word of warning I would like to give you. I've told you that it is best to give suppliers a detailed list of items to price, and I mean it. If you hand out blueprints to three suppliers and compare their bids, I believe you will find many differences in the materials listed and in the total prices produced. I know I've had this happen every time I've relied on suppliers to provide take-offs and prices from a set of plans.

You might expect there to be some differences in the take-offs and prices of competing suppliers, but the discrepancies I've experienced have been beyond minor oversights. I don't know if the estimators actually make such large mistakes or if the suppliers are playing games to make their total price more attractive. I suppose there is no way to tell for sure. What I can tell you is this, if you hand out blueprints and accept bids from suppliers in this manner, your numbers are very likely to be off the mark. You can almost certainly count on your materials costing more than what the estimates indicate. Let me give you an example of what I'm talking about.

A few years back, I was seeking material quotes on three different houses. These were houses I planned to build on speculation, and I wanted tight numbers. I was also in a hurry to see if the project would be feasible. The houses were to be models that would be used to sell other houses. While my lead carpenter and I were making our own take-offs, I sent plans and specs to four suppliers with instructions for them to prepare take-offs and bids. The idea was to come up with a total of six take-offs, one made by my carpenter, four made by suppliers, and one made by myself. Once the six take-offs were complete, I could compare them and chink any holes in them. I was pleased with my idea of assuring the most accurate take-offs I could.

When the take-offs were all in my office, I scanned the bottom-line prices from the suppliers. The range in prices was significant. Then, as I went through the take-offs, item by item, I found many flaws. The take-offs that my carpenter and I had done were very similar. There were minor differences, but this was just a matter of two people who saw the job being done a little differently. The cost differences between the two in-house take-offs were minimal, but the take-offs provided by the suppliers were nowhere near the same.

One supplier failed to include any interior doors. Another supplier forgot to include siding. These items are expensive and account for a significant percentage of the cost of materials. There were other, less glaring, omissions. For example, one supplier had included an allowance for kitchen cabinets, but had not included any countertop. All in all, when I finished working through the take-offs, there was no way I could use the outside versions in a direct comparison. They were so different that no real conclusion could be drawn from them. This same type of problem could occur with your job. If you give suppliers an itemized list to price, you can easily see what each item will cost and you can also make sure none of the items were omitted. Any other method for requesting bids leaves room for mistakes and cost overruns.

COMPARE THE RESULTS

You must be able to compare the results of competitive bids. When you do this, you will find that some suppliers have better prices on some items than on others. For example, one supplier may have the best price on siding but the worst price on windows. If you really want to save money on your dream home, you will probably have to buy materials from more than one supplier. This can be a hassle, but it is usually the only way to save a maximum amount of money.

There is something to be said for buying all of your materials from one supplier. For one thing, you will probably get a little better service. Additionally, it is easier to keep track of your invoices, returns, credits, and so forth if you are doing all of your business with one source. There is also the possibility that you can convince the supplier to lock in the cost of materials for the entire length of the job, like I do, when you buy it all from one place. The downside of this method is paying more for some items than you have to.

In all my years of experience, I've never seen a single supplier provide the best prices for all types of materials. I'm not talking about plumbing, heating, electrical, and building materials coming from one store; I'm talking about basic building materials. I wouldn't expect lumber stores to have excellent prices on electrical supplies, but you'd think that lumber stores would have consistent pricing on lumber. They don't.

In reviewing bids, I've found suppliers who offered great prices on studs, joists, and rafters, only to be extremely high on the price of their plywood. It is not at all unusual for a supplier to have many high spots in a bid. If you want to cut your costs to the bare minimum, you must go through the bids and decide who has the best prices on what, and then create a shopping list of what you will buy from each supplier. You might buy windows, doors, siding, and drywall from one supplier, dimensional lumber from another, and trusses, shingles, and cabinets from a third supplier.

Shopping for the lowest prices from several suppliers will take time. If your time is extremely valuable, the effort may not seem to be worth the savings, but it probably will be. How much money can you save? The amount will vary, but it is likely that you can save more than 10 percent of the total cost of your materials. Of course, you could save more or less, but there will be some savings. I should point out that there are times when it isn't worth the trouble to go from store to store. If you are placing a lumber order and the only item that the supplier is out of line on is nails, you might as well go ahead and get the nails with the lumber order. Running all over town for small items doesn't make much sense. However, if you're dealing with bigger items, such as siding, it does make sense to shop around.

ESTIMATES ARE NOT QUOTES

Estimates are not quotes. When you receive the bid prices from your suppliers, some of them may have the prices labeled as estimates. Before plugging the numbers into your budget, make sure you are working with quotes. Get the quotes in writing and make sure you understand how long the prices are good for. Most suppliers guarantee their prices for thirty days, but I've received quotes, for a whole house, that were only good for seven days. Try to get the quotes locked in for a period of time that will extend to the point where you will be buying the materials. If you can't do this, you can't count on your budget to remain accurate. The prices of building materials often jump up quickly, and this can put you thousands of dollars over your budget.

HOW WILL YOU PAY FOR YOUR MATERIALS?

How will you pay for your materials? Are you going to pay for the materials before they are delivered, when they are delivered, or on an open-account basis? Construction lenders are not going to advance money to you for materials until the materials are on the job, and in many cases, not until the materials are installed. This means one of two things, either you are going to have to pay for the materials out of your own pocket and get reimbursed from the construction loan, or you are going to have to establish an open account with your supplier. An open account is the easiest way to handle this situation. Suppliers will normally be happy to open an account for you once they have documented that a construction loan is in place.

Dealing with suppliers can be a frustrating experience. However, your dealings with suppliers can lead you to some great savings on the cost of your home. It is up to you to determine to what extent you will go in saving money, but building materials are an excellent source of savings.

EXAMINE YOUR DELIVERY AND YOUR BILL

The supplier I'm using, almost exclusively, for building materials is a local company. It has a good reputation, and I've worked with them in the past. I'm dealing directly with the general manager, and even so, mistakes are made. The company has responded to the mistakes quickly, made credit adjustments, and taken good care of me, but only because I brought the problems to their attention. If I had not noticed what was going on, I would be thousands of dollars over budget by now. Let me give you two specific examples of what I'm talking about.

The siding for my house is the first example. It was bought from a well-known supplier. I dealt with an outside salesperson when getting price quotes, and I got the quotes in writing. This is something you must remember: always get your quotes in writing. The siding on my house is wood that has been stained. The supplier had facilities to stain the wood before it was shipped to me. My talks with the salesperson resulted in a price for the siding and a price for the staining, both based on how many linear feet of siding I purchase, with an estimated amount of 8,200 linear feet. The prices I was given were good. My cost for the siding was competitive with the one given to me by my primary supplier. Staining the siding before it got to the job was not only faster, it was much less expensive than on-site staining. I was pleased.

My siding arrived and a few weeks later the bill came in the mail. I was shocked to see that the invoice amount was nearly $1,000 more than the quoted price. I had been give a price of around $3,400, and the bill was for about $4,400. Needless to say, I was upset, but I didn't lose my temper. I called the supplier and confronted them with the cost difference, using my written quote as my leg to stand on. The company apologized immediately and issued a credit, bringing the cost down to the quoted amount. If I hadn't caught this, I would be out a thousand bucks. Did the company do it on purpose? I doubt it, but the damage was done, at least until I got it reversed. By having a written quote in hand, I had my evidence, and there was nothing the company could do but comply with my request. Now, think about this, if they normally charge people that much, that means some poor sucker is paying about 25 percent more for siding and staining than I am. Keep this in mind when negotiating your best deal.

The second story I'd like to share with you involves my primary supplier. This company has been very good to work with, but they have made some mistakes, mostly minor ones, but a few that could have been very costly to me. When the supplier shipped my windows and doors, they shipped three expensive sliding-glass doors that I had not ordered and one window that I hadn't ordered. The cost for these unordered items was just under $1,500.

I had the unwanted doors and window picked up by the supplier, expecting a credit on my bill. When the bill came, there was no credit, but there was a charge for the products I had returned. Looking for $1,500 in overages that are buried in dozens of invoices with a total bill of over $22,000 can get tedious, but I found the glitch. When I approached the general manager, he issued a credit immediately. If I had not spotted the problem, I would have spent nearly $1,500 for items that are not even a part of my home. Just these two material problems would have put me about $2,500 over budget, and there's more.

When my windows were shipped, they were shipped without screens. This is fine; I don't need the screens until the house is finished. However, I was billed for all of the screens when I was billed for the windows. This is a lot less money, but it could be money that would be lost if I weren't paying attention to the invoices coming in. There have been other minor mistakes made, but I believe these examples show the point I'm making; you have to watch suppliers very carefully, even reputable ones.

CHAPTER 7

TAKING BIDS AND SELECTING SUBCONTRACTORS

Working with material suppliers can become frustrating, fast. This chapter gives you the information you need to avoid material substitutions and price quotes that cannot be compared accurately with other quotes. Materials account for a large portion of the total construction cost of a house, so you cannot afford to let your guard down when buying materials.

As a general contractor, part of your job description will be taking bids and selecting subcontractors. These duties are important in two ways, quality and costs. Searching for the best value is what any good general contractor should do. There is, however, sometimes a big difference between a good value and a low price. Accepting the lowest bid can cost you much more than what you think you will save.

Unless your day job involves some type of procurement process, soliciting bids and evaluating subcontractors will be somewhat of a foreign concept to you. Oh, I'm sure you understand that you call up some contractors, give them your plans and ask for prices that you can compare with those of other contractors. This is true, but there is a lot more to it, if you do it right. Selecting the best prices and the best people for the job is not as simple as studying the bottom line of a quote.

If you take an approach of simply hiring the lowest bidder, the odds are high that you will be disappointed. What appears to be the lowest price can creep up with extras. Your thoughts that a subcontractor offered the best deal will change quickly if the quality of the workmanship is below average. When you are dealing with subcontractors, you have to look below the surface, and you must spend some time researching the facts available to you. It is not as simple as requesting three bids and accepting the lowest one.

CONTACTING PROSPECTIVE SUBCONTRACTORS

You can begin contacting prospective subcontractors when your bid packages are complete. This can be done by phone or mail. The first question may be who you should contact. If you know anyone who has had work done recently, you could ask them for names of contractors they were pleased with. Lumber companies might be willing to give you some names to pursue. In general, the phone book will be a logical starting point. You can look up listings for each trade needed, and make contact from there. I would recommend starting with phone calls and following them up with either personal visits or mail.

When you place your initial phone calls, you will get some impression of the contractors you are calling. Some will have answering services, some will use answering machines, others will have employees answering their phones, and you may find a few who allow their young children to answer the phone. First impressions are important, but they can also be deceiving. From a business point of view, you may not look fondly on a foundation contractor whose phone is answered by a five-year-old. Admittedly, this is not good business practice, but the contractor may put in the best foundations in the world. You have to dig deeper, and that is why I recommend a personal meeting. Delivering your bid package is an excellent excuse for getting to meet your prospective workers.

After you have distributed your bid packages, you will have to wait. You may want to place a time limit on the subcontractors who wish to respond to your bids. This does two things. It gives you a timetable to work with, and it sets the stage early for you to take control of the subcontractor. As a general contractor, controlling subcontractors is a big part of your job, and you might as well get started early on.

MONEY MATTERS

Money matters when you are selecting subcontractors and building a home, but it is not the only thing that matters. Selecting suitable subcontractors means getting more than just a good price. What else are you after? Quality work is one requirement you should seek. In addition to a finished product that is acceptable, how and when the subcontractors work can be important to the overall success of your job.

All too often, contractors focus too tightly on the lowest bid. This often buys them trouble. I'm not talking only about first-time contractors, I'm referring to experienced, professional contractors. Has it ever happened to me? Oh yeah, plenty of times, but I don't fall into the trap any longer; I learned my lessons well. My list of experiences is a long one. I've had painters paint roof shingles, by mistake, with spray guns. Plumbers have installed shower surrounds upside down. Electricians have failed to label the circuits in circuit-breaker boxes. Foundation contractors have caused me more than enough grief. I doubt that there is any trade out there that hasn't, at one time or another, caused my hair to turn gray prematurely. We are going to get into specifics of how you can get the best subcontractors for the best value, but first, I'd like to share an experience with you that will point out why what you are about to learn is important.

AN EXAMPLE

My wife and I were building a large volume of homes, and the production schedules were tight. Some of the houses were going to be used as tax shelters by partnerships, and having the houses finished before the end of the year was critical to the deal made with the investors. Since the profit on the investor houses was slim, I looked for ways to trim the fat from bids. I found a drywall contractor who agreed to lower his prices considerably if I would commit ten houses to him at one time. This made sense, so I did it.

As the ten houses committed to the drywall contractor became ready for his work, he was notified. The contractor responded quickly in sending in crews to hang the drywall. I was pleased with my deal. Then I found the hook. After the drywall was hung, the contractor disappeared. It was obvious he was juggling jobs with limited crews to make as much money as he could, and I was unable to stop him. The contracts I used at the time required subcontractors to work on the jobs every workday or risk being removed from the job and replaced with another subcontractor. This drywall contractor beat me at my own game though. He would send someone to each of the jobs each day, but only for an hour or so at a time. The taping and finishing process seemed to take forever, and my hands were tied. The subcontractor was, in legal terms, complying with the contract, so there was nothing I could do.

The result of my bad decision on a drywall contractor cost me plenty. I saved money on the drywall work, but I lost money in construction interest and administrative time. Other subcontractors were thrown off schedule by the delays, and the investors became very nervous. I was able to complete the houses on time, but it was only through the help of loyal subcontractors in other trades and some heavy overtime payments that I was able to do it.

SOLICITING BIDS

Before you begin soliciting bids, there are a few chores you must tend to.

BLUEPRINTS

The first job is to obtain blueprints and specifications that can be provided to prospective subcontractors. Blueprints are expensive, and the temptation to use photocopies of them to reduce your copy costs may be great. Photocopies of plans, as long as you are not violating copyright laws, can be used for some subcontractors, but they should not be used in all cases. When a blueprint is photocopied, the scale of the drawing can be distorted. While the distortion may be minor, it could have a major impact on your pricing.

In laying out my new home, I met with various subcontractors to go over cost-effective plans. My carpet installer requested that I make my office two inches smaller in width. Due to the standard widths in which carpet are sold, the two inches was worth hundreds of dollars. If I had given my carpet contractor a set of photocopied plans, the two inches may have escaped notice, therefore costing me much more money. Your best defense in this situation is to give every subcontractor a true set of blueprints. However, to avoid the cost of unreturned plans, you can ask your subcontractors if photocopies will be acceptable for them to produce accurate bids. Many contractors will not have any problem working with photocopies.

QUALIFICATION

Part of your initial communication with potential subcontractors should include some direct questions. For example, you must require any subs you select to have their insurance companies send you a certificate of insurance. Be sure you ask these questions: "What kind of liability coverage do you carry?"; "What is the expiration date of your state worker's insurance?"; and "Is your local license current?" If the contractors don't carry liability insurance, and worker's comp insurance when required, don't hire them.

You should also ask for work references, but don't rely too heavily on them. If a sleazy contractor wants to fool you, the references you get may be family members or friends who the contractor is in cahoots with. The best way to confirm references is to visit job sites where the contractor is involved. This allows you to see, firsthand, the quality of work being produced.

It's not a bad idea to check credit references of the subcontractor, but contractors will probably not be willing to allow you this freedom. If you were a large-scale general contractor they would, but as a one-time contractor, the subs will probably not be as willing to divulge this information. Check your subs out as thoroughly as possible. Calls to the Better Business Bureau don't hurt, but again, they may not mean a lot. The best protection is to talk with past customers, and to inspect work being done by the contractor.

SPECIFICATIONS

In addition to quality blueprints, you should prepare each bid package with a complete list of specifications much like the specifications that accompanied your list of materials. These specs should be written with great detail, listing brand names, colors, model numbers, and any other identifying information. If you don't have all the subcontractors bidding the job with equal materials, the price fluctuations can be great, and there is no way of determining who is offering you the best deal. Beware of contractors who present proposals with a clause in them that allows the substitution of materials. This clause is typically known as an "or equal" clause.

"OR EQUAL"

If you allow contractors to insert an "or equal" clause in their bid, you are at their mercy. You might specify an ABC front door with etched glass and sidelights and wind up with an XYZ door with plain glass and sidelights. If you had your heart set on an ABC door, you surely will be disappointed to find an XYZ door in its place. It is not unusual for some contractors to use an "or equal" clause to beat out their competition. For example, toilets come in many shapes, styles, and colors, not to mention prices. I can buy a builder-grade toilet combination for less than $50. However, a name-brand toilet, or one similar in appearance, can cost upwards of $100. Toilets in designer colors can double the price. If I were bidding a job with $50 toilets and all other contractors were bidding $100 toilets, I'd have the lowest material price. You might not be getting the toilet you want, but you would be getting the lowest price possible, or maybe you wouldn't. If I were real slick, I might charge you for a $100 toilet in the bid and give you a $50 toilet on the basis of an "or equal" clause.

If an "or equal" switch is made on you and the product is not of an equal value, you might be able to make a case in court. However, the cost of legal proceedings will probably exceed any restitution you might receive from the guilty contractor. The best way to avoid this situation is to not allow an "or equal" clause. Some contractors will argue that the clause must be in their contract, since a particular product may not be available when needed. Don't listen to them. If you want to compromise, name an alternate product that you will accept, and force the bid to be made with the requested items. The key is to protect yourself from as many hidden surprises as possible. Even with the best defense, you are going to face some surprises, but work to keep them at a minimum with detailed specifications.

WHEN THE BIDS ARRIVE

When the bids arrive, you may be surprised. Some bids will be late, some won't come in at all, and of the ones you get, the prices can have a wide range. Another curiosity of the bidding process is the way in which some contractors present their prices. It is truly amazing how unprofessional some so-called professionals can be.

I have received all types of bids over the years, and I'm still shocked at how little respect some contractors have for their businesses. Can you imagine getting a bid proposal that is stained with coffee rings from where a mug has been set on it? I've gotten them. How seriously would you take a handwritten bid, scratched out in pencil, that failed to list anything more than a price and terms? I've gotten those too. Don't expect too many contractors to present their proposals in professional binders with product information included. While I think this is the best manner in which quotes should be offered, I appear to be in the minority.

As irritating as I find casual-looking bids to be, I must say that some of the contractors who use them are some of the best workers. Just as with your phone calls, you can't draw an absolute conclusion by the appearance of a bid. It tells you a great deal about the business or marketing prowess of the contractor, but may say nothing about the work the contractor is capable of. If you ruled out every contractor who used a standardized form for a bid and filled it in by hand, you wouldn't have many contractors to choose from. There are, however, certain elements that must be present in the bid.

Every bid you receive must have a price, terms, and a description of the work to be performed. Otherwise, you cannot rate the bids fairly. If a contractor has left pertinent information out of a bid, pick up your phone and get your questions answered. Don't worry about getting the information in writing, you can take care of that when you enter into a contract. While we are on the subject of contracts, let me interject one quick point. Many proposals will come to you with a time limit on them and a request for your signature of acceptance. Don't sign any of them. *Never use a subcontractor's contract.* Always provide a contract, which was prepared in your best interest by your attorney, to the subcontractor.

Once you have looked over your bids, put them into some type of order. Price is a logical place to start when sorting through the bids. Lay the estimates out beside each other and compare them. Look for any discrepancies in the terms of what you requested, such as "or equal" clauses. After comparing the documents, refer to any notes you may have made in the contact that you have had with the contractors. Rate the bids in order of preference, and prepare for the next step.

FOLLOW-UP COMMUNICATION

Follow-up communication is an important part of the bidding process. You will undoubtedly have some questions pertaining to the prices and information you receive from contractors. Get these questions cleared up, and start to assess the contractors. This is the stage where you will slowly weed through the pile of estimates and reduce your bid list to the best three subcontractors. It makes sense to think that you are only looking for one plumber, one electrician, and so on, but don't limit yourself to just one subcontractor in each trade. You should have at least one backup sub, and I've always preferred to have two backups.

As a professional builder, I make a point of having three contractors in each trade. For example, I have three electricians. My first choice gets most of my work. The second choice on my list gets some work, and the third choice gets occasional jobs from me. This structure keeps me in control. All of the contractors know about each other and the structure in which they are working. If my first-string subcontractors fail to perform properly, they are promptly replaced with the second-string subs. This moves the third-string contractors into second place, and I find some other contractors to take over the third-string position. By protecting myself in this way, I don't get burned by needing a backup on short notice, and all the subs do their best to maintain their positions or to improve upon them.

You are not likely to become a full-time, professional builder, but that doesn't mean that you shouldn't make contingency plans. Suppose your roofer falls off a roof the week before your job needs to be done? If you don't have a backup, you must go back through the entire subcontractor selection process again. By having a second choice selected, you can move ahead on schedule.

CUTTING YOUR BEST DEAL

Cutting your best deal with subcontractors can be fun, if you like negotiating, but it can also be tiresome. Some subcontractors will not be willing to cut their prices at all, others will expect to drop their prices by 5 or 10 percent. This is an area where you can have a direct influence on how much money is saved in the building of your home.

Different contractors bid jobs in different ways. Some contractors will put their best price on the table right up front, others will inflate their numbers so that there will be room to haggle. You may get some idea of where the various contractors stand by comparing competing bids, but

don't count on it. Let me give you an example of what I mean.

When I put the mechanical work for my house out for bids, the spread in prices was more than $2,000, and this is for work where the average price was about $3,500. Can you imagine having one electrical company bid your job for $3,200 when a competing company bids the job at over $5,000? Well, it happened with my house. How can there be such a big difference? This I can't explain, but I know from experience that the lower bid was the more realistic one.

Some contractors underbid jobs. The estimators are either new to the business or they are on the verge of starving to death. If you get a price that is extremely low, be very cautious of it. Inexperienced contractors sometimes bid jobs very high, because they either don't know how to bid them or they have no confidence in their estimating ability. This is another group to steer clear of.

The average drywall price for my home was around $8,000. I believe the low bid was around $6,500 and the high bid was pushing $10,000. I selected all local, known contractors to give me bids. Many of the contractors are people I know, to some extent, and none of them are new to the business. A 20 percent spread is far too much. Five percent is somewhat understandable, but if the prices vary by more than 10 percent, be on your guard, something is wrong. Before you can cut your best deal, you must have some idea of what is a realistic price. I'm going to help you with this in later chapters.

After you have grouped your bids by pricing, you should tag them with personal preferences, subcontractors who made good impressions on you. Once you have narrowed your list, set up a meeting with the subcontractors. Tell them that you are the general contractor for this job and even though you are not a full-time contractor, you are seeking prices that are consistent with the discounted prices given to general contractors. Tell the subcontractors, individually, what you are expecting to pay for their services, and ask if they can meet your budget. For example, if your plumbing bid comes in at $4,400, tell the contractor that you had budgeted $4,000 for the job and that this is the figure that you are looking for. If the subs won't cut their existing prices, thank them for their time and explain that you must keep seeking bids until you find a more agreeable price. Even if this is a bluff, it often works.

There are some key cards that you may be able to put into play to win your hand of showdown poker. If you are dealing with a company that is newly in business (these often give the lowest prices), you can agree to let the contractor use your job as a reference. New companies need satisfied customers and references to grow, and this gives some justification for a lower price.

Another way to trim the cost of subcontractors is to plan the building of your home in the off-season. For example, in Maine, there is not a lot of construction going on in the winter months. If you wanted to maximize your savings in Maine, you would plan your construction so that the shell of the house was completed just before cold weather set in. This would give plumbers, electricians, heating technicians, drywall contractors, and others who do inside work, something to do when the ground was frozen and nothing was going on. This is an excellent way to justify a lower price.

The most important element to cutting your best deal is having a large stable of contractors to choose from. If you live in a small town, one where there are only two foundation companies, expand your search parameters. Reach out and find contractors from surrounding areas. It is very likely these contractors will be competitive with the ones in your community. I've pulled subs in from over fifty miles away to save money. If you live in a highly-populated area, you might do well, very well actually, to seek contractors from the rural areas outside of town. These contractors may not charge as much and they may not be as accustomed to having an abundance of work. These factors can work in your favor. If you have enough people to sort through, you can carve out a good deal.

Finding the right subcontractors is not hard work, but it does require patience, persistence, and good organizational skills. Begin your search well in advance of when you will need workers on the job. If time is on your side, you can pick and choose to suit yourself. Document prices, insurance coverages, references, availability, and your ability to contact the various contractors. Find the ones that best suit your needs, and commit them to solid contracts, which your attorney has prepared. If you do this, you will save money and enjoy a job that runs more smoothly.

CHAPTER 8

MAKING LAST-MINUTE CHANGES

> *Almost everyone decides to make some type of change to their plans at the last minute. It might be adding a skylight in the kitchen or a whirlpool in the bathroom. The change could be something as simple as the paint color for a bedroom, but last-minute changes can wreak havoc with timetables and construction budgets. To protect yourself from lost time, cost overruns, and disappointment, you need to read this chapter. Learn how to make changes before they become too costly.*

Last-minute changes in your building plans are to be expected. Few houses, if any, are ever built without such changes. These deviations can, however, increase the cost of a home beyond what the revisions would have cost if they had been part of the initial building plan. For this reason, and others, it is important to control the changes you make.

If you are able to plan and build your house without some type of change in plans, you will be the first person I've ever known to do so. Plans change, sometimes out of preference, sometimes out of necessity. In either case, changes made at the wrong time can be expensive. Knowing when to make changes in various phases of the job can help you avoid cost overruns, and that is what this chapter is all about.

START AT THE BEGINNING

Let's start at the beginning. You are drawing your rough sketches of a new home. A decision is made to enlarge the kitchen. At this stage of the game, the decision can be made and the change only involves erasing a line and redrawing it. You can make all kinds of changes in the preliminary planning stage. Once you go to the blueprint stage, however, changes get more costly.

When you have your blueprints, you are still free to change paint colors or similar nonstructu-

ral aspects without undue cost. If, however, you suddenly decide you want to add four feet to your garage, the change will get a little more complicated. You might be able to simply note the change on the plans, consult with someone capable of making structural decisions, and move on. On the other hand, the change might create a chain reaction that will require actual revisions to the blueprints. This will add to your design and drafting costs.

After you pass the blueprint stage, you are into the bidding phase. Changes won't have a lot of impact here, as long as you compensate for them in your budget. However, when you get to the commitment stage, you must have all of your ducks in a row. Bankers will get nervous if you make too many changes once your plans are submitted for loan application, and contractors will get frustrated if you are calling day after day with changes. Before you go to your lender, take a hard look at your plans and make sure you are satisfied with them.

ENTERING INTO CONTRACTS

Entering into contracts is serious business. This phase of your job as a general contractor is crucial to the successful completion of your home. You will probably be dealing with a lot of subcontractors, and each of these dealings should be done with a formal contract. The contract should be drafted by your attorney. Avoid signing proposals or contracts submitted to you by contractors. Because contracts typically favor the person presenting them for a signature, you should be the one doing the presentation.

Your attorney will be the person best qualified to advise you on the elements of a strong contract. I'm not a lawyer, and I cannot give you legal advice. However, I can tell you about some of the key elements used in my contracts, and this information may help you when meeting with your attorney.

KEY ELEMENTS

- Start and finish dates
- Amount of money to be paid
- Detailed description of work to be done
- Penalty clause for slow work completion
- Damage/liability clause
- Pay/draw schedule and conditions
- Inspection procedures
- Insurance clause
- Warranty clause
- Procedure for change orders

My contracts are long. They detail the type of work that is to be done and the amount of money that will be paid for the work. A schedule for payment is included in the agreement. There is all the normal contract language, and then there are some special clauses that have evolved over my many years of experience. I've found these clauses are sometimes needed to maintain control over my subcontractors.

TIME AND MONEY

My contracts include a date when the work will be started and a date when the work will be completed. They go on to require the subcontractor to work regularly on my job until the work being done is finished. This helps to avoid having trades show up and work for one day and then move off to other jobs. The clause gives me the power to replace any contractors who do not work consistently on my jobs with a new contractor, and the clause spells out how financial arrangements will be handled if this happens.

DESCRIPTION OF WORK

A detailed list of specifications is included as a part of all my contracts, and the contracts do not allow substitution of materials or deviations from the contract without written authorization in the form of a change order.

PENALTIES

A penalty clause is part of my contract. This clause states, basically, that if a contractor has not finished the contracted work by the contracted completion date, I have the right to assess a per-day charge for each day the work is left uncompleted. My standard daily charge is $100, and the amount can be deducted from any final payment due the contractor. If subcontractors know they can lose a hundred dollars a day for each day they are late, they tend to get the job done on time.

DESTRUCTION

Another clause in my contract deals with destruction. If one trade damages the work of another trade, I have the ability to withhold payment to the subcontractor doing the damage in an amount equal to the damage done. This comes in handy if a plumber cuts out floor joists or if a carpenter saws through electrical wires.

PAYMENT SCHEDULE

How and when subcontractors will be paid should be defined clearly in your contract. If you are going to give the sub a deposit to start the job, and I strongly advise against this, the amount of the deposit should be spelled out. Then you should go on to list the payment schedule for future payments, perhaps including a certain amount when the rough-in work is complete and another payment when all the work is complete. I recommend that your attorney include language that gives you the right to withhold payment until all work has passed local code inspections and an inspection of your own.

INSPECTIONS

All time and date schedules will be altered as the job progresses. I suggest that you define pay periods by events as well as time. If you tell the plumber that he will be paid on June 15 because you *think* he ought to be done by then, but he isn't because of a framing crew problem, then you're stuck with a meaningless contract. Always make inspections and job completion the most important factor in draw payments. Also, carefully outline how, when, and by whom inspections will be made. Not only that, but describe the manner and extent of your inspections. Don't leave anything open to chance or assumption.

INSURANCE

Insurance is another issue that should be covered in your contract. The agreement should require all subcontractors to maintain active insurance for the entire time they will be involved on the job. You should also request certificates of insurance from each subcontractor for your files.

WARRANTY

Warranty work is another issue to cover in your agreement. How long will the subcontractor guarantee the work that will be done? Will the warranty cover labor and materials? Both of these questions should be answered in the contract.

Once you have your fill-in-the-blank contracts prepared by your attorney, you are ready to meet with your subcontractors. Go over the contract terms with them, and make sure there are no misunderstandings. When the contractors sign the agreement, have them initial each page of the document. You should initial them as well. This provides proof that each page of the agreement has been seen and agreed to by all parties. Also have the contractors sign the specifications and blueprints, to indicate that they have been reviewed and accepted. This may sound like a lot of work that is not needed, but if you ever have to go to court, you'll be glad you took the time to do a thorough job in contracting your subcontractors.

THINGS ALWAYS CHANGE

No job will go without a change order being discussed. If you're extremely lucky, the changes discussed might be accomplished without adjusting payments to subcontractors or material suppliers.

But in most cases somebody wants more money to fix the problem. If the change is only a matter of putting up an interior wall six inches away from where the plans call for it, you probably won't have a dollar adjustment to your contract. If the wall is already up when it is determined that your new bay window won't look right in a corner, then your carpenter is going to want some compensation for the extra labor. This means putting it in writing.

Written change orders should be used for every alteration in the original contract. Whether you are changing a paint color, a date for starting work, or the design of your roof, a written change order should be used. This document should be consistent with your original contract, it should cover all aspects of the change, and it should be signed by everyone who signed the original contract. Your attorney can prepare a form for you to use as a change order.

THE TIMETABLE

The timetable for changes can have a direct effect on the cost of your home. We've gotten to the point where contracts are signed and work is about to begin. This is when your decisions about changes in your plans can blow out your budget. To expand on this, let's run through the basic steps of building a house and see when you can make changes without having a major impact on work that has already been done.

Site Work

Site work will be the first phase of work to enter into. This is when you get trees cut down, a driveway cut in, and rough earth work done. You might also install a septic system and well or dig trenches for utility hook-ups.

You can always come back later and cut down more trees, but it makes sense to have them all cut at once. If you don't clear enough space on the first attempt, extra costs will be incurred, and they can be significant. People often fail to clear enough space for their new homes. Anxious to save trees, these people don't allow enough room for concrete trucks to work or to maneuver around the foundation. There are times when the house is framed and homeowners realize that trees are too close for comfort to their new home. Many people forget to clear a path for the utility company to bring the electrical service. Study your site carefully and have all the site work done at one time.

Foundation

The foundation stage is one of true commitment. Once the foundation is installed, it gets very costly to alter it. If you are toying with the idea of expanding a room or adding a concrete front porch, now is the time to do it. Let me add that many people panic when they see the footings for their new homes. They always seem to think the house is too small. This is a natural reaction. If you feel this way, measure the footings to make sure they are installed in accordance with your plans. If they are, wait for the foundation wall to go up, and you will start to see that the footings are not as small as they appeared to be.

Framing

The framing stage is where the majority of changes are made. For most people, this is the first time they can begin to visualize how their home is really going to look. Room sizes look very different on blueprints than they do with stud walls up. A lot of changes can still be made in the framing stage, but it is best to make them before the lumber is installed. This, however, rarely works out. Most changes are made after the wood is in place and people can actually see what they are getting.

I can't count the number of times customers have asked me to make major changes in the framing of their houses. This after exhaustive meetings prior to framing to head off any costly changes. It seems that most people just cannot visualize what their home will be like until they can see walls, windows, and doors in place. Don't be surprised if you suffer from this same type of situation. And hey, it even happens to the pros, I've made last-minute changes in my own framing.

Once you have worked all of the bugs out of your framing, you can look ahead to other trades and see what adaptations will be needed to com-

pensate for your framing changes. For example, if you move a bathroom wall, it can affect your plumber. Adding a door will affect your electrician. By this stage of your building process, almost every change you make can affect some other trade.

Roofing

Roofing is a phase where not many changes are likely. You might change the color of your shingles, and you might even change the style, but these changes will not affect other aspects of your construction.

Siding

Siding is similar to roofing in that changes in it have little effect on other parts of your job. I can't recall ever having a siding change that caused any problems.

Plumbing

Plumbing is a phase where changes are sometimes made. A whirlpool tub is added, a laundry sink is added, a toilet is moved, or a hose bib is added. When you make changes in your plumbing, you can be affecting several things. For example, your electrician will be planning lights and outlets based on your sink location. If the sink location is moved, you have to make adjustments with the electrical wiring. If you are going to make changes in your plumbing, do it during the rough-in work. If you wait until drywall has been hung, many plumbing changes become much more difficult and more expensive.

Heating

You probably won't have any desire to change the layout of your heating system, but if you do, do it during the rough-in. If you wait until the drywall is hung and the heating unit is set, you could be in for some expensive trouble. The same goes for air conditioning.

Electrical

Electrical changes are fairly common. People add extra outlets, move light locations, and come up with needs for extra outdoor outlets. Like plumbing and heating, electrical changes should be made during the rough-in. Once the wiring is concealed, it becomes much more difficult to work with.

Insulation and Drywall

Insulation and drywall are not likely to require any changes. These phases are not normally ones where passion comes into play; therefore, they usually go in according to plan.

Painting

Painting changes in such areas as color and finish can be made without having any effect on other parts of your home. It is best, however, to make these changes before painting begins.

Cabinets

Cabinets are expensive, and they are something that often undergo change during the construction process. You may decide to make a vanity cabinet larger, so that you can have both doors and drawers. You may desire an island cabinet for your kitchen. Most changes made with cabinets will not have a major impact on other parts of your job.

Trim

Changes in your trim won't have much effect on the rest of your job. Adding a chair rail in the dining room or crown molding in the living room won't hurt a thing.

Flooring

Changes in flooring can cause some trouble for other trades. For example, if you planned a vinyl floor in your bathroom and then installed a thick tile floor, the closet flange your plumber roughed in for the toilet may be too low for the toilet seal to work properly. This is not a difficult problem to overcome, but it is an example of how flooring changes can create extra work for others.

Fixtures

Setting fixtures is an exciting time. You know your job is nearing completion, and you've got a good handle on your overall budget. Once people realize that their job is on budget, they often feel comfortable with adding additional fixtures or upgrading the ones they had planned to use. This normally isn't a problem, but it can be. For example, if your plumber roughed in a bathroom lavatory with the intent of installing a vanity cabinet, switching to a pedestal sink can cause two problems. The waste and water pipes probably will not line up with the fixture, and pedestal sinks require special backing to be installed between wall studs for securing the bracket that supports the lavatory bowl. Before you rush out and change fixtures, check with your tradespeople to make sure the change will not create problems.

We've gone through most of the major phases of construction and the changes that may be involved with them. You should now have a better idea of when to make changes and of what to look out for. We're almost ready to start building your home, but first, we must plan for the utilities needed. Let's turn the page and do that now.

CHAPTER 9

PLANNING UTILITIES FOR TEMPORARY AND PERMANENT USE

This is a short, but important, chapter. Many home builders, including professionals, fail to plan far enough ahead for temporary and permanent utilities. If you don't get your job on the right schedules, at the right times, you may have to build with the use of generators, and you may not have phone or electrical service when you are ready for your certificate of occupancy. This chapter makes you aware of what utilities to plan for and when and how to make arrangements for them.

Planning utilities for temporary and permanent use will not require a lot of time, but it is a vital part of building your home. There are several decisions that you must make, a few phone calls to make, and a couple of meetings to schedule. Failure to tend to this phase of your job as a general contractor can result in great disappointment. You might get your house finished, only to find that you don't have any electrical power or phone service. To avoid this, and other complications, you must look ahead and plan your job in advance.

TEMPORARY POWER

Temporary power comes in very handy when building a house. You can build with the use of generators, but a temporary power pole is much quieter and more dependable. There are two catches to using temporary power. One is the cost, and the other is the time it takes to get it in place. I've built houses with the use of generators and with temporary electrical services. My subs have always been happier working with temporary service. Personally, I don't mind working with a generator, but a lot of subs hate to do this.

The time required to obtain temporary electrical service varies, but you should allow several weeks for the process to be completed. You will start by requesting forms from your local electrical utility company. Your electrician will prepare a temporary service and install it on your lot. It will consist of a pole, a circuit-breaker box and an outlet. A code officer will inspect the electrical arrangements and then the power company will send a representative out to look at the work. The next step will be getting service to the temporary pole. This can involve cutting down trees. Once everything is inspected and approved, power will be connected to the pole, assuming that you have paid the connection fee. In the case of my house, the connection fee was almost $400. I elected to use my generator rather than to pay this fee, but in general, I think you will be better off to have a temporary service installed.

In addition to your hook-up fee, you must plan to pay your electrician extra money for setting up the temporary service. You may even have to pay the electrician a monthly rental fee for the use of the pole. And, of course, you will receive monthly billing for the electricity you use. These expenses can add up to several hundred dollars, so don't overlook this cost when setting your building budget.

PERMANENT ELECTRICAL SERVICE

When you begin planning for permanent electrical service, you must decide if the service will come to your home from overhead or from underground. Overhead service is cheaper, but underground service is more attractive. In either case, you may have to clear a path for the utility company to install their wires.

Once your house is "dried in," you can have permanent service brought to the house. A house is considered dried-in when the inside of the home is completely protected from weather. This means having windows and doors in place, a roof on, and it may require siding. You will definitely need siding installed in the area where your electrical service will enter your home. Your electrician will install a meter base, a circuit-breaker box, and a weather head for the utility wires to connect to (if you have overhead service). This work will have to be inspected and approved by the local electrical inspector. Then the power company will look over the work and make their connections.

TELEPHONE SERVICE

Telephone service is usually somewhat easier to obtain than electrical service. Call your local phone company and see what is required to set up a new service. In the meantime, have your electrician run wires during the rough-in stage for the phones in your home. Plan your phone locations carefully, and make sure you rough in enough of them.

CABLE TELEVISION

Cable television has become a way of life for a lot of people. If you have cable in your area, you should have the house pre-wired for cable. Your electrician can do this. All you have to do is determine where you want the connections, and the electrician can do the rest. You will, however, have to contact your local cable company and make arrangements for service.

THE MOST IMPORTANT

Of all the utilities we have discussed, your electrical service is the most important. This is the one that takes the longest to get and that is needed most. Allow plenty of time for getting electricity, and your job should run more smoothly.

CHAPTER 10

PRELIMINARY SITE WORK

Preliminary site work is often required before construction can begin. Cutting trees, roughing out a driveway, and similar work is almost always a prerequisite to building a new home. This chapter shows you what to anticipate and when you should perform various phases of the work.

Preliminary site work is the first real physical work that will signal the building of your new dream home. By the time you see the bulldozer rolling up to your lot, you will probably be so excited that you can't stand yourself. While it may hurt a little to see your beautiful trees being cut down, your mind will swirl with the realization that your dream is coming true.

When the site work begins, your role as a general contractor shifts from administrative duties to on-site responsibilities. You should be on the job when the clearing begins, but stay well away from the actual work. Many construction workers have been injured by heavy equipment and falling trees, so keep your distance. It is your job to direct the work, not to get involved in it.

WHAT ORDER SHOULD THE WORK BE DONE IN?

What order should the work be done in? The removal of trees and stumps is usually the first step in site work, commonly followed by the driveway and rough grading of the lot. Then the foundation trenches are dug. Next is the installation of septic systems and wells, or sometimes the digging of trenches for water and sewer service. After the foundation is installed and backfilling takes place, fill dirt is hauled in and the building lot is shaped into a close proximity of its finished grade.

HOW MANY CONTRACTORS WILL I NEED?

How many contractors will you need for site work? You may only have to deal with one contractor, but it may be more cost-effective to deal with several. It all depends on the type of work required and the contractors in your area. Most professional home builders deal with only one contractor for site work. This is convenient, but it is not always the lowest cost. Your odds for a happy and enjoyable building experience will improve when you keep the number of contractors you must rely on to a minimum. Unfortunately, it often costs more money to allow a single contractor to do all phases of the work than it would to shop around. You must weigh the pros and cons of convenience and control over saving money. How many contractors do you have to depend on for site work? One contractor should be able to handle all of your site work requirements. However, putting together a site work team can save you money. Let's talk about the various phases of site work.

CUTTING TREES

If you have a wooded building lot, cutting trees will be the first step in your site work. Trees will have to be removed for your driveway, electrical service, and your house.

When a lot of trees have to be removed, you

may be able to have the work done without charge. How is this possible? Some people will cut the trees and remove the wood for use as firewood. If you can trade the wood for the labor required to fell the trees, you will save money. Make sure, however, that the workers are insured for the work they do on your property.

STUMPS

Stumps of the trees cut down will have to be removed. Not only will they have to be pulled out of the ground, they will have to be disposed of. Getting rid of stumps has grown increasingly difficult in past years. In the old days, stumps were usually buried, but now, they are hauled away and shredded up. Depending on the size of the tree, it can take a sizable piece of equipment to remove the stump. If you hire one group of people to cut the trees, you must assume that a second subcontractor, probably the one who will do your earthwork, will be needed to extract stumps.

THE DRIVEWAY

The driveway for your new house will require some rough grading and layers of stone or gravel. There will probably be a need for a culvert pipe. This work is usually done by the contractor who removes stumps and does the earthwork.

DIGGING THE FOUNDATION

Digging the foundation might be done by the contractor involved in the site work, or it may be done by another subcontractor. The contractor who will install your footings may prefer to dig the ditches for the foundation. You can talk to the contractor who will do your rough grading and see if the footings will be dug by that contractor or by the foundation contractor.

SEPTIC SYSTEM

If you will be installing a septic system, it is very possible you will have yet another contractor. However, many contractors who do earthwork also do septic systems. You will have to compare prices and decide whether or not to bring in a specialist for your septic work.

TRENCHES

Trenches will be needed for your water service and sewer. These trenches will normally be done by the contractor who is doing the majority of your earthwork. It is, however, possible that the plumbing contractor you hire will take care of these trenches.

FILL DIRT

Fill dirt is often required to backfill a foundation and to rough grade a building lot. This work is typically done by a contractor who specializes in earthwork. While a few contractors use backhoes to perform this work, a bulldozer is more appropriate for the job.

As you have just seen, there is justification and opportunity to involve a number of contractors in your site work. Are the savings worth the effort in dealing with so many contractors? It depends; they can be, but they often aren't. When you attempt to build a team, you must coordinate that team. This can get hectic and troublesome. If your tree-cutters fail to show up and your stump-pullers come in on schedule, only to find that the trees haven't been cut yet, you are going to have some frustrated subs on your hands.

You will have to use your own judgment, as a general contractor, when determining how many subs to involve in your site work. If the price of using just one contractor is not too much more than the price you would pay for using multiple contractors, I would recommend keeping all of your eggs in one basket. When you involve a group of people as a team to accomplish a goal, trouble can arise. If something in the overall job goes wrong, there is potential for the various subs to point fingers at each other. Let me give you an example.

Let's say you've gotten all of your bid prices in and have decided to use numerous subcontractors for your site work. Each contractor has provided you with an itemized bid, and since you are trying to save every dollar you can, you pick through the lists and delegate duties to the various contractors. Your tree-cutters come in and fell the trees. This is the end of their involvement. Your stump-puller comes in and complains that the tree-cutters didn't leave enough tree stump to make the stump-removal process go on in a timely fashion. For this reason, your stump-puller attempts to raise the quoted price. In the meantime, your contractor for the septic system has a septic tank and other materials delivered to the site. These items are in the way of the contractor who is doing your rough grading. A new argument breaks out over this issue. See how quickly this can get out of hand? You will normally be much better off to deal with just one or two contractors for site work.

WHAT CAN I DO?

If you are really into saving money, you may ask yourself what you can do. There are many phases of work in the construction of a home that you may be able to participate in, but site work probably isn't one of them. Unless you own equipment and have experience in using it, your best bet is to stay out of the way. Oh, it's conceivable that you could cut down your own trees, but this work can be very dangerous, and in my opinion, it's not worth the risk. Beyond cutting trees, there really isn't much an average homeowner can do to defray the cost of site work through physical participation. The best you can do is find quality contractors at affordable prices.

PUT THE WHEELS IN MOTION

About all you can do when it comes to site work is to put the wheels in motion. Your main responsibility in this phase is having everything marked and clearly understood by your contractors. For example, you must make sure your tree-cutters know which trees to cut. You can simply spray paint on the trees you wish to have removed. Aside from defining the width and length of your driveway and the area to be cleared for the house, there isn't much else to do. Since this phase of the work doesn't offer much opportunity for you to participate in, let's move to the next chapter and discuss your water and sewer services.

CHAPTER 11

WATER AND SEWER SERVICE

The placement of a well and septic system can influence where a home can be placed on a building lot. Never begin to build before you know where the well and septic system must be installed. If you are building in an area with municipal water and sewer, there may be tap fees to pay, grade elevations to take into consideration, and similar factors that may influence your construction costs. This chapter clears up any confusion you may have about the requirements of getting water and sewer services to your new home.

Water and sewer service is a luxury that most people take for granted in this day and age. It hasn't always been this way, and if you fail to plan properly for your water and sewer service, you may see just how frustrating it can be when attempting to move into a house that is not provided with these utilities. Whether your home will be served by municipal water and sewer or whether you will be installing a well and septic system, you must take some action in order to have the service.

Water and sewer service is something you won't want to be without. Unless you live in an extremely remote area, you won't be allowed to occupy your home until these services are available. Not only are water and sewer services mandatory in most localities, their installation can affect the placement and cost of your home. Failure to plan out these considerations early in your construction can result in big problems.

I've found that many people take time to investigate the placement of their wells and septic systems, but people who will be connecting to municipal utilities are rarely concerned with this. Their sense of security is placed falsely. Even though you may be getting your water from a city water main and tying your sewer into a city sewage system, the placement and elevation of your house may be limited. Unless you don't mind

moving your house after it's built, you had better check into this issue prior to putting in your foundation.

CITY WATER

If city water is available to your new home, you don't have too much to worry about. Where and how you build your home should not be affected by the routing of your water service. There may be, however, a tap fee that is charged to allow you the privilege of connecting to the city water main. This fee can be steep. We're talking thousands of dollars. A tap fee of $1,500 or $2,000 is not at all unusual. Failing to plug this expense into your building budget can call for some quick scrambling for extra cash before your home is finished.

The manner in which various municipalities handle their water taps varies. Some cities will bring a water line onto your property and terminate it at a curb box. Other cities require you to pay for cutting the street and repairing it, as well as making the tap and extending the water line to your home. Obviously, cutting and patching a paved road can get very expensive. Since there is no generic answer as to how your circumstances will turn out, the safest thing for you to do is to talk to your local water authority. Ask how much the connection fees are, and inquire as to what you get for your money. You should investigate this early in the planning stage of your home. Pinpoint your costs and responsibilities before you draft a final building budget.

MUNICIPAL SEWERS

Municipal sewers are available near many building lots. If a sewer is available, you will probably be required to tie into it. Just like water mains, there is usually a tap fee required before service is provided. Also like water lines, sewers may be extended to your property line, or you may have to carry your sewer out into the middle of the street, at your own expense. Check with the official in your city or town.

The same basic precautions that apply to water service also apply to sewers. However, there is an additional concern when it comes to sewers. The most critical question to ask is how deep is the sewer. The depth of the city sewer will influence the elevation of your sewer. If for some reason the sewer in the street is close to the top of the ground, you may run into trouble trying to put your home at some spots on a building lot. Sewers must run downhill, unless pumping stations are used.

Since sewers must be graded downhill and must be covered with a certain amount of dirt, there may be locations on your lot that will not allow you to build with enough height to connect to the sewer. Most locations require a minimum of twelve inches of cover over a sewer when it leaves a house. This means your pipe is a little more than one foot in the ground to begin with. Then the pipe will run with a minimum fall of ⅛-inch per foot. A fall of ¼-inch per foot is preferred. Most sewers don't have to run very far to get from a house to the lateral from the main sewer, but you could have trouble with elevations. There have been times in the past when I've run into very tight situations like this, so it is worth looking into.

A WELL

For those of you who will be building off the beaten path, a well will probably be your source of drinking water. Drilling or digging a well can be a tricky job. A well on one side of the street might be 150 feet deep while a well on the other side of the street might be 400 feet deep. It has been my experience that there is no way to know with any certainty how deep a well will have to be or where water will be found. I've just encountered such a situation at my new house.

When I spoke with my well driller, he estimated a well depth of between 150 and 200 feet for my well. He just finished drilling it yesterday, and the well is 400 feet deep. This is a deep well. Normally, I gamble on wells and elect to pay a per-foot price. In all the times I've done this, I've never lost money. The wells have always cost less than they would have with a fixed price. For some reason, I decided to opt for a fixed-price well with my new house, and am I ever glad I did. If I'd gone with a per-foot price for the well, my installation cost would have been a great deal more than what I'm now paying.

Most well drillers will be happy to provide you with a guaranteed price for drilling your well. The drillers investigate other wells in the area and try to guess at what the depth of your well will be. Once they have an idea of what the cost will be, they factor in a buffer zone of extra money. If you agree to the guaranteed price, that is the price you pay, regardless of how deep the well is. In many cases, like all the previous wells I've ever had drilled and dug, the guaranteed price works out to be higher than the per-foot price. But sometimes, like with my new house, the guaranteed price becomes a blessing. Even though I've always gambled on per-foot prices in the past, I recommend going with a fixed price. If you use the fixed price in your budget, you know you won't run over your anticipated cost. With a per-foot price, you could add hundreds, possibly thousands, of dollars to your construction costs.

Sometimes just striking water isn't enough. In some areas of the country the water that a well produces is unusable because of extreme mineral contaminants. In your agreement with the well driller you should establish what constitutes usable water.

When you install a well, its location is important. Most code officers require wells to be at least 100 feet away from a septic system. On small lots, this can get touchy. Before you put in your foundation or septic system, make sure you have water where you need it. While I've never had a well driller drill a dry hole, it happens. Sometimes there just is no water to be found where you want it. If your septic system is already installed, you could have a very big problem. For this reason, you should have your well installed prior to your septic system, unless you have a large lot and no concerns for running out of room.

DUG WELLS

Dug wells are quite common in the South and rare in the North. When I was building in Virginia, most houses I built had a dug well. In Maine, all the houses I've built have drilled wells. Drilled wells are much more expensive than dug wells, but they are probably worth the extra cost.

Dug wells are relatively shallow, usually less than 30 feet deep, and they have large diameters, usually about three feet. These wells are typically lined with round concrete sleeves or casing as it is normally called. The wells have large diameters to offset their shallow depths. With the big holding area, the well can create a good reserve of water. Even so, this type of well sometimes runs out of water during hot, dry spells.

If you're looking for the least expensive type of well that is feasible for full-time occupancy in a home, a dug well is it. The pump for a shallow well costs less than pumps that are usually used with drilled wells, and the wells themselves can be half the cost of a drilled well. There are, however, a few drawbacks to dug wells that you should weigh.

Dug wells sometimes run out of water. It is not unusual for some dug wells to slowly fill with sediment and become less efficient in later years. The diameter of the well creates a serious danger to children, pets, and adults if the top is removed. Another consideration is the quality of any water produced from the well. Due to a dug well's shallow depth, the water filling the reservoir may not be as pure as water derived from a drilled well. Dug wells are particularly subject to contamination from bacteria. If the ground around your home contains a lot of solid rock, installing a dug well can be very difficult, if not impossible. All

of these factors should be considered before you make a decision on which type of well to use.

DRILLED WELLS

Drilled wells are the best for most homes. These wells tend to be deep, and they can produce a good flow of water even in drought-like conditions. Drilled wells with depths of 125 to 200 feet are common, and some are over 500 feet deep. Unlike a dug well, drilled wells have small diameters, usually only six inches. The pumps most frequently used with drilled wells are submersible pumps. While these pumps are more expensive than the jet pumps commonly used with dug wells, they tend to give better performance, more longevity, and need less repair.

The biggest drawback to a drilled well is its cost. Once you can accept that, drilled wells have many desirable features. The quantity and quality of water with drilled wells is usually far superior to that found with dug wells. It is unusual for a drilled well to fill in with sediment. The small diameter of the well and the bolted-on well cover limit danger for children and adults. It is possible to run a drilled well out of water, but it doesn't happen often. In fact, I've never known of a drilled well that ran dry. I've seen a few dry up due to outside interference, such as blasting rock in the well's vicinity and changing the course of underground water veins, but I've never seen one just run out of water for no apparent reason.

I've owned houses with drilled wells and dug wells. Of the two, I heartily recommend drilled wells. They cost more to install, but I believe they are worth every extra penny. You will, of course, make your own decision on which type of well to use, but consider all aspects before making a firm commitment.

SEPTIC SYSTEMS

Septic systems are used as private sewage disposal facilities when a public sewer is not available. These systems can be simple or complex. They are never cheap, but they can be very expensive, depending on soil conditions and design criteria. If your home will utilize a septic system, you will need a permit for its installation. Before a permit will be issued, the ground around your home must be tested. The test will determine how well your land perks. The percolation rate will influence the size and type of septic system you will be required to install.

There are two main factors that account for the size of a septic system. The first element of the equation is the perk rate. A second factor is the number of bedrooms your home will have in it. The individual designing your septic system will consider both of these factors in sizing your system. Perk tests are generally done by private testing firms or county extension offices. You can check with your local code enforcement office to see who should be contacted to test your land and design your system.

Some septic systems present builders with challenges. For example, my house is situated directly on bedrock. The bedrock runs out from the house site for a considerable distance. Since the rock was only two feet below the ground when we dug our foundation, we knew it would be tricky getting our septic tank installed below grade. By using a low-profile septic tank and some creative placement techniques, we were able to accomplish our goal.

Modern septic tanks are normally made of concrete. A tank for an average house will have a 1,000-gallon capacity. The tank is buried in the ground, somewhere around the house. It is normally required to be at least ten feet from the home's foundation. Just as we talked about grading your sewer for a city connection, the same must be done when connecting to a septic tank. If the tank is placed on a hill or too close to the top of the ground, a pump station may be required. Since pumps are mechanical equipment and mechanical equipment is known to fail, you will do best to avoid a pump station whenever possible. The high cost of pump stations is another good reason to avoid them.

The pipe conveying waste from the septic tank to the septic field should not create many problems, but the field itself can get costly. Some septic fields are built with crushed stone, perforated plastic pipe, and not much else. These simple systems are the least expensive to install. More costly systems use a network of chambers, which may be made of plastic or concrete, to disperse septic waste. A chamber system can get very expensive, costing two to three times what a pipe-and-stone system costs.

Before you can establish your building budget, you must have a septic design drawn. Once you have the layout on paper, contractors can give you quotes for the cost of installation. Since these prices could range from less than $4,000 to over $10,000, you cannot afford to guess at what the figure will be. Request quotes from competent contractors, and get the prices in writing.

When you have your land tested for a septic system, it would be wise to request tests be taken at various locations around the house. While one spot of ground might require an expensive chamber system, another location, perhaps on the other side of the house, might be suitable for a less expensive, stone-and-pipe system. The extra test holes and testing will not cost nearly as much as installing a chamber system when it could be avoided.

ADVANCE PLANNING

Advance planning is your best defense against runaway costs related to water and sewer service. Find out early if you will need a well or septic system. Research the manner in which you will obtain your water and sewer services and their costs. Don't wait until your house is under roof to begin your planning for utilities. By looking ahead and planning carefully, you can save some money and a lot of headaches.

THE SECOND STAGE

PUTTING YOUR HOUSE TOGETHER

Once all the pieces of the machine are in place and scheduled, the excitement begins. From the moment the heavy equipment shows up on your property to the moment the drywall finishers head out the door, you will see rapid and dramatic changes occur. Take plenty of pictures, because it all happens so fast that you'll have a hard time remembering each new phase. Your home will go quickly from a hole in the ground, to a pile of lumber, to a box, to a cavernous, mixed-up-looking barn, to a collection of actual rooms. Before the trim is up and the flooring is down, you will have learned more about houses than you had ever suspected. You will also have learned to do some fancy juggling and orchestrating.

CHAPTER 12

THE FOOTING AND FOUNDATION PHASE

The footing and foundation phase is the first step you take that makes you feel like your house is going to be a physical reality. Many soon-to-be homeowners panic when they see the size of their footings. Footings always make a home's foundation appear much smaller than it actually is. This chapter tells you what is required during the footing and foundation phase and how you can take an active interest to ensure this critical step in your home's construction is done correctly.

The footing and foundation phase of your building project will be exciting. You will thrill at the site of your foundation hole being dug. Seeing the first building block of your dream home going into place will make your heart race with enthusiasm. This is a happy time. However, some aspects of this phase may put you into a mild panic.

I have seldom built a house when the homeowner wasn't concerned about the size of the footings. Footings are the concrete foundation pads or trenches that support the foundation walls of a home. A ribbon of concrete laid out in the expanse of a building lot can be hard to visualize as a house. The common reaction to footings is that they are too small. And I admit, footings do give a visual impression of being smaller than what they really are.

When you see your footings for the first time and feel that they are too small, measure them. They will probably be the right size. As long as the footings are the right size, don't worry about the appearance. It will change quickly as the foundation walls and framing are done.

MATERIALS

Materials for foundation walls generally fall into a narrow range. Wood and cinder blocks are common materials for pier foundations. Cinder blocks and brick are very common foundation materials,

depending on the part of the country you are building in. Concrete is also frequently used. It has been my experience that the materials used for foundation walls are often set by local standards. By standards, I'm not talking about building codes, but rather local preferences.

Almost every house in Maine has foundation walls made of solid concrete. Forms are set up on footings and concrete is poured into the forms, creating solid, eight-inch walls. In Virginia, brick and block were much more common for foundation walls. Concrete was used for some tract housing and for a lot of townhouse projects, but a quality home was determined by its brick-and-block foundation. Personally, I think a brick foundation is much more attractive than a stark, gray concrete wall. It is also more expensive, but probably not as sturdy.

If you are building on a basement, I believe poured concrete walls are better; they are less likely to leak than a cinder-block wall is. For a crawl space, a brick-and-block foundation works fine. If you can't afford the price of brick, you can have your foundation made of cinder blocks and then parge over the block with a mortar mix. The parging can then be painted, giving a swirled stucco look that is attractive. This is the cheapest route for a foundation finish.

In terms of market value, brick will fetch a higher appraisal than block or concrete. When it comes to maintenance, concrete is the winner. Brick foundations sometimes must be pointed up. This means that the mortar joints must be touched up. Parged block foundations have to be painted now and then. Raw cinder blocks are not attractive, so they should not be considered a finished foundation. In a pier foundation, pressure-treated lumber may be your material of choice. If it is, you have a maintenance-free foundation for many years, but a time may come when the posts must be replaced.

If you are unsure of what type of foundation material to use, look around the area where you will be building. What types of materials have been used on the houses in your new neighborhood? This is always a good way to start in making your decision. Another effective way is to consult with a local, licensed real estate appraiser. By talking with an appraiser, you can determine what your return on an investment in your home will be. Do your homework, and the problem should solve itself.

DIGGING AND POURING FOOTINGS

Digging and pouring footings is a job that some handy homeowners-to-be can do themselves, but the task is usually best left to professionals. The footings are the root of your home. If they are not done right, your whole house can suffer. In case you are contemplating the possibility of installing your own footings, let's discuss the work required.

THE TRENCH METHOD

Most of the houses I've built have been built with the footings installed in a manner that I refer to as the trench method. Until I moved to Maine, very few of the homes I built had basements. They were typically built over a crawl space. For this type of construction, I used to dig trenches to hold the concrete footings.

Footings must be installed in the ground at a depth that is below the local frost line. In Virginia, that depth was eighteen inches, in Maine, the depth is four feet. To install footings, a backhoe is normally used to dig the trenches, although I've

seen hearty souls digging them with a pick and shovel. The frost line determines the depth of the footing. You can establish your local frost line by consulting a code enforcement officer.

The width of a footing is dictated by the width of your foundation wall. A footing should be somewhat wider than the foundation wall will be. There will be some local code requirement for the exact overage on a footing, so check this out with your local building inspector. As an example, if you were going to install a foundation wall that had a thickness of eight inches, your footing would probably be about twelve inches wide. The depth of the concrete used to create a footing is also determined by local code requirements.

Once your trenches are dug and cleaned out so that there is no loose dirt lying around, the trench should be inspected by a building inspector. If you are building a house with government financing, you may also have to have a representative of the lender inspect the footing trench. Once the inspections are approved, you can pour your concrete. The trench acts as your concrete form, and the finish on the concrete doesn't have to be trowled smooth. Grade stakes, pieces of wood or metal, will be stuck into the ground in the trenches to allow you a reference point for how deep the concrete should be. When the wet concrete reaches the top of your grade stakes, you know it is at the proper depth.

While the finish of a footing doesn't have to be smooth, the footings should be level. This can be accomplished with a string and a string level, a transit, or in a pinch, a long board and a level. If the footing is not level, adjustments will have to be made when the foundation walls are installed.

As far as saving money is concerned, there aren't many ways to do this with footings. You could dig the trenches by hand, but it wouldn't be worth it to me to do this. You can't skimp on the quality or quantity of your concrete. It is feasible to shop for the best concrete prices in town, and you can negotiate hard with any subcontractors who will be involved in the process. Beyond this short list, there isn't much else you can do.

WHAT KIND OF FOUNDATION?

Your options in this matter may be many or they may be limited to just a couple. Topography, soil composition, ground water, weather, and local conventions are as important to consider as personal preference. Let's look at the possibilities.

The foundation walls of your home might be made of solid concrete or block and brick. If you're building a weekend retreat, you might not have any foundation walls at all. Pier footings and foundations are common on seasonal cottages. Most of the homes I built in Virginia, with the exception of townhouses, had foundations made of block and brick. In Maine, all of the houses tend to have solid concrete foundations, like the ones I used for townhouse projects in the South.

It is possible to build year-round homes on pier foundations, but it is seldom done, especially in areas where freezing temperatures are common in winter. However, let's discuss this type of foundation along with more conventional methods.

PIER FOUNDATIONS

Pier foundations are the least expensive type of foundation you can choose. The footings consist of several concrete pads that will accept the foundation piers. These pads can be square, round, or rectangular. They are installed below the frost line by digging holes and filling them to a certain point with concrete. Since less concrete is normally used with a pier foundation, the cost is less.

Foundation piers can be made of cinder block, concrete, or wood. If concrete is used, a form must be made to hold the concrete until it sets up. Cardboard-like tubes are normally used for this purpose. Wooden support posts are the least expensive way to construct a pier foundation. Posts that have been pressure treated to withstand moisture and insect infestation are the material most frequently selected for wooden piers. The dimensions of the posts depend on the engineering of the house, but post sizes of 6″ × 6″ are a common choice. If you are handy, you can build your own pier foundation, from footings to posts.

While a pier foundation is attractive in its cost, it is not so pleasing to the eye. Aside from leaving a lot to be desired visually, there are some significant disadvantages to a pier foundation from a practical point of view, especially if you live in a climate that experiences cold temperatures.

Pier foundations do nothing to block wind and cold temperatures. Even if the underside of your home is well insulated and sealed with some type of insulation board or plywood, the floors of your home may get very cold in winter. Plumbing pipes can freeze, due to their lack of protection. Not having a crawl space or a basement can make it hard to install mechanical equipment, like heating and air-conditioning equipment. All in all, pier foundations give you a cost advantage and several possible disadvantages. Do the disadvantages outweigh the advantage of a lower cost? Not necessarily.

A pier foundation in an elite subdivision would not go well. In fact, covenants and restrictions in the deeds of the building lots would probably prohibit them. On the other hand, if you're building a rustic home in the country, especially if the house is being built on the side of a hill, it might be an ideal time to opt for a pier foundation. Mechanical equipment can be placed in closets and storage areas, plumbing can be boxed in, and pipes can be protected with heavy insulation, boxed chases, heat tapes, and other means of frost prevention. You have to gauge the pros and cons for yourself. I've almost built a few houses for myself on pier foundations, but I never have. At the last minute, I've always decided on a closed-in foundation.

CRAWL SPACES VERSUS BASEMENTS

When you are ready to build, you may be faced with the question of crawl spaces versus basements. Much of this issue will be decided, by where you are building. For example, very few homes in Virginia have basements, and almost every home in Maine has a basement. While building a house with a basement in an area where crawl spaces are dominant wouldn't be a problem, building a house without a basement in a region where basements are standard features could be.

I broke the rules with my own new home. Personally, I don't care for basements. In my opinion, they are a waste of investment dollars. Most homeowners in Maine don't agree with me, and this means that if I ever decide to sell my home I may have to pay for my preference because of the limited pool of local buyers willing to accept a basementless house. Appraisers back up my personal opinion in terms of retail value. If you spend $10,000 for a basement, it's worth $10,000. Spending the same $10,000 for a fourth bedroom or some additional kitchen and bath features could transform the ten grand into $15,000. I like to build equity and see a return on my investment, and that's hard to do with a basement. I will admit that from a resale point of view I might lose some prospective buyers by not having a basement. But, I believe that investing the money into a more attractive, desirable, above-ground living space was a wiser move to make.

Crawl spaces are much less expensive than basements. If you are building on a tight budget, a crawl space is your best overall choice. Most building codes require a minimum of eighteen inches of distance between untreated wood and raw earth. This means that crawl spaces, depending on the depth of your local frost line, can have very short foundation walls. This, of course, reduces your building costs. There are, however, some trade-offs in choosing a crawl space over a basement.

Basements, if they don't leak, provide good storage space, and they can give you inexpensive living space. If you can build a daylight or walk-out basement, the money you invest will not be spent foolishly. Taking a buried basement (one with no full-size windows) and converting it to finished living space is more than likely going to result in lost money. Public opinion and local building practices have a lot of influence in the decision of whether to build on a basement or a crawl space. Cost is another factor. Basements cost about twice as much, or more, than crawl spaces. To put all of these cost factors into an understandable format, let's look at them individually.

BURIED BASEMENTS

Buried basements are the least expensive basements to build; they are also of the least value when it comes time to reap the rewards of your building effort. What can you do with a buried basement? You can put your laundry facilities down there, but then you are going to have to lug laundry up and down steps. A buried basement provides plenty of space for mechanical equipment, and this is a desirable feature. Storage is another feature a buried basement brings. However, if the items being stored require frequent movement in and out of the basement, the process can become tiring. As an example, I've used basement storage in the past for my various contracting businesses, most specifically plumbing business. It is a real pain toting plumbing parts up and down the basement steps. I would much prefer to have outside storage that I can drive right up to and load and unload without climbing stairs.

Many people decide at some point to finish off part of their buried basement, to use as living space. This is a job a lot of people can do themselves, but the money invested is difficult to recover. Whether you finish an office, a play room, or any other type of room, most appraisers will not value the space for as much as you spend to have it converted. Putting bedrooms in a buried basement is almost never legal, since there are no full-size windows for a means of egress. Unless you have an outside entrance that can be considered an emergency escape, bedrooms are out of the question, unless you are willing to go against code requirements, and I do not recommend this.

DAYLIGHT BASEMENTS

Daylight basements are basements where full-size windows can be installed. This type of underground living space is more viable than that created from a buried basement. With full-size, egress windows, you can have bedrooms in your basement legally. Ventilation is another big advantage with a daylight basement. Buried basements typically receive very little cross ventilation, and can become damp and musty. Daylight basements, on the other hand, have regular windows that can be used to avoid mold and mildew.

Real estate appraisers look much more favorably on daylight basements than they do on buried basements. Building lots that offer topography for daylight basements often lend themselves to split-foyer homes and split-level homes. With either of these designs, you can maximize your appraised value.

WALK-OUT BASEMENTS

Walk-out basements are usually quite desirable. Not only does this type of basement appraise well, it offers a lot of potential. Walk-out basements are found under homes on sloping lots. Their big feature is the fact that full-size doors can be employed for access. This makes the basement very user-friendly for storage or living space. It is not uncommon to find in-law quarters or teenager space built into walk-out basements. Some people even put their home offices in walk-out basements.

If you have a steep lot, a walk-out basement should be a safe investment. The living space will not cost as much per square foot as your upstairs living space, because you need a foundation in any case. Combining your foundation with extended living space is a cost-effective way to get the most out of your home and building lot.

SLAB FOUNDATIONS

Slab foundations—foundations consisting of a footing and a concrete floor—are uncommon in some areas and popular in others. Slab foundations are very cost-effective. There are, however, many drawbacks to this type of floor system. For example, there is no way to access plumbing and other mechanical systems that are installed in a concrete slab, unless the concrete floor is broken up. If problems with one of the mechanical systems arise, gaining access to make repairs can be very expensive. Let's take a close look at both the good and bad points of slab foundations.

The Good

The good news about a concrete slab is the initial cost. Slab foundations provide a foundation and a floor in an inexpensive package, assuming that topographical limitations don't create problems. Footings are required for all quality foundations. In most cases, footings are trenches in the ground that are installed below the local frost line. One

exception is the pier foundation. When piers are used, holes are dug in the ground to a point below the frost line. With other types of foundations, such as crawl spaces and basements, the footings are dug into the ground as trenches and filled with concrete. If you assume that you will be digging trench-type footings, there is no less expensive way to go than a slab foundation.

The footings for a slab foundation are installed with the same procedures used for a basement or crawl space. Since the cost of the footings are the same for any one of the three types of foundations, it is easy to see why a concrete slab is the least expensive. After footings are installed for a crawl space or basement, foundation walls must be built, then a wood floor system must be installed. When a slab is used, the foundation walls are eliminated—or at least greatly reduced—and the concrete slab serves as a subfloor, doing away with the need for a flooring system made of wood. The time and materials saved with this procedure can be substantial.

Most slab foundations are done with a monolithic pour. This means that the concrete for the footings and the floor are poured at the same time and that the floor becomes an integral part of the footing. Another form of slab foundation is the floating slab. Short foundation walls are built on top of the poured footings and the concrete floor is poured within the foundation walls. In my opinion, a monolithic pour is the best way to go, and it is cheaper. The advantages of a slab include a low cost for installation, a rapid rate of completion, and a solid subfloor that will not squeak in later years.

The Bad

One of the biggest problems encountered when building a house on a slab is the inability to have access to mechanical systems. This problem surfaces when the systems are being installed, and can really fester if problems arise with the operation of the systems after the home is completed. Many homes are built with crawl-space foundations that allow room for electrical wiring, plumbing, heating and air-conditioning equipment to be installed beneath the house. This is also true of houses with basements. Slab homes, however, don't offer this potential. Pipes, wires, and ducts become surrounded by concrete after they are installed. Heat pumps, furnaces, water heaters, and other equipment must be installed in a mechanical room or closet, using up valuable living space.

Installing siding on a home with a slab foundation can be difficult. Exterior siding should not be installed too close to ground level. Moisture from the ground can cause the siding to rot or its paint to peel. Most building codes have set requirements that mandate the siding not be installed within a certain number of inches of the ground. With a slab house there may not be any foundation wall, and this means the siding is going to be installed too close to the ground.

If you got cold feet about taking the plunge into home ownership, you may be sad to discover how cold your feet really are on a slab foundation—especially in rooms with vinyl flooring. Concrete is not known for its warmth, and a slab floor can be very cold.

Cracking and leaking can become problems with slabs that are not installed properly. If a slab is not protected from frost, the ground beneath the concrete can heave up and crack it. Water infiltration can follow, causing mold, mildew, odors and damage to your finish flooring.

Can you install your own slab foundation? It is very possible that you could dig your own footings and pour your own slab, but the work is hard on your back. The most difficult part of the job is keeping the concrete level and smooth. This is a job that many people can do, but that few should attempt.

DRAINAGE (PRECAUTIONS)

There are some precautions you should take when installing a walk-out basement, and these same precautions can apply to other types of basements. Many basements are haunted by water problems. If the basement is unfinished, rising water can be a nuisance. When your basement is finished, rising water can be a disaster. With this in mind, you should take some steps to avoid water problems in your basement.

The most effective way to protect your underground space from water is to use perimeter drains. To do this job right, you will want drains on the outside of your foundation and on the inside. The ideal basement will also have provisions for accepting a sump pump.

An outside perimeter drain is normally made with crushed stone and perforated pipe. A layer of stone is installed in a trench that surrounds the foundation, at the footing level. Perforated pipe is laid on top of the stone. Choose a pipe that is equipped with a fiber filter. Without this filter, the holes of the pipe can become clogged with dirt or other sediment, rendering them useless. The outside drain will be installed so that gravity will drain the pipe into a location where excess water will not affect the home. Once the pipe is in place, a layer of stone should be installed on top of it. This stone helps prevent sediment blockages.

Inside perimeter drains are installed with the same basic materials and procedures used for outside drains. There is, however, one key difference. Inside drains, which are installed beneath the concrete floor of a basement, are run to a central discharge point. This point is a location where a sump pump can be installed if ground water becomes a problem. A plastic sump is set in place, along with the drainage pipe, prior to the floor being poured. If water collects in the sump, a pump can be installed to evacuate the unwanted water. Almost anyone can install perimeter drains and sumps.

WATERPROOFING

All basement walls should receive coatings of waterproofing. Here is another part of your job where you can get your hands dirty, not to mention your clothes. The waterproofing material used for basements is normally black, and it comes in buckets. The application process can be done with a paint roller, a paintbrush, or even a broom. This is messy work, but it should be done, and you can do it yourself.

When you build your house on a crawl-space foundation, there isn't a lot of room for people in the mechanical trades to work. Plumbers, electricians, and HVAC mechanics will have to spend a lot more time in their rough-in stages, due to the slower working conditions. This will drive up the costs of your mechanical systems. There will also be a need to insulate the floor of your home. This is an expense that is not required with a basement. You might still need perimeter drains to avoid water build-ups under your house, and you will definitely need a moisture barrier (sheets of plastic) installed over 80 percent of the exposed ground under your home. You may or may not be able to install your mechanical equipment, such as a water heater and furnace, in your crawl space. If you can't, additional living space will be surrendered to provide a home for the equipment.

Aside from the cost factors dividing basements from crawl spaces, there is also the issue of storage. Most families require a good deal of storage. Basements can provide a lot of storage. Crawl spaces don't give much room for storage, and the damp conditions are not ideal. Without a basement, you must look to outside sheds, attic storage, or possibly an over-sized garage. In any case, you should keep the issue of storage in mind.

INSULATING YOUR BASEMENT

Insulating your basement walls is a good idea, especially if you plan to use the subterranean space for anything beyond storage. This is normally done with rigid boards of foam insulation. The insulation can be installed on the inside walls, the outside walls, or both. Putting insulation boards on the outside walls of your foundation before backfilling will give you a considerable edge when the heating season rolls around. This is a job you can do yourself.

WHAT SHOULD YOU DO?

What should you do for a foundation? Well, the choice is mostly a personal one. My new house is built on a crawl space. Crawl spaces are very common in many parts of the country. If you're tight on money, a crawl space is the most feasible type of foundation to go with. Pier foundations are cheaper, but their use is more limited, due to building restrictions and climates. Basements are nice, but I'm not sure they are worth their cost. In an unfinished condition, you shouldn't lose any money on a basement, but it is doubtful that you will make any either. Basements do, however, give you an edge in resale value and market demand.

Much of your decision on what type of foundation to choose may be based on your building lot. In my case, the lot I chose to build on has bedrock about two feet below ground level. I wasn't keen on a basement to begin with, but the rock made my decision for me. If your land drops off quickly, it would probably be foolish not to build your home on a walk-out basement. A sloping lot can practically demand a daylight basement. The choice is yours, but you should pay attention to your building costs, your appraised value, and local customs. All of these issues can influence the type of foundation.

CHAPTER 13

FRAMING THE SHELL AND INTERIOR PARTITIONS

> *The framing phase is fun. This is when you start to see the house take shape. It is also a time when many people decide to make on-site changes to their plans. Making changes at this time is okay, as long as you make them at the appropriate time. This chapter walks you—one step at a time—through the framing of your new home.*

When your subcontractors begin framing the shell and interior partitions of your new home, you will most likely become ecstatic. Watching the body of your house take shape is an experience you will never forget. I must warn you, the framing phase can become addictive; you may never want to leave the job site. Watching walls go up and ridge poles or trusses being set is a peaceful way to spend a day. You have an opportunity to see all of your hard work with administrative duties pay off.

As much fun as the framing stage is, it is also a pivotal point in your building process. This is when you can see enough of your plans to know if the house is what you want. If it is not, you can act quickly and make some changes in the interior layout. If the changes are not of a structural nature, you won't incur a lot of costs or lost time.

WHAT CAN I DO?

What can I do? Unless you are a skilled carpenter, there isn't a lot that you can do with the framing. There are, however, some odd jobs that you can do to participate. Let's walk through the framing of a standard house and see where you might be able to save some money. Before we start with the hands-on stuff, let's cover some potential problems that may arise with your subcontractors when you decide to get in on the framing act.

SUBCONTRACTORS

Subcontractors prefer to take on a job where they are responsible for doing all of the work. Whenever a professional has to work in a hands-on capacity with a homeowner or other unknown partner, the risk of problems increases. Don't feel bad. It is not just homeowners who the pros don't want to share work with. Let me explain.

The carpenters who are building my house have a lot of experience in many phases of construction. Unlike my building practices in Virginia, where every subcontractor specialized in a specific phase of work, tradespeople in Maine tend to do many types of work. It's practically the only way they can stay busy. Anyway, my carpenters are also my roofers, my siding contractors, my painters, my cabinet installers, my trim carpenters, and my drywall hangers.

The carpenters are competent to finish the drywall, but they don't want to do the taping and sanding. They are not fast enough to be competitive with crews who do nothing but drywall work. While they can keep up with the specialized crews in the hanging stage, they can't run the same race in the finishing phase. Because of this, I have had to find subcontractors who are willing to come in behind my hangers to do the finish work on the drywall. This task has, at times, been troublesome.

AN EXAMPLE

My most recent building job is my own house. The house has a lot of angles, high ceilings, and difficult aspects when it comes to drywall work. To give you an example, the ceiling in my living room and master bedroom is nearly thirty feet above the floor. When you consider that an average ceiling is about eight feet tall, mine is nearly four times higher than average. Obviously, working at such heights slows down the process. The many angles in the house are also a potential for problems. When I sought drywall finishers, I found several who were happy to bid the whole job, but few of the contractors were willing to come in behind my hangers. The finishers didn't want to offer any guarantee on their work, because if the hangers didn't do a good job, it would be hard to determine if the problem was the fault of the hangers or the finishers. Anyway, I did get some quality finishers to come in behind my hangers. The point is, I had to sort through several drywall contractors to find a couple who would do the job the way I wanted it done. If this is a problem for me, a professional contractor, you can imagine how frustrating it might be for you.

In my house, the subs were reluctant to come in behind professional contractors. If I were an average person who was hanging the drywall in my home, it might have been next to impossible to find good finishers who would do the taping and sanding for a reasonable price. I've faced this type of problem many times in the past, and sometimes I've been the subcontractor who didn't want to do half of the job. If I'm going to be held responsible for work being done, I want to be in total control of it. I tell you this so that you will not be shocked if you want to do some of your own work in a specific phase and find it difficult to connect with cooperative contractors to pick up where you leave off.

SPECIALISTS

If you are building in an area where demand for trades is high, you will have the opportunity to work with specialists. When building in Virginia, I had over 100 subcontractors and vendors. In Maine, I can get by with less than 20. Why is this?

If you remember our discussion about my carpenters, you will recall that these people do a lot more than just one form of carpentry. In rural areas it is not uncommon to find plumbers who do heating or even electrical work, and carpenters do everything that involves the extensive use of hammers. In progressive building markets, specialists prevail. Plumbers don't do anything but plumbing, and many of them break plumbing down into specialized areas, such as drain cleaning, remodeling, service work, new homes, and commercial work. The same is true for other trades. Carpenters specialize in framing, siding, and trim work. Roofing is done by roofers, not carpenters. This type of competitive marketplace can give you some cost advantages. If you hire a carpenter to do everything, you can't expect all aspects of the work to go as quickly or as inexpensively as it might with the use of multiple specialists.

Now, let's get on with our step-by-step look at the framing process.

THE FRAMING PROCESS
SILL PLATES

The sill plates are the first step in the framing process. Sills are the boards that are installed flat on the top of a foundation wall. Most good contractors use pressure-treated wood for sills. This type of wood discourages damage from insects and moisture. There is usually a foam gasket that is installed between the bottom of the sill and the top of the foundation. If you can find a framing contractor who will let you participate in the framing of your home, you can install your own sills. However, if you do not have a lot of experience, be prepared for an uncomfortable moment when you bring this issue up with the framer.

The sill may look like a simple element, but to the framer it is the most basic step in his job. Can you deal with warped boards, drill for anchor bolts, control overhang and joint matching, walk an 8"-wide path with an 8' drop on either side? If you have any doubts about these things, then let your framer do the work. If you have a burning desire to saw and hammer and be part of the crew, offer your labor to the subcontractor as an apprentice, then be willing to learn. I don't want to encourage you to get into the middle of your own framing, unless you have some carpentry experience. If you don't know what you're doing, you can create extra work for your carpenters and waste expensive wood. However, I know some of you will want to do as much of your work as possible. On a scale of one to ten, installing your own sill plates is a two, and from our previous discussion of sill-installing tasks, you can probably imagine how difficult some of the other parts of framing might be.

THE GIRDER

The support girder for your home is another part of the framing phase that you can probably manage. The girder is normally two or three 2×10s, 2×12s, or 2×14s nailed together. The girder sits on piers that are spaced along the middle of your foundation. Aside from making the girder the proper size, you must be careful to get the girder set at the right height. Check your blueprints and don't allow the girder to get too low or too high.

FLOOR JOISTS

Floor joists are your next adventure. If you've done your own sills and girder, you can probably cut and install your own joists. If you have a detailed set of professionally drawn blueprints, there will be a page dedicated to floor joists. The page will show you what size joists to use and where to put them. Your joists will sit on top of your sill plates and girder. In most cases, houses are wide enough to have joists reaching from the two outside walls to a central location on the girder. The joists are nailed to the girder and sill plate. They are also nailed to each other where they meet at the girder. If your house is less than twenty-four feet wide, you can get by with a long joist that spans the house with the girder providing a center support. The tailends of your joists, where they sit on the sills, will be nailed into a band board. The band board is a board with the same dimensions of your joists. It sits on its edge, on the sill plate, and runs all the way around the floor structure. The ends of your joists will butt into the wide part of the band board and be nailed to it.

Installing your own floor joists is not a difficult job, in terms of technical abilities, but it can be a laborious job. It certainly helps to have an extra set of hands available when taking on this task. Basic carpentry skills are all that are needed, but allow yourself plenty of time, and expect to sweat. If you are building a two-story house, the joists for the second floor can't be installed until the partition walls are in, and this may be a job you should leave to professionals.

SUBFLOORING

Subflooring is a job that anyone who is comfortable with a saw, a hammer, and a tape measure can take on. Subflooring is the first layer of plywood or particle board that is installed over floor joists. The sheets of subflooring may be butted together or you can use tongue-and-groove (T&G) material. If you butt the wood together, you will have to install a second layer of subflooring before you are done. When T&G material is used, there is no requirement for a second layer. T&G subfloors are usually made with ¾" material.

T&G subfloors, where only one layer is used, are normally less expensive than butted subflooring. However, fitting T&G material together can require the use of a sledgehammer and a good deal more work than butted joints. You will have to weigh the differences in your labor and the cost of materials. If you're hiring the work out, you should see a lower price by going with a ¾" T&G subfloor. You will still want an underlayment (second layer) in the kitchen and bathrooms, where vinyl or tile is the finished flooring being installed. Whether you do your own subflooring or sub it out, make sure it is nailed down frequently and well. Floors that don't get nailed down properly are going to give and squeak. I should add that if you decide to use two layers of subflooring, the second layer should be installed perpendicular to the first.

OUTSIDE WALLS AND INTERIOR PARTITIONS

Outside walls and interior partitions can be done by hardy homeowners, but the skills needed to build these walls properly may elude some do-it-yourselfers. Unless you have framing experience, you should probably hire professionals to frame your walls. There is not enough space in this book for me to tell you all the intricacies of framing walls, but let me tell you that the job is not as easy as carpenters make it look. If you set your mind and study framing procedures, you can do your own walls, but this is not a job to be taken lightly.

OUTSIDE WALLS

Due to the cold climate in Maine, outside walls are typically framed with 2×6 studs, rather than the more common 2×4 studs. Since the state has cold, make that very cold, winter temperatures, wider wall cavities with more insulation makes plenty of sense. Spending some extra money on studs and insulation in the construction stage can save much more in heating costs.

EXTERIOR SHEATHING

The exterior sheathing used on walls in Maine is typically plywood. It is common practice to cover all the exterior walls with plywood. This was a big difference from anything I've been used to. In all other areas I have worked, plywood was only used on the corners of outside walls. A fiberboard material was used for the remaining sheathing. In many houses, corner braces were used and no plywood was needed on the corners. Since plywood costs more than twice what fiber-type sheathing does, it doesn't take long to run up the cost of a house when plywood or particle board is used for wall sheathing.

THE ROOF STRUCTURE

The roof structure is not a complicated matter on paper, but it can be a tough job in the field. If you build your roof structure with rafters, you will need a ridge pole. Getting a ridge pole into place requires some skill, some athletic ability, and a lot of nerve. If you're afraid of heights, this is no job for you. Blueprints that are detailed extensively will show you what must be done to build a roof, but doing the job is more than most amateurs should attempt.

Trusses are an alternative to rafters. A lot of framing crews pull trusses up and set them by hand. Other crews hire a crane to set the trusses in place. In either case, the balancing act required to set trusses, and keep them from falling, is more than a casual carpenter should attempt. If I were you, I wouldn't even consider building my own roof.

Once the rafters or trusses are in place, roof sheathing must be nailed into place. Again, the job is not for the faint of heart. It can be a long and dangerous fall from the top of a house to the ground below. I recommend that you sub this part of your job to some insured professional.

WINDOWS AND DOORS

Windows and doors are a part of the framing process. Unless you are building your own exterior walls, I don't believe you should install your own windows and doors. The installation of these items is dependent on the rough openings framed for them. In my opinion, whoever frames the rough openings should install the window and door units.

To sum up what we've covered, most handy homeowners can do their own framing up through the subflooring phase. Beyond that, professional help should probably be engaged. Everyone's abilities are a little different, and you may be able to frame your own walls. You may even be able to complete your whole shell. If you assess your skills, you will develop a good feel for how far you should go.

LOCAL CUSTOMS

The biggest unexplained mystery I have encountered in Maine is the use of strapping. Strapping is basically a furring strip that Maine carpenters install on ceiling joists and rafters. To me, this is a big waste of money. The cost of installing strapping in a house can easily exceed $800 in labor and material. I cannot understand the need for strapping, and I've done a lot of research to find a viable reason for it.

There is no requirement for strapping in any building code that I know of, and I know most of the codes. There is no code requirement for it in Maine. I've asked carpenters why they use strapping, and I've never gotten a good answer. Most people simply tell me that they have always done it. After interviewing appraisers, code officers, carpenters, and other builders, no one has been able to give me a valid reason for the strapping. If no one knows why they install strapping, why would anyone pay $800 for something that is not needed? This a good example of unusual building practices increasing the cost of your home.

On the other hand, roofing felt was used on every house I can ever remember working on until I moved to Maine. Felt roofing paper is sometimes used in Maine, but the occasions are rare. Most Maine builders install roof shingles on the roof sheathing directly. I've been told by other local builders that the felt deteriorates shingles. This is difficult for me to believe, especially since most shingle manufacturers not only recommend roofing paper, they won't warranty their shingles if felt is not used.

MATERIAL

Framing material is a big part of your overall building expense. Not only will you be concerned with board-for-board prices, you must decide on windows, doors, and building procedures. The procedures can account for a lot of money. It might seem that building is building, but that simply is not true. I found this out in a big way when I moved to Maine.

I've worked in Colorado, South Carolina, West Virginia, Maryland, Washington D.C., Virginia, and Maine. Most of my time has been spent in Virginia and Maine. When I moved to Maine, I found a lot of things to be very different than they were in any other place I've ever lived. Many of the differences were business related. In the building business, procedures in construction have proved to be very different from any I've ever witnessed. Most of the differences in Maine wind up costing home buyers more money. Are the changes in construction mechanics needed? Are they justified? Some may be, but some aren't. Let me expand on this.

CHOOSING MATERIALS

Choosing materials for your framing can make some difference in your overall building costs. Obviously, building 2×6 outside walls with extra insulation will cost more than 2×4 walls. Even though the initial cost is more, the expense may be justified in the money saved by having a more energy-efficient home. Other types of material upgrades are not as worthwhile.

Sheathing for exterior walls is a good example of a way to spend a lot more money than you have to. Particle board costs more than fiberboard, and plywood costs more than particle board. Any of these materials will serve the purpose of wall sheathing. I don't doubt that plywood will make a stronger wall than fiberboard, but is it necessary or worth the extra cost? I don't think so.

Some people will want to overbuild, but a lot of people are only concerned with having quality construction at an affordable price. This has always been my preference. When you plan your home and shop for materials, you will have to make some of these types of decisions. I don't suggest that you cut corners that will lead to problems down the road, but I'm sure you can trim some fat from your building budget with enough thought and shopping.

SAVING MONEY

When it comes to professional labor, about the only thing you can do to save money is shop around and negotiate. Shopping and negotiating are two simple words, but doing either of them can get complicated. One of the first decisions you must make is whether to hire one company to do all of your framing or do some of the work yourself. You should have enough information by now to decide if you will be doing any of your own framing. After making this decision, you are left with finding the best subs at the best price. This requires a lot of administrative time. You must check references, prices, personalities, and other elements that we talked about in earlier chapters.

CHAPTER 14

FIREPLACES AND STOVE FLUES

Many homes are built to accommodate fireplaces and stove flues. If you are planning either of these options for your home, read this chapter before you contract the masons. Not only will this chapter show you how fireplaces and flues are installed, you will discover the many options available to you.

I t is not unusual for homes to be equipped with fireplaces and stove flues. If you are planning either of these items for your home, there is some advance planning that may be needed. For instance, if you're going to install a masonry fireplace, you are going to need a footing, pad, or reinforced location to install it. With either a fireplace or a flue, you must look ahead to where the chimney will penetrate your roof or how it will run up the side of your home. You will also have to consider the various materials that these improvements can be made with.

IS A FIREPLACE A GOOD INVESTMENT?

Is a fireplace a good investment? From my experience, I'd say that it is. According to appraisers who I've consulted with, masonry fireplaces will almost always return their cost in appraised value. Prefabricated, metal fireplaces are not such safe bets, but even they can do well on an appraisal and at the time a house is sold.

Costs vary across the country for building materials and trades, but you can pretty much count on spending several thousand dollars for a masonry fireplace. Of course, if you are building a two-story home, the cost will be more than if you are building a house with just one level of living space. The taller the house, the taller the chimney and the steeper the cost.

If you are thinking of a fireplace for supplemental heat, it is hard to justify the expense. Open fireplaces simply are not efficient in terms of heating. If the fireplace is large enough to accept an insert-type stove, you can gain a lot of secondary heating potential, but you loose the romantic, peaceful aspect of an open fire. Why build a fireplace just to put a stove in it when you could build a flue for a lot less and still have the benefits of a wood stove?

I love fireplaces. I like the smell of wood smoke, and I enjoy being mesmerized by the flickering flames. My daughter, Afton, likes to play a game we call imagination whenever we build a fire in the fireplace. This is when the whole family gathers around the fire and imagines all sorts of images being made in the flames. Sometimes we see little animals, sometimes it's a fairy, and sometimes it's just a wave of relaxation. In any event, we enjoy our open fire immensely.

As much as my entire family loves to watch a fire in the fireplace, we chose not to install a fireplace in our new home. This was a difficult decision, but one that we made based on financial options. A masonry fireplace would have cost us over $3,500, probably closer to $4,000. Given our budget, we weighed the cost of the fireplace against other options available to us. For example, we could buy a whirlpool tub for less than $700. Since both the fireplace and the whirlpool were desires, rather than needs, we could compare their value equally. Both investments will be returned on the appraisal, and both are objects we could enjoy. In the long run, we opted for the whirlpool and some extra living space. We used the same amount of money we would have for a fireplace, but we got benefits that we could use year-round. If money was of no concern, I would have put a fireplace in the master bedroom, the living room, and in my office. However, money is a factor so I'm doing without a fireplace. I may, however, add a wood stove with glass doors at a later date.

FIREPLACE OPTIONS

When you begin to look at fireplace options, you will discover several. Many of these options will affect the cost of the fireplace. For example, it is less expensive to place your chimney on an inside wall than it is to run it up on the outside of your home, assuming that you want brick in all locations that are exposed to view. Let's take a little time to do some comparisons of the options available to you.

OUTSIDE CHIMNEYS

An outside chimney is typically more expensive to construct than a chimney installed within the house. The reason for this is the extra expense of covering the rough chimney with a nice finish, such as brick or stone. If you are going to have an outside chimney built, do it before you do the siding on your home. It is much easier to get a nice looking job when you can butt siding to the chimney than it is to cut the chimney into the siding. Outside chimneys should be set on a concrete pad and footing. Otherwise, frost in the ground can shift the masonry work and cause problems with the chimney pulling away from the house.

Not all chimneys are made of block, brick, or stone. Many chimneys are made of metal pipe. This pipe is usually made with two or three layers, basically like a chimney within a chimney. This design allows the pipe to be placed closer to combustible materials. If you are running a metal chimney, you can leave the metal exposed, or you can enclose it in framing that will be covered with siding. This is the more attractive way to do it.

Under these conditions, you want to get your framing done while your framing crew is on the job, and you want to get your pipe installed before the siding contractors finish their work.

When metal chimneys are installed on the outside of homes, they are usually attached to the homes with special mounting brackets and hardware. Most stove shops sell insulated chimney pipe, also known as double-wall, triple-wall, or multi-wall pipe. This pipe is expensive, but it's a lot cheaper than masonry work, and you can install it yourself. The metal pipe is normally only used for prefab, metal fireplaces.

INSIDE CHIMNEYS

Inside chimneys are less expensive than outside chimneys. When an inside chimney is to be installed, your framing contractor must make arrangements for it. In the case of a metal chimney, this involves only framing a chase for the pipe. When a full masonry chimney is going to be installed, the framing work can get more involved. If your house is going to have an inside chimney, talk it over with your carpenters and your masons.

CINDERBLOCK

Cinderblock is the material most often used in the construction of unseen chimneys, such as those located in interior walls. There is, of course, mortar, flue liners, and other odds and ends, but cinderblock is what makes up the outside of the chimney. Most people don't want a cinderblock chimney running up the side of their home or sticking out of the top of their roof. It is common practice to cover the cinderblock with a more attractive finish when it is visible.

BRICK

Brick is the most common material used for hearths and exposed chimneys. Brick is not cheap, but it is attractive. While the brick plays no significant role in the operation of a chimney, it is a desirable finish. Brick, however, is not the only choice you have.

STONE AND OTHER OPTIONS

Stone is sometimes used for hearths and chimneys. A stone fireplace, in a rustic home, is a delight. In addition, slate, flagstone, and other types of finishes can be used in your fireplace and chimney. You must shop around and decide what you like. I will say this, brick is the most common material used, and it is well accepted. If you get too crazy in your choice of materials, you may damage the appraised or resale value of your home. It is usually best to stick with materials that are used in other houses around the neighborhood.

WOOD STOVES

Wood stoves have been extremely popular in the past, and they are still in demand, although the demand seems to have weakened with the energy crisis waning. Nevertheless, people still look for a flue for their wood stove when buying a house. Should you install a flue in your home? Well, the answer to this question depends on you, your family circumstances, and your feelings about burning wood. I wouldn't install a flue just for resale value, but appraisers have told me that the cost of a good flue will be returned on an appraisal work-up. Unless you plan to install a wood stove, there is not much cause for installing a flue. However, if you will be using an oil-burning heating system, such as a boiler, you will need some type of flue or venting system. So, even if you are not going with a wood stove, you might want a flue for your heating system.

The principles that apply to the chimneys of fireplaces are mirrored when you look at wood stoves. There are no great differences, except that multi-wall metal pipe can be used for all wood stoves, and it is a cost-effective solution to any problem you are facing with a flue. A lot of houses have cinderblock flues, but I wouldn't hesitate to use a multi-wall metal flue.

OUTSIDE FLUES

One advantage to an outside flue is that it doesn't consume your living space. This, however, is the only advantage I can think of, and the additional cost for running a flue up the outside wall of your home may not be worth the little bit of space you will lose by installing it inside.

INSIDE FLUES

Inside flues, like the chimneys for fireplaces, can be run with rough material, such as cinderblock, until they penetrate the roof, and then they can be covered with a desirable finish, such as brick. If you opt for a metal flue, your overall costs will be much less, probably less than one-half the cost of a masonry flue.

Anyone with average physical abilities can install a multi-wall flue pipe. Special collars are sold that mount between ceiling joists and support the flue pipe. Once the collar is put in place, during the framing phase, it is simply a matter of putting the pieces of flue pipe together. Then you will have to cut a hole in your roof, install another collar and extend the chimney to a point where local fire codes are satisfied. Your carpenters can build a chase wall around the flue pipe. This allows drywall to be installed on the framing, hiding the pipe from view. When the pipe exits the roof, you will install a chimney cap. This can be the end of the process, or you can have your framers extend the chase above the roof and have your siding crew cover it. This gives a nice finished look to the chimney.

There are fire codes that control how close your metal pipe can be to various types of materials, such as wood and drywall. Check with your local code office or fire department to determine the clearances required. The clearance needed will only be a few inches when multi-wall pipe is used.

POWER VENTERS

Power venters are venting devices that can be used with oil-burning equipment, in place of conventional flues. A quality power venter works well, and it costs a fraction of what the cheapest flue does. I'm using a power venter in my new home. If you have a need for a power venter, such as an oil-fired boiler that provides your heat, your heating contractor will be the one to supply and install it. The power venter is mounted so that it is in an outside wall, but there are no special framing requirements for its installation.

PROS AND CONS

There are pros and cons to both masonry and metal chimneys. Both should be cleaned regularly, at least once a year. Metal pipe is smoother than a masonry chimney, so there is less risk of creosote building up. The cost of a metal chimney is considerably less than that of a masonry chimney, and you can probably install a metal chimney on your own. Masonry chimneys are not something that most people have the skill to build. From a resale point of view, a masonry chimney is often considered to be better than a metal chimney. It may be, but I wonder if this belief is not just a mental image that isn't based on facts. All in all, if I were installing an oil burner, a wood stove, or a pre-fab fireplace, I would vote for a metal chimney, or in the case of an oil burner, possibly a power venter. I believe a metal chimney is a better choice than a power venter for an oil burner, but I used a power venter due to the design of my home and the inconvenience that a chimney would have caused.

Now that we have covered the topic of fireplaces and flues, let's move onto windows and doors. We want to cover all the aspects of the framing stage before we get into mechanical work, so let's turn to the next chapter and see what to look for, and what to look out for, with windows and exterior doors.

CHAPTER 15

INSTALLING WINDOWS AND DOORS

Windows and doors give your home a personality. These items are expensive, and it can be hard to decide what units offer the most for your money. This chapter gives you an item-by-item description of the features to look for in windows and doors for your home. In addition, you are told all about proper installation procedures. Even though you may not be installing the units yourself, it helps to know how the job should be done, so you can keep your contractors honest.

Installing windows and doors is a part of the framing process. Once the wood shell of a home is complete, the rough openings made for windows and exterior doors can be filled. This is a job that you might be able to do yourself, but I wouldn't recommend that you do it unless you have some experience in this type of work. If windows and doors are not installed properly, they will not work well, and if it is your fault that the units don't operate smoothly, there will be no one to blame but yourself.

Windows and doors account for a significant percentage of your material costs. If you use an overall average of $250 per unit, you will see that it doesn't take a lot of windows and doors to add up to thousands of dollars. If you move into unusual shapes and designs, you can pay over $1,000 for a single window. This type of spending can burst your budget quickly. With so much money at stake, let's spend some time examining the various types of windows and doors you might choose to have installed.

WINDOWS

When you begin to shop for your windows, you will be given so many options that you are likely to become confused and frustrated. Should you buy single-pane, double-pane, or triple-pane glass? Check the U-factor for the windows you are considering, and let it tell you how efficient

each window is. Most suppliers don't put the U-factor of a window into plain view. You will probably have to ask for, and possibly demand, specifics on the U-factor.

THE U-FACTOR

The U-factor is to windows what an R-factor is to insulation. It is a unit of measurement that allows consumers to compare windows for their efficiency in energy conservation. When you deal with insulation, the higher the R-factor is, the more insulating quality you have. The exact opposite is true when dealing with windows. The best windows, in terms of being energy efficient, have the lowest U-factor. For example, a window with a U-factor of four is more efficient than a window with a U-factor of six.

DOUBLE-HUNG WINDOWS

Double-hung windows are the most common type of windows used in homes. In a double-hung window, both the top and bottom half of the window will move. This allows you to ventilate your home with either half of the window. Single-hung windows have only one movable sash. They look like double-hung windows. They are less expensive than double-hung windows, but they aren't the same as double-hung windows. If you don't care to have both sashes capable of movement, you can save some money by purchasing single-hung windows without sacrificing the look.

CASEMENT WINDOWS

Casement windows are windows that open one side to the other with the use of a crank. Unlike double- or single-hung windows, where only one-half of the window area can be open at a time, casement windows open completely, giving a ventilation area the full size of the window. This can be a real advantage. Not only do casement windows give more opportunity for air movement, they are generally more energy efficient than double- or single-hung windows. There is one catch. Casement windows cost quite a bit more.

The appearance of casement windows does not suit every person's eye. This is another consideration in choosing windows. Since windows are the eyes of your home, they should be attractive and inviting. If you want double-hung windows with mullions and fanlights, then that is what you should buy. When you want maximum ventilation and energy efficiency, you should consider casement windows.

AWNING WINDOWS

Awning windows work on a principle similar to casement windows, except that instead of opening from one side to the other, they open from bottom to top. When you crank open an awning window, it opens from the bottom and rises as you crank it. The window can be stopped at any point along its route. This gives you an ability to open the window and receive fresh air, even when there is a pouring, blowing rain. Like casement windows, awning windows are not cheap.

Very few houses have awning windows installed throughout them. However, this type of window can be used in any room of a house. There is another advantage to the design of awning windows, especially when they are used in bathrooms. Awning windows can be installed high enough in a wall to afford visual privacy while they still give light and ventilation. You probably won't want to outfit your entire house with awning windows, but there are certainly some places where you might wish to use them.

SLIDING WINDOWS

Sliding windows have been around for years, but they are not used much anymore. Aluminum sliding windows are probably the least expensive type of window you can buy, but I wouldn't recommend using them. In addition to lending a cheap look to a house, aluminum sliders come with some problems.

Condensation is frequently a problem with aluminum windows. Since condensation occurs when warm air mixes with cool air, this gives you a hint that aluminum windows allow a lot of heat loss. In cold temperatures, aluminum sliders can freeze to a point where they cannot be opened. You may not have much desire to open your windows during freezing weather, but it would be nice to know you could.

All in all, sliding windows, in my opinion, should not be used in a year-round home. If you are building a summer home, that little getaway cabin in the woods, a storage barn or a tool shed, sliders are fine, but avoid them in your primary residence.

OTHER TYPES OF WINDOWS

There are many other types of windows. They come in all shapes, sizes, and styles. Most building suppliers will be more than happy to supply you with free catalogs to shop for your windows. There are certainly plenty to choose from, but you may need deep pockets to pay for them.

When my wife and I were designing our new home, Kimberley had her eye on a big bay window and two windows that had rounded tops. The windows were attractive, but we both knew they would be expensive. Kimberley argued with me when I expressed my guess at what the windows would cost. She claimed that they couldn't possibly cost as much as I was thinking. Guess who won the debate? I did. All three of the windows were over $1,200. We didn't buy any of them. I worked out a compromise using fixed glass, and this is something you may want to consider for special applications.

FIXED GLASS

Fixed glass can give you a lot of light and wonderful views for a fraction of the cost of operable windows. The sitting room that adjoins our master bedroom has a window opening in it that is six feet wide and the same height as the other windows in our home. Our breakfast room also has a glass opening of about this same dimension. Then there is a five-foot piece of glass installed above our whirlpool. We bought all the fixed glass for these openings for about $600. It is tempered, insulated glass with a thickness of about one inch. If we had used windows in these spaces, the cost would have more than doubled, and might have tripled. Since we wanted the glass for light and views, and didn't need ventilation from it, fixed glass was a sensible solution to a potentially expensive proposition.

Fixed glass can be used in many applications to give your home some unique appeal. The glass can be purchased in custom sizes and shapes. It is held into the rough opening with pieces of wood trim, and it can be installed in one large piece or in several smaller pieces. In our case, we used three panels of glass to fill in the six-foot opening. If the glass will be low enough that it may be run into or broken, you should buy tempered glass. This is glass that will crumble into little, relatively harmless pieces when it is broken, rather than shattering into large, sharp shards. Fixed glass can be purchased through any glass company.

EXTERIOR DOORS

Exterior doors, like windows, come in a variety of sizes and designs. You can get doors made of wood, fiberglass, metal, or mostly glass. Some doors are sold with etched glass in them, but these begin to get expensive. When you are shopping for exterior doors, you must keep many factors in mind. Let's go over some of these factors now.

WOOD DOORS

When you begin to price out wood doors, it won't take long to find out what a wide range there is in prices. A simple, six-panel door is very affordable, but a door made from some exotic wood with deep grains and a warm finish can cost more than what you expected to spend on all of your exterior doors. Since price is a direct reflection of personal preference and taste, it is difficult to put the price range into perspective. You can get wood doors that will be priced competitively with any other type of door, or you can spend many hundreds of dollars for one. The decision will be yours.

One problem that is often encountered with wood doors is their tendency to swell during damp weather. All wood does this to some degree, but cheap wood doors can swell to a point where they cannot be opened or closed. Obviously, you don't want a door that you can't use, so this should be one of your criteria when selecting a wood door. Buy a quality door from a name-brand manufacturer to reduce the likelihood of excessive swelling.

Another downside to wood doors is their insulating quality. Wood doors have low R-values, when compared to metal, insulated doors. If you are trying to make your home as energy efficient as possible, strike wood doors from your shopping list.

METAL DOORS

Metal doors, which have insulated interiors, are very good in terms of energy efficiency. They don't swell in damp weather, and they are inexpensive. A solid, six-panel, metal, insulated exterior door, including its jambs, can be purchased for less than $150 and a price between $99 and $125 is not uncommon. One drawback to a metal door is that it cannot be stained. It can be painted, but not stained. If you have your heart set on staining your exterior doors, you will have to go with either wood or fiberglass doors.

GLASS PATTERN

Many exterior doors have some type of glass pattern in them. This allows extra light into a home at the expense of some security. While having glass in an exterior door does decrease the security potential of the door, the result may not mean much. If your house has glass windows in it, why do you need an impenetrable door? When burglars want to get into a house, they will. Professionals can pick locks and open your door as if they had a key to fit it. Sloppy bad guys will just break out a window and climb through it. Security, in many ways, is a state of mind. It is true that you can reduce risks with security-type doors and locks, but I've always figured that if there were windows in a home, the best door in the world wouldn't keep a determined thief out. For this reason, I think it is fine to use doors with glass patterns in them. The only other disadvantage to having glass in your door is the amount of heat or air conditioning that is lost through the glass.

SLIDING GLASS DOORS

Sliding glass doors are frequently installed in breakfast rooms, sun rooms, and where the door opens onto a deck. A sliding glass door brightens a room with a lot of light, but it can also create a drafty, cold spot in a room. Doors with aluminum frames will often be plagued with condensation, and it is not unusual for cheap doors to stick in their tracks. You can buy a six-foot slider for around $200 or you can spend over a thousand dollars. What makes such a big difference in price? Quality and name recognition are two influencing factors. Cheap doors often don't have the same energy efficiency as more expensive doors. In addition to a lack of energy conservation, cheap doors frequently fail to move smoothly, and their appearance can be detrimental, when compared to more expensive doors.

Aluminum sliders are the least expensive type of sliding glass door. If you are willing to put up with a metallic look, some condensation, and an occasional fight to open the door, an aluminum unit will give you what you pay for.

Wood frames are another option when shopping for a sliding glass door. The problem with this type of door is that the frame requires regular painting. Wood-framed doors don't condensate, but they can still be a chore to open and close.

Vinyl-clad sliders are the most expensive units you are likely to run into. These doors are said to be maintenance free, meaning that the frame never needs painting. Windows are also available with vinyl-clad frames, and if you don't like to

paint, these no-maintenance units are just the ticket.

When I was shopping for the three sliding glass doors that went into my sun room, I found that the price range had three primary levels. The least expensive door that I could find was just under $200. The next step upward in quality put the price at about $500. Vinyl-clad doors were fetching $1,200. Having been a builder and a homeowner for a long time, I've had my share of experience with sliding glass doors. I installed windows with vinyl-clad frames, but I couldn't see my way clear to spend $3,600 for three doors if I could obtain about the same goal with only $600. I bought the cheap, aluminum sliders.

One reason why I decided to buy cheap doors is because these particular doors won't be used on a daily basis. One of them leads into the sun room and two of them open to the outside deck area. If the doors were intended to serve primary ingress and egress functions, I probably would have bought the mid-range doors. You see, I feel that you must spend your money based on need and use.

GLIDERS

Gliders are doors that look like sliding glass doors, but that operate much more smoothly. They also cost somewhat more. If you are afraid that a large, sliding glass door will be too difficult to open and close, a glider could be ideal for you.

FRENCH DOORS

French doors are pretty. They are also expensive. These doors have a wood frame with numerous glass panes in them. With true French doors, both doors can be opened. Less expensive versions have only one door that opens. The accompanying panel remains in a fixed position at all times.

French doors add a touch of elegance to a home, such as when they close off a formal dining room. There are a few disadvantages to this type of door, beyond its cost. If you have small children, you may be concerned about having so much glass that is accessible to the children. Since the glass goes almost to the floor, it is easy for accidents to happen. A child can fall into the door or toss a toy through the glass. You can also spend a good part of your day cleaning fingerprints from the panes.

TERRACE DOORS

Terrace doors are normally used as an alternative to sliding glass doors. These doors have two panels, but normally only one opens. Terrace doors are available with full glass panels or partial glass. If you go with a full glass panel, you have about the same amount of light that is offered by a sliding glass door, but you have the ease of a door that opens like a standard exterior door. Terrace doors can be drilled for deadbolt locks that sliding glass doors cannot accept. In terms of energy efficiency, terrace doors have a decided edge over sliders. I have found that terrace doors are well liked by most home buyers.

GARAGE DOORS

Garage doors can be big and heavy. Most modern houses with garages are equipped with automatic garage door openers. This is not only convenient, it takes the strain out of lifting a heavy door. I remember one of the houses that I lived in as a teenager. The house had a two-car garage with a single garage door. The door was big. My mother has never been a strong person, physically, and she used to have a devil of a time raising the garage door. Back in those days, automatic openers were not nearly as common as they are today. I guess they existed, but I can't remember ever knowing anyone who had one.

My father fumed over what could be done about the heavy wooden door. He did some research and decided to have the big wooden door replaced with an aluminum one. After the replacement was made, my mother could open and close the garage door without any problem. Even though you will probably rely on an automatic opener to raise and lower your garage door, you still might want to keep the weight of the door in mind.

Do you want windows in your garage door? There's no problem if you do, and the glass will add a bit of light to the garage. Do you have a beam in the middle of your garage, on your blue-

prints, that will give you problems with clearance? If so, you can order a door with low-clearance hardware. Do your plans show a door that is tall enough for your tallest vehicle to pass under it? Not all doors are tall enough to accommodate full-size vehicles, especially if the vehicles are four-wheel-drive trucks. Check your plans to make sure the door is tall enough. It would be a shame to build a garage that your truck couldn't fit in.

When you shop for a garage door, there isn't a lot you have to worry yourself with. Pick a door that you like and can afford. However, if you choose wood as your material, remember that you will have to paint it from time to time. A door with a no-paint finish will cost more, but the reduced maintenance will be a welcome relief in years to come.

THE NUTS AND BOLTS OF INSTALLATION

The nuts and bolts of installing windows and prehung exterior doors are not difficult to understand. The framing crew frames a rough opening. Your crew will know what size to make the opening by reading literature from the manufacturer of your window and door units. Assuming that the rough opening is the right size and has been framed plumb and level, installing the windows and doors is not very difficult. The exact methods vary from brand to brand, but overall, none of the brands are difficult to work with.

WINDOWS

The basic procedure for installing a window involves first setting the window unit into place. Many windows have a nailing flange on their outside edges. If the window is level and plumb, all you have to do is nail the unit into place. This, however, is rarely the case. More often, some shims are needed to level and plumb the window units. Cedar shims are driven between the window frame and the rough opening until the entire unit is plumb and level. Then nails are driven through the frame and shims, into the wood making up the rough opening. The exterior nailing flange is also nailed to the stud walls.

One person can install a new window, but the job is much easier when there are two people working together. In this way, one person can steady the window unit while the other person shims it and nails it. I might add that windows above the first floor of living space get a little tricky, due to the height at which they are installed. If you're not comfortable on a ladder or scaffolding, leave the windows on your second or third floor for the professionals to install.

DOORS

Installing an exterior, pre-hung door is not very different from installing a window. The one main difference is that the door frame will not have a nailing flange. All nailing will be done through the frame and into the rough opening. The basics for setting the door are the same. Get it level and plumb, using shims if necessary, and nail it into place. It is very important that windows and doors be installed level and plumb. Windows and doors that are not installed in this way may not open and close properly.

It is customary for framing contractors to install windows and exterior doors. When you get your framing bids, this work should be included in the price. However, if you have the desire and ability to do this work yourself, you can save a few bucks, maybe even a bundle of bucks, if you have a lot of windows in your home.

We have covered all the normal elements of the framing stage. Windows and doors were the last items to work through. Now we are ready to go up on the roof and install some shingles, or at least watch a professional roofer do it. So, let's turn the page and see what goes on over your head.

CHAPTER 16

ROOFING

> *When you first think of roofing, you might think this phase of your job is simple and deserves little thought. Think again; roofing protects your investment and plays a large part in the overall appearance of your home. Should you use fiberglass shingles or asphalt shingles? Are cedar shakes a fire hazard? The answers to these questions—and a lot of others—are in this chapter.*

Roofing is one part of building your house that should almost always be contracted out to a professional. Installing shingles properly is not as easy as roofers make it look, and working on a steep roof can be very dangerous. Even professional roofers occasionally come off a roof more quickly than they plan to. Not only is roofing somewhat complicated and potentially hazardous, it is an important part of your home. If the roof doesn't do its job, your house will pay the price. A leak in the roof can do a lot of damage before it is noticed.

While it is certainly possible for many people to roof their own homes, I'm not an advocate of it. I've seen people get in trouble on roofs. I've had my own share of bad experiences on roofs. I nearly slid off the roof of a three-story house one morning when the shingles were wet with dew. I did fall off a tin roof when I was first getting into the construction trades, and I even had a bunch of bricks chasing me to the ground. You see, the chimney where I had my safety rope attached gave way, and I was sent sliding, with the bricks right behind me. Wet earth, covered with autumn leaves, helped to break my fall, and fortunately the roof wasn't very high.

I've shared my roofing experiences with you to make a point. If professionals can loose control on a roof, do-it-yourselfers who have little to no experience can certainly wind up in some messes.

If you are planning to do your own roofing, you must take plenty of safety precautions, such as installing walk boards on the roof, wearing proper footgear, and paying strict attention to what you're doing.

WHAT TYPE OF ROOF?

What type of roof should you have installed on your new home? Asphalt shingles are the most common roofing material, but they are far from your only choice. Fiberglass shingles have caught on in recent years, and they are giving their asphalt cousins quite a run for their money. Cedar shingles, or shakes as they are often called, are expensive, but they are also a possibility for your roof. Depending on the style of home you will be building, a tin roof might be nice. Once you get beyond these options, you are moving into roofing materials that are not used very often, such as slate. So, which one of these materials should you select? Well, let's examine your options more closely and see what we come up with.

LIGHT VERSUS DARK

When you are thinking about a roof color, you may wonder about the advantages of light versus dark. Light colors tend to keep the upstairs of a home cooler than dark colors. This is an advantage in the summer and a disadvantage in the winter. My preference usually leans toward a mixed color, one with dark, light, and middle-range shades in it. With all the insulation that normally goes into an attic, I don't think roof colors are as important as they once were to heating and cooling expenses.

ROOFING FELT

Roofing felt, or roofing paper as it is often called, is common in some parts of the country and not so common in others. I had never seen a house built where roofing paper wasn't installed between the roof sheathing and shingles—until I moved to Maine. A large percentage of the roofers in Maine don't use the felt. This seemed strange to me, so I started asking questions.

Most people who I asked why they didn't use roofing paper gave me simple answers, such as that they had never used it and saw no reason for using it. One roofer told me that the paper got hot and caused the shingles to deteriorate more quickly. In my opinion, roofing paper should be installed under shingles. In fact, some roofing manufacturers will not honor their warranties if felt is not installed under their shingles.

Roofing paper is not expensive or difficult to install. I can't see why anyone would throw away a twenty-year warranty on their shingles to save a few bucks on roofing felt. It just doesn't make sense to me. You can do what you want, but I would strongly suggest that you have your framers or your roofers install a layer of felt on your roof before the shingles are put into place.

ASPHALT SHINGLES

Asphalt shingles have long been an industry standard for residential roofs. These shingles are affordable, attractive, durable, and dependable. With warranties of twenty years and more, asphalt shingles don't leave much to discuss in the way of disadvantages.

FIBERGLASS SHINGLES

From the ground, fiberglass shingles look very much like asphalt shingles. Their patterns and colors are similar, and their size appears to be about the same. Fiberglass shingles have become fairly popular in recent years, but they do have charac-teristics that may cause you some trouble if you live in a cold climate. Many roofs in Maine have been covered with fiberglass shingles, and several of them have suffered some damage. It seems that the cold weather makes the fiberglass shingles brittle enough to break. When the shingles become fragile, wind can get under them and rip them off the roof. The barn roof outside my window is evidence of just such occurrences.

When I was shopping for a roofing material for my new house, I talked with local building suppliers about the use of fiberglass shingles. I wanted to see if there was any clear advantage to using them. In the past, I had always used asphalt shingles. I had heard of the problems associated with fiberglass shingles and I had seen the results of such problems, but I wasn't sure if what I knew was enough to rule out fiberglass shingles.

It seems that a lot of people in Maine have had similar problems with fiberglass shingles. Many customers had called the building suppliers with complaints of cracked, broken, or missing shingles. I was told by one supplier that a high percentage of the fiberglass shingles sold by the supplier were reported to be defective. When I asked about the manufacturer's response to warranty work, I was told that some manufacturers were very quick to stand behind their product and that others were not.

After my investigation, I couldn't come up with any reason that provided enough justification for me to switch from my time-proven asphalt shingles to fiberglass shingles. My new house is roofed with asphalt shingles. I'm not trying to tell you that fiberglass shingles are no good. However, I want you to know that my research on them in the cold climate of Maine produced results that were not flattering. I recommend that you talk with local roofers and roofing suppliers to see what is normally used successfully in your area for roofing materials.

CEDAR SHAKES

Cedar shakes, and their installation, are quite expensive. Not only are cedar roofs expensive, it takes a special kind of house for the shakes to look appropriate. Many house styles simply are not complimented by a shake roof. There is also the risk of the shakes discoloring over time. Add to this the added fire risk, and you've got some good reasons for avoiding cedar shakes.

Are cedar shakes a fire risk? Many manufacturers treat their cedar shingles to make them somewhat fire resistant. Still, they are thin wood, and thin wood can make great kindling for a fire. If I were building a house where a cedar roof would set it off nicely, I wouldn't worry about the roof posing any great threat of fire. It would be wise, however, to check out the cedar shingles you are thinking about buying to see if they have been treated for fire resistance. You may also want to check with your insurance provider to see if your homeowner's insurance policy will tag the shingles as an unusual fire risk.

SLATE

Slate was a common roofing material many years ago. It is still used on some upscale houses; however, finding roofers with the skills and experience to work with slate can be a problem. Slate is heavy, very heavy actually, so your roof structure may have to be beefed up to carry the heavy load. If you decide on a slate roof, you may find yourself with some maintenance problems. It is not uncommon for slate roofs to become spotted with a growth of green cover. If the roof is in a shaded area and stays damp, mold and other living matter can begin to take over the roof. This requires cleaning, and cleaning a roof isn't the easiest job in the world. The price of a slate roof will stop most people from pursuing the idea, and like cedar shakes, it takes a special type of house to give a slate roof its deserved appearance.

A TIN ROOF

A tin roof can be quite an eye-catcher when it's installed on the right style of home, such as a farmhouse design. Personally, I love to listen to rain on a tin roof. My grandparent's home had a tin roof, and there were many times when I dozed off for a nap while listening to the pitter-patter of raindrops on the roof.

Today's tin roofs are a little different from the ones used in the old days. You can still find tin roofs being installed on commercial buildings and now and then on a house. Tin is more expensive than asphalt or fiberglass shingles, but there is no other type of roof that looks or sounds like a tin roof.

OTHER TYPES OF ROOFING

There are, of course, other types of roofing. If your home has a Mexican style, you might use a tile roof. Depending on your design, you might choose roofing panels made of fiberglass. In a sun room, it would not be uncommon to use a glass or heavy plastic roof. Rubber roofs are even available. All in all, though, asphalt and fiberglass shingles are the most common types of roofs being installed on homes. Not only are these shingles affordable, they are readily accepted for any style of home.

ROOF METALS

Your roof will need edging, flashing, venting, and guttering. This can be pretty straightforward stuff, or you can get fancy with ice control and venting devices.

DRIP EDGE

Drip edge is a finish trim that is installed between the last roof shingles and the exterior trim boards. Aluminum material is often used as drip edge. The advantage to aluminum is that it doesn't rust and discolor. A disadvantage is that the flimsy material is difficult to install in a straight line, and the finished product often gives a less-than-perfect appearance. A more rigid metal, like galvanized drip edge, will give cleaner lines, but it tends to rust after exposure to the elements. As much as I hate the rag-tag look of aluminum drip edge, I use it, because I think a few imperfect seams are better than a rusted galvanized drip edge.

FLASHING

Flashing is an important step in any roofing job. Your house is going to have plumbing vent pipes coming through the roof. These pipes must be flashed to avoid water damage inside your home. The flashing of these pipes may be done by your plumbing contractor or your roofer, but someone has to take care of the job. Vent pipes aren't your only need for flashing. If you have skylights or chimneys, flashing will be required. When two separate roof lines meet to form a valley, flashing is needed. I can't imagine a roofing contractor who would overlook flashing, but this is one step in the roofing process that you should make sure is done and done properly.

GUTTERS AND DOWNSPOUTS

Not all houses are equipped with gutters and downspouts, but most should be. Water cascading off the roof of a home can do a lot of damage to both the grounds surrounding the home and the home itself. Failure to plan for runoff water can be a costly and inconvenient mistake. The steady pounding of raindrops bouncing off of shingles can dig deeply into the ground destroying expensive landscaping and causing moisture problems such as cracked and peeling paint and siding, wet basements, and mold and mildew growth.

Entryways and steps that are positioned under runoff locations can be miserable to use in wet weather and dangerous to use in freezing weather. Water that falls off a roof onto steps and stoops can freeze during winter months. As snow melts from a roof, it can slide down onto the steps and stoops.

Rain diverters—small pieces of metal installed on a roof to divert water off to the sides of steps and stoops—can greatly reduce the problem of water, ice, and snow falling on a traffic area. However, rain diverters do not carry water away to a desired disposal site. Choosing rain diverters is better than not addressing the issue of roof runoff, but it is not as wise as installing gutters and downspouts.

Types of Gutter Material

There are many types of gutter material available. Some of these materials are all but obsolete, and others are quite common. Each type has its own place.

You can build gutters with *wood*, but the only time to use wood in modern gutter construction is when the architectural demands on a home are

to make it authentic to a certain historical period. Many historical districts require builders to bring buildings up to modern requirements while maintaining historic appearances.

Wooden gutters are expensive, heavy and difficult to maintain. If they don't drain properly, the wood will rot. The rough surface of a wood gutter can trap all sorts of things, and it is not unusual to see small, sprouting trees growing from gutters filled with debris.

Copper gutters are still found on many older buildings. The cost of using copper in today's construction is prohibitive. Copper gutters are no longer practical, but the material does stand up to the test of time.

Steel gutters are inexpensive, but there are trade-offs for the low cost. Most people agree that steel gutters are not very attractive. Rusting is a problem, and the life of a steel gutter is short when compared to other materials available.

Aluminum is the most popular gutter material available. It offers many advantages and few disadvantages. One of the most appealing aspects of aluminum gutters is the ability to make the gutters in any reasonable length without seams. This is not only practical—since it eliminates leaking joints—it is also attractive.

Aluminum can be purchased in a variety of colors and can be fabricated into custom-made gutters—sometimes on the job site. The costs range from inexpensive to moderate. If you want a gutter that is durable, attractive, practical, dependable, and relatively inexpensive, aluminum is your answer.

Plastic gutters are inexpensive, easy to install and normally quite durable. Their appearance appalls some people, but the look fits in with many types of houses. If you are not opposed to the round look of plastic gutters, they can be an excellent, affordable way to avoid water problems around your home.

Installing Gutters

Installing gutters and downspouts is not hard work, but it can be dangerous and often requires the help of one or more assistants. Since gutters are installed just below the edge of a roof, the use of a ladder is required. Working from a ladder can be dangerous at any time, and the risk escalates when handling long, awkward pieces of gutter material. Also, stay away from power lines when working around your roof. A close brush with a main power feed could result in death, so make sure you avoid any contact with electrical wires.

When installing or supervising the installation of gutters and downspouts, the first decision you must make is one of practical use or appearance. Some people install gutters level, so that they will be more appealing to the eye. While this type of installation is attractive, it is not as functional as when gutters are installed with a slight pitch or grade to allow water to flow more freely. Since gutters are meant to drain water to a disposal location, it makes sense to grade the gutters in the direction of disposal.

The number of downspouts you need depends on the size and pitch of your roof. Short sections of gutter can be served by a single downspout. Longer sections should be equipped with a downspout at each end. The gutter should crown at its center to allow water to fall off from the center in both directions. In cases where a length of gutter is very long, downspouts should be installed at each end and at intervals along the gutter. Failure to supply adequate downspouts will cause a gutter to overflow.

The attachment of gutters can be done with spikes, hangers, or a combination of the two. The key is to get and keep the gutters secure. If you're using spikes, they should be nailed in locations where they will enter rafter tails. If you just drive the spikes into plywood, the weight of the gutter and its contents can pull the spikes loose. Once you select the type of material you wish to use, follow the manufacturer's recommendations for attachment.

While you are installing your gutters, you may want to install gutter guards. These prevent leaves, twigs, nuts and other debris from clogging a gutter. Wire mesh is often used for this purpose. Ideally, the guards should be hinged so that they can be tipped—with a pole—from ground level for cleaning. Otherwise, you will find yourself on a ladder frequently to keep the gutters clear.

What Happens to the Water?

What happens to the water after it has traveled through the gutters and downspouts? If the water is allowed to rush out of the downspouts unchecked, there is still the risk of moisture damage and erosion. There are a few good solutions to this problem.

Splash blocks are one of the simplest ways to deal with water leaving a downspout. The splash block—a concrete block formed to direct the flow of water—is placed beneath the outlet of a downspout. Water hits the block, preventing immediate erosion, and is run off in a direction away from the home. These blocks stop on-the-spot erosion, but unless the exterior grading around the home causes the water to run away naturally, puddles can develop. You could have a bug breeding ground near each of your downspouts, not to mention moisture problems.

Some people use *roll-out* devices on their downspouts. These inexpensive items are made of a light vinyl-type material. The units remain rolled up until water enters them from a downspout. The water pressure causes the device to unroll, diverting the water farther away from the home. Some are perforated to act as lawn sprinklers.

Sub-soil drains are the ideal solution to dealing with excess roof water. These drains are installed below ground and connect directly to the downspouts. Water travels out of the gutter and into the underground drain piping. The pipe (often an inexpensive, flexible, plastic material) carries the water to a proper disposal site. This site could be a place away from the house or a dry well.

DON'T GET CARRIED AWAY

Don't get carried away with your choice in roofing material. While a slate or cedar roof will add a little to your home's appraised value, it is not likely to add enough to warrant the cost. More often than not, the cost of such a roof will be much more than the value returned on an appraisal. I would keep the roof covering simple. Either asphalt or fiberglass shingles should produce the best return on your investment.

DO IT YOURSELF?

Should you do it yourself? Can you install your own roofing? You probably can, but I would advise against it, especially if your house has a steep roof. There is the obvious danger of falling off the roof and getting hurt, but my hesitation in recommending that you tackle the job goes beyond that. Roofing is a complicated job. I know it looks simple, but the planning and layout of a roofing job is not nearly as easy as it looks. Getting all the shingles in proper alignment is a lot more difficult than you might think.

Should you install your own gutters? It depends on how much your time is worth. Many professional installers will supply and install gutters at prices that may not make it worthwhile to do the work yourself. For example, if you choose aluminum as your gutter material, a qualified professional will come equipped to make the gutters right in your yard. You would have to take measurements and have the gutters made up at some supplier's shop. Obviously, it is easier to get a perfect fit and a better looking job when the gutters are fabricated right on the job site.

If I were you, I'd hire a professional roofer to install my shingles and gutters.

Once your house is framed and roofed, you can turn your attention to siding and exterior trim. To find out more about them, turn to the next chapter.

CHAPTER 17

SIDING AND EXTERIOR TRIM APPLICATIONS

> *Cedar siding, pine siding, and vinyl siding are all popular forms of modern siding. Which type will you elect to use? Did you know that maintenance-free vinyl siding is not really maintenance free? Are you aware that the wrong treatment of pine siding can result in ugly black spotting? What type of nails are needed for a good siding installation? How can you keep nails from rusting and leaving run marks on your new siding? This chapter educates you in the facts regarding siding and its installation.*

Siding and exterior trim applications are done after a house is framed. There are many types of siding available, and siding is a job that some ambitious home-owners can do themselves. However, siding is not always a simple job, and it can be best to leave this phase of work to professionals. Before you can have your siding installed, you must know what type of siding you will use. And that is where we will begin this chapter, discussing the various types of siding.

SIDING CHOICES

What features are you looking for in siding? For example, if you don't enjoy painting, you might want to install vinyl siding on your new home. If your house is of a rustic design, a pine or cedar siding might be ideal.

Are you planning to paint your siding, or will you stain it? Will you choose a siding with a horizontal pattern or a vertical pattern? What's the easiest type of siding to work with? Which type of siding is the least expensive?

All of these questions, and probably a lot more, will come up as you shop for siding. Different people will answer the questions differently.

To help you find your own answers, let's look at the many common types of siding.

PINE SIDING

Pine siding is the least expensive type of conventional wood siding that you can buy. This doesn't mean it is of low quality or that it gives your home a poor appearance. In fact, once pine siding is stained or painted, you'd be hard pressed to tell it from cedar siding, which is much more expensive. I love pine siding, and I've used it on all my personal homes and on countless houses for customers. There are, however, a few rules that must be followed when using pine siding.

If pine siding gets wet, and stays wet, before it is stained or painted, it will turn black. Once the siding turns black from moisture, staining it is no longer an option. You must seal it and paint it. This problem is, however, easy to avoid. All you have to do is stain or paint it before it gets wet for an extended period of time. I should add that this is a job almost anyone can do themselves, but you might want to consider the option I'm about to give you as an alternative to staining your own siding.

I put pine siding on my new house. With past houses, I've always stained my own siding. I've done this before the siding was installed. My approach has been to set the siding up on sawhorses and stain it with rags and staining mitts. If you do this, you must be careful of the splinters that can come out of the siding. Paintbrushes can be used when staining pine siding, but rags and mitts give a better overall coverage with less splotching. Spray guns can also be used. The sprayers are the fastest way of covering siding, but it can be difficult to get a uniform coverage when using a power sprayer.

On my newest house, I didn't stain my own siding, the lumber company did it for me. That's right, the supplier stained the siding and then delivered it to my job site. The company has a special machine that stains the siding very inexpensively. I figured my cost to buy stain and the time it would take to stain the wood. When I compared my costs of doing the work with the cost for having the machine do it, I was pleased to see that it was more sensible to have the machine stain the siding. The machine's labor rate was only a few pennies per linear foot, and I could not hire someone to do the job anywhere near that cheaply. Nor could I afford to lose time from income-producing work to stain the siding myself. Not all suppliers have staining machines, but it can be worth your while to investigate this option when buying your siding.

Since my siding was stained before it was delivered, I didn't have to worry at all about it getting wet and turning black. If you are going to stain or paint your own siding, do it as soon as the wood is delivered. The longer you put it off, the more likely you are to have problems with discoloration.

If you stain or paint your siding before it is installed, the job is much easier and goes much faster. There will be some touch-up work needed after the siding is installed, but at least the bulk of the work can be done on the ground.

The nails you use with your siding are also important. If you use regular nails, you are going to be disappointed a few months down the road. The nails will rust, and their rust streaks will run down your siding, ruining its appearance. Some contractors use galvanized nails, but I insist on stainless steel nails. The stainless steel nails cost quite a bit more per nail, but the total extra cost for a whole house is normally less than $200. For a few extra dollars, you can assure that the exterior of your home will not be tainted with rust stains.

If you decide to side your house with pine, your supplier will need to know what grade of wood you want. Stay away from the cheapest grade. It will have too many knots and bad grains in it. A number-two pine will have quite a few knots, but in my opinion, this adds to the appearance of a home. It shows that the siding is real wood. If you want a minimum amount of knots, go with a number-one grade. This will cost more, but it will give you the clearest pine you can get. I've always used number-two pine, and none of my customers have ever been disappointed with its appearance.

CEDAR SIDING

Cedar siding costs much more than pine siding. It is a harder, more durable wood, but I've never seen the justification in its cost. If you plan to leave your siding untreated, unstained, or unpainted, cedar will last longer than pine. However, if you seal the wood, pine will last a very long time. I've seen a lot of people choose cedar siding for a natural, rustic look. They leave the siding untreated, so that it can weather naturally. You can do this, but I don't think you will be happy with the results. When cedar ages, in an unprotected state, it tends to turn gray, sometimes very gray. If this is what you want, go for it, but I think you will regret it.

It seems senseless to me that anyone would pay two or three times as much for cedar siding only to cover it up with paint. There is some justification in upgrading to cedar when the siding will be stained, but I can see no reason to do so if the wood will be painted. Painted cedar looks the same as painted pine, as long as the knots in the pine are sealed so that they will not bleed through the paint.

Both cedar and pine siding are sold in the same widths and shapes. They are both normally installed horizontally, in a clapboard style, but either can be installed with a herringbone look. The point is this, if pine siding is painted properly, you probably won't be able to tell that it is not cedar. You can save a good bit of money by using pine, and I know that if it were my house being sided, it would get pine.

HARDBOARD SIDING

Hardboard siding is sold in sizes and shapes comparable to pine and cedar. This siding is about the same price as pine, although it may be cheaper at times. You can't stain hardboard siding; it must be painted. It is easy to tell that this siding is not wood, but that doesn't mean that it looks bad. Overall, from an appraisal point of view, wood siding will bring in a higher house value than hardboard siding will. Since hardboard and pine siding cost about the same, I can't see why you wouldn't go with pine and get a higher appraisal, but a lot of people do use hardboard siding.

One problem that is often encountered when working with hardboard siding is its tendency to get wavy. The material is soft, and if it is not stored and installed on a flat surface, the siding can get a lot of humps and bumps in it. You also don't want to store the siding where it will get wet. Hardboard siding, unlike most wood siding, is very smooth. If you want a very smooth, painted finish on the exterior of your home, hardboard siding can be a good choice, as long as you store and install it properly.

VINYL SIDING

Vinyl siding is very popular as a replacement siding for older homes, and it is also used on a large number of new homes. Vinyl siding has its advantages, but appraised value is not one of them. Most real estate appraisers are not kind when it comes to putting a price on vinyl siding. For whatever reason, vinyl siding is considered by many to be a low-grade finish for the exterior of a home. In reality, there are a lot of advantages to vinyl siding, but when it comes to having your home appraised or selling it, you could be forced to face the reality of public opinion.

You know, the people in this great country are not always moved by logical and practical emotions. All you have to do is look around you, at cars, boats, houses, and other big-ticket items. The ones that are the most practical are rarely the best-sellers. People frequently buy on impulse. They are also guided by tradition and flair. When you look at vinyl siding in this light, it doesn't fare so well.

I thought about installing vinyl siding on my new home. I liked the fact that it would not have to be painted, and the fact that it was cheap. After evaluating all of the pros and cons, I went with pine siding. The wood siding cost more and it will need some routine maintenance from time to time, but I still chose it. Why? Because I like wood siding, and my home is nestled into a remote wooded section of the Maine woods. It seemed almost wrong to build a house in such a natural setting without putting wood on the outside of it. Consultations with local appraisers also influenced me to stay away from vinyl siding. Then there was the mold and mildew issue.

My land has 800 feet of river frontage. Maine is typically a damp state. While vinyl siding is said to be maintenance-free, this is not always the case. Mold and mildew can build up on vinyl siding, requiring the use of a high-pressure washer to clean it. In some parts of Maine, this can be an annual responsibility. This was not my main reason for choosing a wood siding, but it did play a role in my decision-making process.

All in all, I chose wood siding because I like it and I trust it to give many years of good service. This trust has developed over a twenty-year career in the trades. I've got nothing against vinyl siding, except its low appraisal potential. You might feel better with vinyl siding, and there is certainly nothing wrong with that.

There are two big advantages to vinyl siding. It is inexpensive, and the upkeep of it is minimal. If you have your exterior trim wrapped in a maintenance-free material and use vinyl-clad windows and doors, you have no exterior painting. Unlike aluminum siding that can be dented and damaged easily, vinyl siding is resistant to damage. The color is made into the material, so it doesn't scrape off. The only routine maintenance will be power washing, and you may not even have to contend with this. If you're on a tight budget or just don't want to worry about painting, vinyl might be the best siding for you.

T1-11 SIDING

T1-11 siding is sold in large sheets, usually with dimension of 4′ × 8′. This siding resembles a sheet of thick plywood, except that it is grooved and has a rough, but fairly consistent pattern in the wood. T1-11 siding has long been the homeowner's friend when it comes to do-it-yourself siding. Since the siding is sold in large sheets, it is generally perceived to be easier to install, and in some ways, it is.

I used T1-11 siding on my first house, and I installed it myself. The installation of this siding is pretty easy. Starting at a corner, you must simply make sure the top of the siding is level and the side edge of the siding is plumb. Then it can be nailed into place. The next adjoining sheet of siding is put in place. It fits over the first piece in a groove and is attached. This process continues until all of the siding is attached. At some point during this installation you are going to realize something you probably hadn't thought of. I know I did on my first house. Since the sheets of siding are only eight feet tall, they will require additional pieces of siding to be installed on top of them. Ah, the easy job just got more difficult.

When you have a gable or a wall where an eight-foot sheet of siding won't cover it all, you're going to need some flashing. If you don't install flashing where two pieces of T1-11 siding butt together vertically, water will run into the seam and rot your walls. Don't worry, the flashing is not difficult to work with. You will, however, need a pair of tin snips or aviator snips to cut the metal flashing.

Your flashing will attach to the exterior studs of your home. It will be covered by the siding, but a small lip of the flashing will stick out between the two sheets of siding. This protruding flashing will be turned down, to keep water from finding its way into the seam between the siding. I've got to tell you, having a seam of flashing running around your entire house does nothing to improve your curb appeal. T1-11 is often thought of as a second-rate siding, and the exposure of flashing helps to cement this opinion.

Once the flashing is in place, you can install your second level of siding. It will be installed with the same techniques used on the first level. The key is to keep all of the vertical grooves lined up and to make sure the siding is installed level and plumb. If you're working on a windy day, be advised, large sheets of T1-11 can be difficult to hang onto in the wind, and they can cause you to fall off your work station.

SHIPLAP (OR BOARD AND BATTEN) SIDING

Shiplap and board and batten siding is what T1-11 siding is supposed to simulate. Shiplap siding, however, is far above T1-11 in prestige and cost. Basically, shiplap siding consists of wide boards that are installed vertically on the sides of a home. The boards fit together by means of rabbeted edges, while board and batten is vertical boards installed so that they butt together at their edges, and the seam is covered with another board, one that is much more narrow. These sidings can be expensive, depending upon the quality of the wood used, but the vertical orientation does make for a nice looking job when installed on a house with an appropriate design.

EXTERIOR TRIM

Exterior trim describes many different pieces of trim. It includes soffits, corner boards, cornice boards, and so forth. The style and type of exterior trim that is used on a house varies with the taste of the homeowners and the design of the house. People who want a house that is completely paint-free on the exterior use trim that is wrapped in a color-coordinated aluminum or vinyl. Homes with wood siding normally use wood trim. There are many options available to you for exterior trim. Either your siding contractor or supplier can provide you with details on what's available for the type of siding you are working with.

CORNER BOARDS

Corner boards are part of your siding job. These boards are narrow and are installed at all corners, both inside and outside corners. Your siding butts up against the corner boards to give a finished look. It is customary to caulk the joints between siding and corner boards, but this is not always done. If you are installing vinyl siding, you can use either wood corner boards or no-maintenance corner boards that are meant to be used with vinyl siding. If you're using vinyl siding to avoid painting, you should invest a little extra and install maintenance-free corner boards.

J-CHANNEL

If you are installing vinyl siding, you will hear talk about J-Channel. This is a special strip that is used to attach vinyl siding. It normally is installed anywhere vinyl siding starts and stops, such as at the bottom of your outside walls, and around your windows. J-Channel is not used with wood siding.

CAN YOU INSTALL YOUR OWN SIDING?

Can you install your own siding? You probably can, but you may not want to. The work can be tedious, it should be done by at least two, if not three, people, and the work areas can be high off the ground, especially up in the gable areas. T1-11 siding is probably the easiest type of siding for novices to install. The horizontal siding materials, such as pine, cedar, and hardboard, are not difficult, in theory, to hang, but the actual work requires a lot of planning and attention to detail. For example, chalk lines should be struck across the exterior sheathing to mark the location of each and every piece of siding. You should maintain an even and constant exposure on horizontal siding, such as a four-inch exposure. Seams in the siding should be staggered, to avoid unsightly lines running up the side of your new home.

In a lot of ways, siding is like roofing. There is not much to nailing it in place, but keeping it in the right place can be frustrating. Unless you are really pressed for money or have a strong background in construction work, I would recommend that you hire someone to install your siding for you. On the other hand, this is a job that can be done by people with only average skills, so if you have the time and patience to do it, you can install your own siding and save a few thousand dollars.

CHAPTER 18

EXTERIOR PAINTING AND STAINING

Exterior painting and staining is often taken for granted. Many people feel they are qualified to paint or stain their new home, and some of them are, but many are not. This chapter gives you all the facts on painting and staining the exterior of a new home. You find out how to estimate your material needs, how to reach gable ends, and when the weather will have an adverse effect on your efforts. There is, of course, much more covered on the principles of painting and staining in this chapter.

Exterior painting and staining is a phase of your job where you might very well be able to exert some effort and save a lot of money. While painting and staining the exterior of a home is not as easy as many people believe it is, this is a job that is within the capabilities of most people. If you are not afraid to work from a ladder or scaffolding, you can do your own paint and stain work. In fact, there are some ways to get the job done without ever leaving the ground.

The cost of exterior paint and stain work does not make up a huge portion of your construction budget, but it's worth enough money to make doing it yourself attractive. Everyone values their time differently. For some people, it makes no sense, whatsoever, to spend time on a construction job when they could be doing the work they normally do. Other people will find that they can save more than they normally make by doing some of the work on their homes themselves. Then there is the group of people who want to tackle the job for more than the money that can be saved. They want to participate in the building of their dream home. Well, painting and staining is a good place to get your hands dirty.

PAINT OR STAIN?

Should you paint or stain the siding on your home? This is largely a matter of personal taste and the style of home you are building. I lean towards rural locations and semi-rustic looks, so I like stain.

However, when building spec houses in dressed-up neighborhoods, I often have the homes painted. Some of your decision will be made based on the type of material being covered. For example, stain would not work very well on hardboard siding.

Personally, I believe it is much easier for an average person to obtain professional-looking results with stain. I don't care how easy painting looks, it is an art, and it is a job that few amateurs can do and fool the pros. Staining, on the other hand, is as simple as rubbing a stain-laden mitt over the siding. It's a piece of cake. Maybe that's why I prefer staining to painting.

Maintenance is another factor in deciding between paint and stain. When paint ages, it becomes dull and often cracks and peels. These are sure signs that some attention must be paid to the condition of the home's exterior. Stain doesn't crack or peel. It discolors, but nobody can ever be sure what color the stain should be, so they don't know that it has faded. All in all, I would choose stain over paint in most instances. As proof of this, I've used stain on every house I've ever built for myself, and I've never had to restain any of the homes.

WHAT DOES AN APPRAISER THINK?

What does an appraiser think about paint versus stain? I've never interviewed an appraiser who showed any preference between the two. In terms of appraised value, there seems to be no noticeable difference between staining and painting. However, since staining is easier for an inexperienced person to do, it offers a better advantage in saving yourself some money.

ESTIMATING YOUR MATERIAL

Estimating your material will be one of the first steps in getting started as a painter. Paint is sold in containers that indicate approximately how many square feet of coverage you can hope for out of each can. For example, you might study a can of paint and see that it should cover 400 square feet. This, of course, is under optimum conditions. If you're acting as your own estimator, you must allow some loss to waste, thirsty wood, and similar situations.

How can you figure out how much paint and primer is needed? You measure your house and find the surface area to be covered. This is not difficult. Let's assume that you are building a one-story house that has dimensions of 24' × 44'. To find the square footage of your siding, you would multiply 24 by 8. Next, you would multiply 44 by 8. When you had the sums of these two equations, you would double the number, to allow for both ends of the house and both the front and back of the home. You still need to figure the gable ends.

The width of your gable ends, at their lowest point, will be twenty-four feet. Stand so that you can measure vertically up the middle of the gable end. Let's say that from the baseline of the gable to the uppermost peak is seven feet. You would multiply the width (24') by the height (7') and divide the answer by two. You would either have to do this for both gables, or you could just find the total of 24 times 7 and not divide it, to give you the approximate total square footage of both gables. Once you have your square-footage numbers, you can divide them by the amount of coverage that can be expected from your paint.

When you figure the square footage of your siding, the windows and doors become variables. Obviously, these items are not going to be painted, and they consume a portion of your overall square footage. If you want to get very precise, you could back out the footage that they occupy. To be safe, ignore the presence of windows and doors to make up for waste factors in your paint needs. In other words, figure the house as if it were all going to get painted. What paint is not used for windows and doors can hedge against mistakes in the take-off.

When you are estimating your needs for painting trim, you will use similar formulas. By measuring the width and length of various trim areas, you can come up with a measurement of square footage. Since house trim is normally painted a different color from the rest of the house, you will need to do this separately.

VARIANCES

There will be variances in the coverage you obtain from paint. The first variance can come from differences in the paint itself. You must check the can to see what coverage the can is rated for. Beyond that, you must take into account how the paint will be applied. Typically, a power sprayer will get more coverage out of a can of paint than a paintbrush will. Another factor is the type of surface you are painting. Hardboard siding will consume less paint than wood siding will. The supplier who sells you your paint can determine what the approximate rate of coverage will be.

WHERE SHOULD YOU BUY YOUR PAINT OR STAIN?

Where should you buy your paint or stain? Building supply centers normally sell name-brand stains and paints. Paint stores also sell both, but a paint store offers some advantages over a general supplier. For one thing, employees in a paint store should be more knowledgeable in the field of painting and staining than employees in a building supply center. This may not be true, but it should be. Another reason to lean towards a paint store is the help you can get in creating custom colors. If you don't want a stock color, a good paint store can mix colors to give you the look you want. While general suppliers may have some mixing capabilities, they probably are not as advanced as a full-service paint store.

How often have you seen advertised specials at department stores for paint and other building materials? Well, you probably won't find roof trusses at your local department store, but you might find cans of paint and stain. It's okay to buy from these outlets if you are buying a name-brand material. Personally, I would shy away from any brands that were not known to be of professional quality. If you buy from a department store or a discount warehouse, you will probably be on your own. You might get some help loading the cans into your car, but I doubt that you will gain any valuable insight into what to do with the paint or how to do it. Advice is another key asset of professional paint stores.

I usually buy my stain from basic building suppliers and my paint from paint stores. This may not be the most cost-effective way to buy paint, but I'd rather spend a few extra dollars to get quality paint from a supplier who will stand behind it. As much as I like to save money, I never attempt to do so if I feel the effort may result in unsatisfied customers.

You can probably paint your own siding, and you can certainly stain it, if you have average physical capabilities. By doing this work yourself, you can save thousands of dollars. The exact amount of your savings will depend largely on how big your house is, but it would not be unusual to save two or three thousand dollars in labor by painting or staining your own house.

My mind is rushing with a whirlwind of tips to give you on painting your own home. Ideas like mixing your paint in a five-gallon bucket, rather than in a one-gallon can. There is so much to be said about cutting in trim, preparing surfaces, applying primer, and creating a smooth finish coat. Unfortunately, we just don't have the space in this book to cover all of the intricacies involved with doing a professional paint job. I wish we did, but we don't. Even though we don't have the space to cover all aspects of painting and staining, there are some tips that I can give you.

PAINTING

Painting the exterior of your home with your own two hands can be exciting, rewarding, or somewhat disastrous. Much of the outcome will hinge on the preparation you put into the job. If you just stick on a painter's cap and start spreading paint with a brush, you're probably not going to be happy with the end result. Matters could get worse if you decide to use a power sprayer and accidentally paint your roof shingles. Hey, I've seen professional painters do it, so don't think it can't happen.

I'm not sure why, but a lot of people feel confident that they can produce professional-looking results as a painter. These same people wouldn't consider plumbing their own house or putting the roof on it, but they will jump right in with a can of paint. Well, painting is not the same as roofing or plumbing, but it does require more than a brush and an enthusiastic arm, if you want a quality job. Painting is such an extensive trade that entire books have been written on the subject. I'm not going to attempt to make you a professional painter in just one chapter, but I am going to give you a primer, no pun intended, on what to expect if you act as your own painting contractor.

PICKING UP A BRUSH

Picking up a paintbrush does not make you a professional painter. Sure, you can slap paint around and call it painting, but if you want the work to turn out well, you're going to have to prepare for the job. How you prepare will depend, to some extent, on the type of siding and trim you are painting and the type of paint you are using. The list of options for paint and primers is a long one, and it is one you should discuss, in detail, with your paint supplier or painting contractor.

You will have to determine what type of paint will work best in your local climate and with the type of wood you are covering. Will you need a sealer? What type of primer will work best for your circumstances? These are questions your local paint professionals can answer for you. How many coats of paint will you use? Will you use one coat of primer and one coat of paint, or will you need two coats of paint? A lot of these questions can't be answered with authority until you have decided what type of siding you are using. For example, painting pine and hardboard siding are two very different jobs. Pine siding can bleed through paint, and it soaks up paint like a sponge. Hardboard siding, on the other hand, doesn't bleed or require as much paint.

SPRAYING

When you are spraying your home with paint, you will need a little time to get accustomed to your sprayer. If you hold the sprayer too close to your siding, paint will be applied too heavily and it will run. When the sprayer is too far away from the siding, you will not get enough paint on the siding.

A power sprayer requires its operator to move it continuously during painting. It takes a while to get into the proper rhythm, but once you do, a sprayer makes the job go much faster than it would with a brush.

STAINING

The staining of your siding can be done with a brush, a power sprayer, a rag, or a staining mitt. I normally use a mitt. If you are working with wood siding, you must be careful of splinters. When using a rag or a mitt, you should wear heavy gloves to protect your hands. I always prefer to pre-stain my siding, before it is installed. This has always seemed easiest to me.

When you pre-stain your siding, there will be some touch-up work needed after the siding is installed. As the siding is cut and handled, some bare wood will show. You could climb a ladder to touch up these areas, but there is an easier way. All you need is a long pole, a rag or brush, and some way to attach the rag or brush to the pole. I find that a piece of plastic plumbing pipe, some duct tape, and a two-inch brush work very well in doing touch-ups. The pipe can be purchased in ten-foot and twenty-foot lengths. If you desire a length that measures more than ten feet but less than twenty feet, you can custom cut your pole with a standard handsaw.

I normally used PVC pipe that has a diameter of one and one-half inches. This type of pipe is rigid, but lightweight. The handle of the brush is taped to the end of the pipe, and I have an instant touch-up tool. With this tool, I can avoid climbing a ladder and work more quickly.

HITTING THE HIGH SPOTS

If you do your own painting, hitting the high spots can get a bit shaky, especially if you are working from a light-duty ladder. An eight-foot stepladder will allow you to reach all the areas needing paint on the first level of a home. The gable ends, however, will be far out of reach from the ladder. If you have a two-story home, the stretch is considerably more. What are your options for getting to these elevated areas?

Extension ladders are commonly used for exterior painting. These ladders scare me. I've known people who have been hurt badly when working from tall ladders. If you're going to work from a ladder, make sure the ladder is a heavy-duty one, rated for professional use. Homeowner-grade ladders increase your risk of injury. You should rent or buy a ladder that has braces on it. These braces extend from each side of the ladder, near its top rungs, and they stabilize the unit very well. Of course, be very careful when using your ladder around electrical wires.

A safer, although more troublesome, means for reaching second stories and gables is the use of staging or scaffolding as it is often called. Staging is a series of pipe sections that are put together with cross brackets. When the staging is set up, it provides a means for climbing and an area for standing. When set up properly, staging is much safer than a ladder, and it can be added to, in height, to reach the highest parts of a house.

While you might go out and buy a good ladder, it's unlikely that you will purchase staging for just building one house. You can, however, rent pipe staging and walk boards from most tool rental stores. You can also rent wheels that mount in the bottom ends of the first piece of staging. This makes moving the platform much easier. If you decide to rent staging, make sure the supplier renting it to you instructs you in the proper way to set it up and use it. Staging is stable and relatively safe when used properly, but it can be dangerous if it is not set up right.

SPRAYERS AND WINDY DAYS

Windy days and paint sprayers don't mix. If there is a strong breeze blowing, avoid using a paint sprayer. This may seem like common sense, but many painters have learned about the wind in an embarrassing way. I once had a professional painter spraying one of the houses I was building for a customer. The house we were building was a large two-story, and the painter was working on the upper level. As I recall, the paint color was a light gray.

I drove into the subdivision to conduct a routine inspection of the work crews. As I pulled up in front of the house, I could see paint being blown to the painter's right side by the wind. With my eye following the cloud of paint, I was horrified to see that it was landing on the house next door. The neighbor's black roof was growing old. At least that's the way it looked, since it was turning gray. I could hardly believe what I was seeing, but sure enough, the painter was getting nearly as much paint on the roof next door as he was on the siding of the house I was building. The painting contractor and I had a few choice words, and he assumed full responsibility for the roof.

In addition to the painted roof, I've seen paint blown onto trees, shrubs, cars, and other items that were never intended to be targets of the paint sprayer. Take my word for it, if it's windy, don't use a paint sprayer.

Now that we have the outside of your home finished off, let's turn to the next chapter and get into the mechanical trades. We will start off with your heating and air-conditioning needs.

CHAPTER 19

THE HVAC INSTALLATION

Ductwork can cut you in the blink of an eye. If you are going to be your own tin bender, you need to heed the safety advice in this chapter. The installation of an HVAC system is not difficult to understand, and the mechanical layout is often detailed on the blueprints of a home. There are, however, some tricks of the trade you should know, and they are in this chapter.

The heating, ventilation, and air-conditioning (HVAC) installation in your home can cost a lot of money. It can also be an area where you can save a lot of money. HVAC installers normally must be licensed to perform their work. Even though you are probably not a licensed HVAC contractor, you can probably perform your own installation. Most code enforcement offices will allow homeowners to do their own work, even when a license is normally required, so long as the homeowners actually do the work and will reside in the house where the work is being done.

When you build a house, several permits are required. There may be a need for a septic permit. A building permit will be required, and you can obtain it yourself. Then there are the mechanical trades: plumbing, heating, air-conditioning, and electrical. These trades require special licensing. Standard procedure requires a master of the trade to obtain a permit and be responsible for the work being done. Most jurisdictions are willing to waive this requirement when homeowners want to do their own mechanical work. However, the rules routinely require that the permit holder, in this case it would be you, do the work and then reside in the property. It would be a code violation for you to pull the permit as the homeowner and then allow your brother-in-law to do the work.

He could help you, but you should be actively involved in the work.

There are states and local jurisdictions that do not waive the requirement of a master's license. For an example, New Hampshire will not allow homeowners to install their own plumbing. Check with your local code office to see if you will be allowed to do your own mechanical installations. If you get clearance from your code office, you can do most of your own mechanical work. I say most, because some areas of the work are likely to be beyond your capabilities. However, the more you do, the more you save.

MECHANICAL EQUIPMENT

Buying mechanical equipment can be difficult for unlicensed people. Some trade suppliers will not sell to the public. These suppliers will only sell wholesale, and only to licensed professionals. This may not be the case in your area, but it is not uncommon. You should plan on some hassles in the acquisition of your mechanical equipment.

When you start shopping for a heat pump, furnace, or boiler, you are likely to be amazed at all the technical data that must be compared before you can determine where the best value is. Should you buy a cast-iron boiler or a steel boiler? Both have good warranties, but steel boilers cost hundreds of dollars less than cast-iron boilers. Cast-iron boilers retain their heat better than steel boilers. Both types of boilers can develop leaks, but steel boilers are said to be more likely to leak. When you look at efficiency ratings for boilers, you may be surprised to see that none of them are 100 percent efficient. A normal efficiency rating will be somewhere in the range of 85 percent.

There are so many factors involved in mechanical equipment that it is not feasible in a single chapter to list all of the possibilities to look for in a value test. The best you can do is look at every detail available to you for as many models as you can find. When you do this, make notes on each model. Create a comparison chart. For example, have a column for efficiency ratings and fill it in with the ratings for each model you are investigating. Use this approach for every aspect of your potential system.

Look beyond the sales hype when shopping for a heating or cooling system. The fancy brochures you pick up at suppliers are only going to tell you the best points about a system. Ask to see a copy of an owner's manual. If you run into resistance with this request, contact the manufacturers directly. Most manufacturers will be glad to supply you with an owner's manual. You may have to spend a little money to obtain the information, but it is money well spent. Having all of the facts contained in an owner's manual is the only way to make a clear-cut choice on where the best value lies in mechanical equipment.

Your heating and cooling system is going to be expensive, and it is going to have to last a long time. With so much at stake, you should dedicate enough research time to avoid making a mistake that you will have to live with for years to come.

HEATING AND AIR-CONDITIONING SYSTEMS

Heating systems can take on many different looks. You might install a heat pump. This can give you heating and air-conditioning from a single unit. Another option might be a boiler and forced hot-water heat. A third option, though not used too often anymore, is electric heat. If you have any type of heating system other than a heat pump, you may also wish to install an air-conditioning system. There are plenty of options to consider when shopping for an HVAC system, and your decision can result in a lot of money, either saved or spent. Let's expand on this topic by taking a closer look at the options available to you.

HEAT PUMPS

In many parts of the country, heat pumps are the number-one choice for both heating and air-conditioning requirements. These systems are economical to install (considering that you are getting both heating and air-conditioning service) and very affordable to operate, under the proper climatic conditions. Your local climate is a big factor in determining if a heat pump will be advantageous to you.

There are different types of heat pumps. The most common type is an air-to-air heat pump. These are the least expensive to install and they are used throughout states that have moderate climates. Water-source heat pumps are cost-effective to operate in any climate, but the cost of installing a water-source heat pump is much more than that of an air-source heat pump.

Air-Source Heat Pumps

Air-source heat pumps are what most houses are equipped with when a heat pump is used. This type of system pulls in outside air and conditions it for heating and cooling. These units work magnificently in climates where winter temperatures don't normally drop below 27°F for long periods of time. If your winter temperatures dip well into the teens or even below zero, as they do here in Maine, an air-source heat pump is not your best heating choice.

Heat pumps have what is called a balance point. For most air-to-air units, the balance point is somewhere in the upper twenties. This means that when the outside temperature gets into the low twenties and below, the heat pump loses its efficiency. Supplemental, electric heaters are used to compensate for temperatures that linger below the balance point. As you probably know, electric heat is expensive. If you live in a cold climate, such as Maine, where the outside temperatures often drop into single digits and stay there, you're going to spend a bundle on electric bills. However, if you live in Virginia, or some milder climate, an air-source heat pump can save you a good deal of money in operating costs.

Water-Source Heat Pumps

Water-source heat pumps pull their heat source from underground water, such as a well or a closed-loop piping system. Since well water maintains a fairly constant temperature all year, the efficiency of a water-source heat pump is as good in Maine as it is in Virginia. However, the cost of installing a water-source heat pump is much more than an air-source unit. The initial cost can outweigh the benefits when installing a water-source system.

It is possible to use the same well that you use for drinking water to supply a water-source heat pump. However, a high volume of water is required, and only drilled wells that have high recovery rates can be considered for this. A drilled well, not including any pump equipment, will cost over $2,000.

A closed-loop system involves a network of underground piping. The piping is installed below the local frost line, and it takes up a lot of space. The excavation work for this type of system, not to mention the pipe and pipefitter labor, adds up quickly. These costs can put a water-source heat pump out of the budget ballpark.

People who live in areas with extreme winter temperatures usually have a minimal need for air-conditioning. For example, there are usually only a couple of weeks out of the year where air-conditioning is needed in Maine. This past summer was unusual in the fact that hot temperatures were sustained for a longer period of time, but this situation is uncommon. Since air-conditioning is not a need, justification for the expense of a water-source heat pump is difficult. I toyed with the idea of putting such a system in my new home, but I decided against it. I went with an oil-fired boiler and hot-water baseboard heat. This heating system is an industry standard in Maine, and I didn't want to damage my resale potential. I also didn't want to spend a small fortune for air-conditioning that is rarely needed.

Heat pumps, where they are feasible, are a good investment. Even though they may cost a little more at the time of installation, they will usually repay that amount, and considerably more, in reduced operating costs. Unless you live in an area where very cold temperatures are dominant, you owe it to yourself to investigate heat pumps.

FORCED HOT-AIR FURNACES

Forced hot-air furnaces are not as common as they once were, but they are still being installed. These furnaces share some of the characteristics of heat pumps, in terms of their rough-in installations. Both types of units rely on ductwork to transport conditioned air to living space. Furnaces, however, differ from heat pumps in many ways. For example, they do not offer air-conditioning options. They also are not as efficient in energy use.

Dust is a problem with any type of forced-air system, and this includes furnaces and heat pumps. Since conditioned air is forced into the home through ductwork, a lot of dust is stirred up and relocated. If you have allergies, this can be a serious problem. Dry air is another frequent complaint associated with forced-air systems. Unless a humidifier is installed in the ductwork, dry air will normally cause a lot of static electricity in carpets and some health problems, such as breathing difficulties and sore throats.

The house I live in at the moment is equipped with an oil-fired hot-air furnace. This is not a house I built, it is a rental I'm living in until my new house is finished. I've lived in other rental properties in the past that were equipped with forced hot-air heat, and I've got to tell you, I don't like it. I don't like the static electricity, the stuffed-up nose, the sore throat, or the lack of efficiency, not to mention the dust. Some people swear by hot-air furnaces, but I swear at them.

To be objective, I should give you some of the good points of a hot-air furnace. They are cheaper to install than a heat pump or a forced hot-water system. The ductwork used with the furnace can serve double duty as a conduit for air-conditioning, but you will need a separate air-conditioner to connect to the ducts.

FORCED HOT-WATER SYSTEMS

Forced hot-water systems are the prime choice of homeowners who live in cold climates. There is no air-conditioning included with this type of system, but if you need constant heat, a hot-water system is hard to beat. Hot-water baseboard heat is the standard for cold spots. The system consists of copper piping, radiant heating units, and a boiler. The boiler can supply hot water for your culinary and bathing needs as well as your heating. This eliminates the cost and need of an electric water heater.

Most boilers are either oil-fired or gas-fired. The strong selling point of this type of system is its ability to beat any amount of cold. You can get into a lot of options with such a system. For example, your hot water that is used in bathing, cooking, and drinking can come from what is called a domestic coil. This gives a nearly endless supply of hot-to-warm water, depending upon the demand. A hot-water storage tank can be coupled to the system to give you nearly unlimited hot water. If you've ever been frustrated with an electric water heater that only allows two hot showers before it goes on vacation for an hour, you'll love the hot water supply from a boiler.

The baseboard heating units used with a boiler are normally made up of copper pipe and little fins that collect and radiate the heat. If you want a super system, you can use cast-iron baseboard heaters. They cost more, but they store up a lot more heat. Older hot-water systems used radiators. They are not seen much in modern construction, but cast-iron baseboard units work on the same basic principle as radiators.

As good as boilers and hot-water systems are, there are some drawbacks. You will need either a flue, chimney, or power venter for your boiler. This is an expense that is not incurred with other types of heating systems. The cost for venting your boiler can range from less than $500 to well over $1,500, depending on your choice in venting options.

As I said earlier, there is no air-conditioning option with hot-water heat. At least with a furnace, you already have the ductwork. If you want air-conditioning, hot-water heat is going to run your costs up. There is also the issue of appearance. Baseboard heating units are mounted on the walls of homes, near where the wall meets the floor. Heat pumps and furnaces use grills that are mounted in the floor. If you don't like the idea of heating units running along your walls, you won't like baseboard heat.

ELECTRIC HEAT

In terms of initial installation cost, electric heat is the cheapest alternative. You simply can't beat the acquisition and installation cost of electric baseboard. You will, however, pay a price for this early savings as you use the heat. If you live in Florida, or some other warm climate, electric baseboard may be your best bet. But, if you live in an area where your home must be heated for several months out of the year, you may spend many months regretting your decision to install electric heat.

I remember one of my parents' new homes. It was built just as I was entering my teenage years. At that time, the fad was to have an all-electric home. My parents bit on the hype and had electric heat installed. It was never my job to pay the electric bills, but I know they were high. When my parents sold that house, they never bought another one with electric heat. They always went after homes with heat pumps.

When Kimberley and I moved to Maine, we weren't ready to build or buy a house. We wanted to get a feel for the lay of the land, so to speak. Our first inspections of potential rental properties appalled us. Having been used to owning our own home and coming from an area where two and a half bathrooms was standard procedure, we were shocked at the rental market in coastal Maine. All of the houses we looked at had two bedrooms, one bathroom, and not much more. A thousand-square-foot house, according to the rental agents, was considered good. We were used to houses twice that size, and then some. Culture shock set in on us.

Well, we held our breath and holed up in a rented cottage, on a day-to-day rental basis, as we sought satisfactory housing. Many of the houses were ancient. They had 60-amp electric services, with fuses. Some didn't even have inside plumbing. We both like rustic, but not at the prices people wanted for these properties.

After a few days, we found a house that fit our style. It was a contemporary home with frontage on salt water. The house had three bedrooms, two and a half bathrooms, a basement, a modern kitchen, and wall-to-wall carpet. I know this probably sounds like an average house to most of you, but from what we were looking at, it was a palace. We rented it immediately.

The house was equipped with electric heat and two wood stoves. At that time in our lives, Kimberley and I were used to heating with wood and were not intimidated by the electric heat. However, our circumstances changed after the first winter. We had a baby. All of a sudden, a hot wood stove was not an acceptable option. We had to depend on the electric heat. Our electric bill soared between $300 and $400 for most of the intense heating season. To put this in perspective, the house we live in now is about the same size as our first rental house in Maine, but it heats, with an oil-fired furnace, for about one-half the cost of what the electric heat proved to be.

As you can see from this example, there is more to consider than just installation cost. You won't beat the installation cost of electric heat, but if you live in a cold climate, you will pay a price for every day you heat your home. If you're building in the Deep South, electric heat is probably the most cost-effective way to go, but in colder locations, you must look beyond your installation costs.

INDEPENDENT AIR-CONDITIONING SYSTEMS

Independent air-conditioning systems are becoming more and more a thing of the past. Heat pumps have pretty much dealt them a death blow. However, if you want to install such a system, you might want to give serious consideration to a forced hot-air furnace for your heating needs. The same ducts used to convey heat to your registers can be used for air-conditioning. By getting

use out of your ducts year-round, you can offset their cost considerably.

I think that if air-conditioning were important to me, I would opt for a heat pump, even if it had to be a water-source heat pump. In my opinion, the system should save enough money over a period of time in operating costs to offset its initial extra expense. I'm sure that I wouldn't install a duct-less heating system if I were planning an independent air-conditioning system.

INSTALLING YOUR OWN

Now that we have hit the high spots on the various heating and air-conditioning systems that are available to you, let's see how much of the work in each type of system you might be competent to do. We'll start with heat pumps.

HEAT PUMPS

Installing your own heat pump is certainly possible, but some parts of the job may be beyond your capabilities. One of the first questions you must address is the type of heat pump you will be installing. An air-source heat pump is much less complicated than a water-source heat pump. Both types of heat pumps will present challenges that the average person is not well prepared to deal with.

Most heat pumps are split systems. This means that one piece of the heat pump is installed outside of a home, and a second piece of equipment is installed inside. There is copper tubing that connects the two units together. Conditioned air from a heat pump is conveyed through ductwork, to outlets in various rooms. To install a heat pump, a person must be capable of working with electricity, tubing, ducts, drains, and other things.

It is doubtful that you will want to install your heat pump from start to finish. You may, however, find that you are perfectly capable of installing some, if not all, of the ductwork. Depending upon what trade skills you have, you might be able to do a lot more. In my opinion, you should hire a professional contractor to check your work and put the system into operation. Heat pumps are complicated, and mistakes in the installation could do costly damage to the unit. Paying an expert to check over your work, install parts of the system, and put the heat pump up and running is a good investment. If you decide to install your own heat pump, always follow the manufacturer's recommendations. I also recommend that you obtain books that are written specifically on the subject of installing heat pumps.

HOT-AIR FURNACES

Hot-air furnaces are easier to install than heat pumps. In the case of a furnace, there is only one major piece of equipment to deal with, and it will be located inside your home. Once the furnace is put into place, the rest of the job is mostly a matter of installing ducts. There is some electrical work involved, and there may be a need for gas piping or tubing for fuel oil. The basic installation requirements for a furnace are pretty simple. This, however, doesn't mean that the job can be done by just anyone. If you can read and follow instructions well, you should be able to install your own furnace. It is wise, however, to hire a professional to check your work before the furnace is fired up.

Whether you are installing a furnace or a heat pump, ductwork is a major part of the job. Just knowing how to size the ducts can get complicated. If you're going to do the job yourself, it would probably be well worthwhile to hire a professional to advise you in areas such as sizing the heating unit and ducts.

When you install a furnace, or a heat pump, there is a big box of ductwork that basically sits on top of the equipment. This is called a plenum. The plenum is the point where all other supply ducts originate. This is usually done with the use of a trunk line. A trunk line is a large, usually rectangular, piece of ductwork that extends for some distance. The distance varies with the size of the house. As the trunk line extends through the house, its size diminishes. By cutting back the cubic area of the trunk line, good air flow is maintained. From the trunk line, supply ducts extend to the register outlets in various rooms. A cold-air return will be installed in some central location of the living space. Ductwork will be run from this back to the furnace.

We don't have time to get into all aspects of installing ducts and furnaces, but we should spend a little time on what is involved. The ducts can be made of different types of material. For example, the plenum and trunk line may be made of sheet metal while the supply ducts are made of flexible duct material. Sheet metal has very sharp edges. Experienced professionals often manage to cut themselves badly on it. Metal duct is held together with drive strips, which are pieces of sheet metal that have been formed so that they can be driven over the lips of two adjoining pieces of ductwork. Take-off fittings for supply ducts are cut into the trunk line and screwed into place. If you do your own duct installation with metal ducts, there will be a lot of cutting and handling of the duct involved. This increases your chances of getting sliced open, so be careful.

You can avoid a lot of the risk associated with sheet metal by using fiberboard ducts and flexible ducts. Neither of these materials are as difficult to work with, and they don't possess the same sharp edges as are found on sheet metal. Talk with your local supplier or HVAC professional to see which types of ducts you can use to your best advantage.

BOILERS

Boilers for forced hot-water heating systems require a lot of plumbing expertise to install. You will have to cut and thread steel pipe, screw the pipe and fittings together, and solder copper tubing and fittings. If you are intimidated by soldering, don't even consider installing your own hot-water heating system.

If you elect to install your own boiler, you're going to need some specialized equipment. You will need a pipe vise, a steel pipe cutter, and pipe threading equipment. This can all be rented from a tool rental store. It may be tempting to rent an electric pipe threader, but I recommend that you don't. These devices can grab hold of a finger or shirt sleeve and make a mess of you. Rent a rachet-style, manual threader. You will have to work a little harder, but you will be safer.

Most of the work done in a hot-water heating system involves copper tubing. Joints must be sweated (soldered). Only work right around the boiler will involve large-diameter steel pipe. In addition to plumbing skills, you must have knowledge of controls and electrical wiring to put a boiler on-line. There will also be the possibility of having to install gas piping or an oil tank and oil tubing.

If you can solder copper joints, you can rough-in your own heat lines and install your own heating units. The boiler connection may confuse you, but you can hire a master heating technician to take care of trimming out the boiler. You will also need either a chimney or a power venter for the boiler. You can run your own smoke pipe to a chimney, and you can probably install your own power venter.

With any of the heating systems we have discussed, you should plan on having an expert assist you in some ways. At the very least, you should have a professional inspect your work and put the system into operation for you. Most contractors will be happy to help you on a consultant basis.

ELECTRIC HEAT

Electric heat is the easiest of all types of heat to install. It is simply a matter of attaching the heat to a wall and making a wiring connection. As long as you are sure the power is turned off to the electrical feeds, you can do all of this job yourself. Follow manufacturer's recommendations and wiring diagrams to make sure you connect the heat to your wiring properly.

INDEPENDENT AIR CONDITIONERS

Installing independent air conditioners is very similar to installing a heat pump or furnace. If you are installing a furnace and an air conditioner, you may be able to use the same ductwork. However, the sizing of ducts is different for heating than it is for air-conditioning. The placement of supply registers can also be different. Consult with local professionals to confirm the feasibility of using one duct system for both heating and cooling. It

can be done, but you should get all the facts before installing any ductwork.

MAKING THE CHOICE

Deciding upon the system you will use to heat and cool your home is serious. You will not be able to change it without turning your home inside out. Consider your future plans for the house and your future needs. Will you ever sell the house? If so, how will potential buyers like your choice?

PUBLIC OPINION

Public opinion affects the value of various types of heating and cooling systems. Electric heat is almost always looked upon as a bad investment. The exception to this may be locations where heat is rarely needed. Heat pumps are accepted in all but the coldest regions. Hot-water heat is considered top-of-the-line in climates where extreme cold is commonplace. Furnaces and independent air-conditioning systems are not scorned in the way that electric heat is, but they don't enjoy the wide appeal that heat pumps do. To determine which type of heat is best for your home, you must do some local research. You can start by looking around to see what types of systems are prevalent in your area. If you want to be really safe, you can consult with a licensed appraiser.

MAINTENANCE

The maintenance and upkeep of the various systems we have discussed are minimal. None is required for electric heat. Heat pumps require filter changes, which are not expensive and that can be done by almost anyone. The same is true of forced-air systems. Boilers need to be cleaned every now and then, and this is a job you won't want to do yourself. All heating systems, with the exception of electric heat, should be cleaned on a regular schedule and tuned up. A lot of people do this annually, right before the heating season. In most cases, outside professionals are hired to do the cleanings and tune-ups.

CHAPTER 20

THE PLUMBING INSTALLATION

If you can do your own plumbing installation, you can save some serious money. With today's modern plumbing materials, it is easier than ever for average people to do their own plumbing. This chapter introduces you to the plumbing procedures required on average homes, and gives plenty of detailed examples to help you install your own plumbing. Even if you don't want to tackle the job yourself, you will enjoy being able to carry on an intelligent conversation with your plumbing contractor.

The plumbing installation for your home is an area where you can potentially save a lot of money. Plumbing is not as hard as it used to be, and it is not as complicated as people often think it is. The plumbing trade is a technical field that requires a lot of experience to understand completely. However, plumbing a house is no big deal. With the modern plumbing materials available today, you can plumb your whole house without ever sweating a joint or caulking a cast-iron pipe.

Plumbing is a trade that is normally done only by licensed plumbers. A master plumber is normally required to obtain plumbing permits. In many jurisdictions, however, homeowners are allowed to install their own plumbing. This is not always the case, so you should check with your local plumbing inspector before getting too far into your own plumbing installation. You must obtain a permit for the work before starting.

Assuming that your local code authorities don't object to you being your own plumber, there is a lot that you can do to reduce the cost of your new home. There may be some parts of the job that you will want professional assistance with, but you can do a lot of the work yourself.

There are three basic phases to plumbing a house. Two of them occur during the rough-in stage. This is when the house is all framed up but none of the walls have been covered with drywall.

The first phase is the rough-in of drains and vents. When this work is done, water pipes must be roughed in. The third, and final, phase is the setting of fixtures and the connections to a water service and sewer. This work is usually done when the house is nearing completion. There can be one other phase. If you are building a house where plumbing fixtures will be set on a concrete floor or where plumbing for any purpose will be installed beneath such a floor, you have what is called a groundworks phase. This is when you install all plumbing that will go under the floor, prior to the floor being poured.

ROUGHING IN DRAINS AND VENTS

Roughing in drains and vents is the most complicated aspect of plumbing your own house. There are many code requirements that affect this work. For example, some fittings can be used when turning a pipe from a horizontal position to a vertical position, but not when going from a horizontal position to a horizontal position. As complicated as the code requirements are, there are some basic ways to simplify them for your purposes.

For example, a short-turn elbow fitting can be used when going from a horizontal run to a vertical run, unless the fitting will be concealed under concrete. These short-turn fittings cannot be used when turning from a horizontal position to another horizontal position. Long-turn elbows can be used to make turns either horizontally or vertically and concealed under concrete. The simple solution is to use all long-turn elbows in all applications.

There are some basics to follow in plumbing, such as having all of your drains installed so that they drain by gravity. Normally this is accomplished by installing the pipes with a slope of ¼″ per foot. Drains and vents should be supported at four-foot intervals. No more than two toilets should drain into a common three-inch pipe. All fixtures should be vented. The list of code requirements go on and on.

If you are planning to install your own plumbing, you should buy a book that deals only with plumbing installations. A step-by-step installation guide will be a necessity for the drains and vents.

Drains and vents in modern homes consist of plastic pipe. The pipe is a schedule-40 plastic, in either PVC (polyvinyl chloride) or ABS (acrylonitrile-butadiene-styrene). PVC is white and ABS is black. There are some cost savings in the use of PVC, but ABS is easier to cut and to work with. Both pipes are approved by all major plumbing codes, and either of them can be cut with a hacksaw, handsaw, or other type of saw.

WATER PIPE

For years, the water pipe in homes has been mostly copper tubing. Old houses were fitted with galvanized steel piping. Today, copper is still used in a large number of new houses, but it has met with some strong competition.

The competitor is polybutylene (PB) pipe. PB pipe is a gray plastic pipe that can be purchased in rolls or in straight lengths. By using PB pipe, you avoid having to make soldered joints. This can be a real plus for most do-it-yourselfers.

I've worked with PB pipe for well over ten years, and I don't have a bad thing to say about it. Some people don't trust it, but I've never had a leak with it and the pipe has never caused me to go back to a job for warranty work. In my opinion, PB pipe is the way to go. It costs about one-third of what copper costs. It is fast and easy to install. It is not affected by most water problems that can destroy copper pipe, and it gives you an option of eliminating joints in concealed locations.

My new house has three bathrooms in it. There is a laundry room, a kitchen, a whirlpool, and a darkroom for my photography work. With all this plumbing, the only concealed joints in the whole house are the ones that are necessary at the filler valves for the bathtubs and shower. If I had plumbed the house with copper, there would be dozens of joints that could cause me problems in the years to come. By using 100-foot rolls of PB pipe, I didn't have to use any elbows, tees, or other offsets. In my opinion, this is a significant advantage.

If you choose to use PB pipe in your home, you will need a special tool. The pipe can be cut with a hacksaw, although there are special cutters designed for cutting the pipe, but to make joints you will need a crimping tool. You can use compression fittings and avoid the crimping tool, but I don't recommend it. A crimped joint is much stronger and more dependable than a compression joint.

When I install PB pipe, I use barbed, copper insert fittings, copper crimp rings, and a crimping tool to make my joints. In all my years of doing this, I've never had a leak or a problem with the joints. There are horror stories about how PB pipe joints blow apart for no apparent reason. I've never seen this happen, but I would guess that the cause is a joint that was made in haste or simply not made well.

Code requirements for water pipe are much less complicated than they are for drains and vents. Copper tubing must be supported at a minimum of six-foot intervals. PB pipe must be supported at thirty-two-inch intervals. No more than two fixtures can be served by a half-inch pipe. There are other code requirements, but these are the ones that will come into play the most. I should note that code requirements can vary from place to place. Every local jurisdiction has the authority to amend the plumbing code adopted for their region. Before you depend on any code requirements that you read about, you should confirm them with your local plumbing inspector.

HOW MUCH MONEY CAN BE SAVED?

How much money can be saved by plumbing your own house? It depends on the size of your home, its layout, and the number of plumbing fixtures being installed. At a minimum, you should save at least $1,500. Larger homes with more plumbing fixtures can provide savings of more than $3,000. Of course, trade rates vary from state to state. A plumber in Northern Virginia charges much more than a plumber in Maine. A rule-of-thumb in most trades is that labor is equal to the cost of materials. In other words, if you get a plumber's bid for labor and material where the amount is $6,000, you can assume that you might save up to $3,000 by doing the work yourself. This equation doesn't always work out, but it works often enough to make it worth mentioning.

Should you decide to tackle your own plumbing, plan on having someone available to help you, at least some of the time. The job is difficult for one person to do alone. You will need a second set of hands to help in making some connections and possibly in setting the bathing units. It is also common sense to have someone on the job with you whenever you are working, in case you are the victim of an accident.

WHAT TYPES OF FIXTURES SHOULD I BUY?

What types of fixtures should I buy? There are a host of fixtures available to you. Some are cheap, some are not. I can buy a cheap toilet for around $55. If I purchase a name-brand toilet, in a competitive grade, the cost will be closer to $80. Should I decide to buy a name-brand toilet in a designer color, I can spend well over $200 for it. The fixtures you buy will depend, at least to some extent, on your personal tastes. There are, however, some aspects of fixture selection that we can discuss on a monetary level.

TOILETS

Toilets don't all look or work the same. Appearance is one of the main factors when buying a toilet. If the fixture is ugly, nobody wants it. However, ugly is in the eye of the beholder. Some toilets are made so that their integral trap is evident and outlined on the outside of the fixture. People sometimes object to this type of unit. You will know if you like the looks of a toilet or not, so let's concentrate on some other elements of your buying decision.

Price and appearance are easy for you to deal with, but not all aspects of buying a toilet are so clear. Most toilets are made out of china, but some are made from plastic materials. I've seen plastic toilets, but I've never installed or worked on one, so I can't attest to their qualities. China is the industry standard, and the material I recommend.

Toilets are sold with round bowls and elongated bowls. Round bowls are normally used in homes and elongated bowls are typically used in commercial buildings. This doesn't mean you can't have an elongated toilet in your house, if you want one. If you have trouble using standard toilets because they are so low, you might want to buy a taller toilet. Toilets that are eighteen or twenty inches tall are much easier to use if you're not as spry as you once were.

When you buy a toilet, you may be surprised to find that it is not sold with a seat. Seats have to be purchased separately. If you buy a round bowl, you need a round seat. Elongated toilets need elongated seats. Elongated toilets cost more than round-front toilets. High-rise toilets also cost more than standard toilets and high-rise toilets are normally sold only in elongated versions.

The vast majority of toilets in use are two-piece toilets. The tank is one piece and the bowl is a separate piece. The two pieces are bolted together at the job site. You can buy one-piece toilets, where the tank and bowl are formed as one piece. Many people consider these toilets to be more fashionable. They are also more expensive and the extra cost is not normally recovered on an appraisal.

White plumbing fixtures are traditionally less expensive than fixtures that are sold in other colors. Standard colors, like blue, almond, green, and so forth, are normally only a little more expensive than white fixtures. Almond, bone, and off-white are the most universal colors. They are a step above white, and they are neutral enough to go with most decors. If you get into flashy colors, like red, black, chocolate, and so on, you are increasing your fixture cost tremendously. These high-fashion, designer colors can more than double the cost of your fixtures. Again, the additional expense is rarely recouped on an appraisal.

BATHTUBS

Bathtubs come in different configurations. Bathtubs can be just bathtubs, or they can have surrounding walls that allow the use of a shower head. One-piece fiberglass units are the most common in new construction. If you fail to get your one-piece unit into the house while you still can (early in the framing stages), you can buy a two-piece, three-piece, or four-piece unit that can be carried through most standard doors. One-piece units are advantageous in that they don't have any seams to leak. The wholesale price of a one-piece, fiberglass tub/shower unit will run between $225 and $300.

An upgrade over a fiberglass unit is an acrylic tub. These two tubs look very similar, though the acrylic may have a slightly better finish on it. The cost of an acrylic tub is somewhat more than that of a fiberglass unit, and personally, I don't see the extra value.

If you don't want a one-piece tub, you can buy bathtubs made of fiberglass, enameled steel, or enameled cast-iron. Steel tubs are the least expensive. Cast-iron tubs weigh the most, tipping the scales somewhere in the range of 400 pounds. There are pros and cons to each of these types of tubs.

Steel Tubs

Steel tubs can be bought for less than $100. Once installed, it is difficult to tell a steel tub from a cast-iron tub, if you're just looking at it. There are two main advantages to a steel tub. The bathing unit is lightweight and easy to handle. It is also cheap, without looking cheap. Now for the disadvantages. Steel tubs can be awfully cold to sit in. The enamel on the tub can be chipped just by dropping a shampoo bottle. Noise can also be a problem with steel tubs, especially in houses where the tubs are not located on the first floor.

If you have a steel tub in a bathroom that sits over your living room, you will hear water bouncing off the tub every time it is filled. This can be annoying, and embarrassing if you are entertaining while someone is preparing a bath or taking a shower. The noise can be reduced by installing insulation or sand under the tub, but some ping-ping-pings will still slip through.

Cast-Iron Tubs

Cast-iron tubs are expensive and very heavy. They look very much like a steel tub, and for the life of me, I can't see why anyone would install a cast-iron tub with the many options available to them in other types of tubs. The enamel on a cast-iron tub can be chipped and cracked, just like the enamel on a steel tub. Since cast-iron is stronger than steel and doesn't flex like steel, there is less chance of the enamel cracking, but it can, and it will if something is dropped on it. Due to its mass and material, a cast-iron tub will not give you the noise problems associated with a steel tub. But if I wanted a standard bathtub and was debating between a cast-iron tub and a steel tub, I'd put my money into the steel unit.

Fiberglass Tubs

Fiberglass tubs, like steel tubs, are lightweight and easy to handle. The color is built into them, and there is no enamel to pop off or crack. Fiberglass units are much warmer to sit in than steel or cast-iron tubs. The cost of a fiberglass tub is more than a steel tub and considerably less than that of a cast-iron tub. There is some noise generated when a fiberglass tub is filled, but the distraction is not nearly as great as with a steel tub. Given the choice of a steel, cast-iron, or fiberglass tub, I'd take the fiberglass unit.

Plastic Tubs

Plastic tubs are also on the market. These tubs are flimsy. The few that I have ordered for customers have normally arrived at my shop damaged. These tubs are cheap, and by cheap, I don't just mean inexpensive. They are poorly made, at least all the ones I've seen have been.

SHOWERS

Showers, like bathtubs, can be purchased in an array of choices. The most popular showers seem to be one-piece, fiberglass models, usually with dimensions of no less than three feet by three feet. Larger units are available with built-in seats, and there seems to be a good demand for these units. One-piece fiberglass showers, however, are only one of many types of showers available.

Fiberglass showers are available in take-down units. You can get two-piece showers, three-piece showers, and four-piece showers. If you don't want fiberglass shower walls, but do want a molded shower base, you can have it. Shower bases can be bought separately and any type of waterproof surround can be installed for walls.

Fiberglass shower stalls are the industry standard, but your shower walls can consist of ceramic tile, plastic surrounds, or other more exotic (and more expensive) materials. The cheapest showers on the market are made of metal. I would never install one of these showers in a home. The units are flimsy, ugly, and they rust after a few years. Most of the units are not large enough to meet plumbing code requirements. My best advice on metal showers is to stay away from them.

The least expensive route for a shower that will serve you well is a molded base and plastic walls. I'm not keen on plastic walls, but at least they won't rust. Unless you are scraping the bottom of your budget for a shower, try to stick with a fiberglass or tiled shower.

Tiled showers can be done in either of two ways. The least expensive way is to use a molded base with tile walls. This method is perfectly acceptable, and probably less likely to give you problems down the road. An alternative is to form up a shower base out of waterproof material. Concrete is poured into the form and tile is laid over the concrete. Then the walls are tiled. This gives a completely tiled shower. This method was popular years ago, but it is not used much in today's homes. Fiberglass rules the roost when it comes to tubs and showers.

If you want a tile surround for your bathtub or shower, you can probably do it yourself. Installing ceramic tile is not very difficult, and tile suppliers will often loan you tile cutters and other special tools needed to work with tile, as long as you buy your tile from them. The suppliers will also be happy to give you detailed instructions on how to install tile. You can save a few hundred bucks per bathing unit by doing your own tile work.

When it comes to recovering the value of your bathing unit, keep it simple. Fiberglass units typically are worth every penny you spend. Steel tubs don't cost much, but they are valued similarly to cast-iron tubs. Tiled surrounds, whether in a shower or around a tub, are usually a safe investment. You aren't likely to build any equity with a bathing unit, but in most cases you won't lose any money. If you're going to lose money, I think it will be with a cast-iron tub or plastic surrounds.

KITCHEN SINKS

Most kitchen sinks are made of stainless steel. These sinks are durable, easy to clean, and often cost less than $75. This is a combination that is hard to beat. However, not all stainless steel sinks are created equally. Some sinks are so flimsy that the installation of a garbage disposal will pull the bottom of the sink bowl down. You can tell the thickness of a stainless steel sink by its gauge. A 22-gauge sink is not as sturdy as a 20-gauge sink. The lower the number of the gauge, the stronger the sink is.

If you don't want a standard stainless steel sink, you might be interested in a cast-iron sink. These sinks come in a variety of colors. I must warn you, the cost of a cast-iron sink will make you dig deeply into your pockets. If you plan to install a cast-iron sink yourself, arrange to have some helpers on the day of installation. Cast-iron sinks are very heavy.

Other types of kitchen sinks are available. For example, home builders who are planning to have the look of a country kitchen might be interested in large soapstone-like sinks. Again, you have to brace yourself to face the cost, but this is one of the only ways to get the big, deep sink that was common in country kitchens from years gone by.

Aside from material choices, you will have to decide on what style of sink to get. Do you want a single-bowl sink or a double-bowl sink? Double-bowl sinks are the most common, and they are not much more expensive than a single-bowl version. Perhaps you want a triple-bowl sink, where one of the bowls is meant for some special use, such as washing vegetables or housing a garbage disposal. Your preference is yours alone, so I'm sure you can decide on what type of sink you want. I will tell you this, anything other than a standard stainless-steel sink will probably not recover its full value on an appraisal.

LAVATORIES

Bathroom lavatories, like most plumbing fixtures, are available in numerous sizes, shapes, and materials. There are drop-in lavatories, self-rimming lavatories, wall-hung lavatories, pedestal lavatories, and molded lavatory tops, just to name a few. The type of lavatory you choose can affect the cost of your plumbing installation.

Your choices in materials for a lavatory range from plastic to cultured marble, and beyond. China is a standard material, but it is not your only option. The type of lavatory you buy will have some effect on the material. For example, I've never seen a plastic wall-hung lavatory. Plastic models are usually drop-ins or self-rimming lavatories. Cultured marble is reserved for molded lavatory tops that are fitted to vanity cabinets. I recommend molded lavatory tops when vanity cabinets are used, and china lavatories for all other uses. However, many of the plastic versions are acceptable, and very inexpensive.

Under $30

If you're looking for a lavatory for under $30, you should investigate plastic units and china wall-hung lavatories. Most of these, in an economy grade, can be bought with less than $30. As you move up the price scale, your options broaden. China drop-ins and self-rimming lavatories are available for less than $100 and often for less than $75. The next step is a pedestal lavatory or a cultured marble top. These up-grades may cost more than $100. An average price will probably be somewhere around $150, with larger and better units tipping in between $200 and $300.

Pros and Cons

Let's discuss the pros and cons of various types of lavatories. Wall-hung lavatories are inexpensive, but very serviceable. They are not attractive, but neither are they ugly. They can be installed with, or without, chrome support legs. Backing must be installed in the wall where a wall-hung lavatory will be hung. This is done during the framing stage. For pure simplicity and economy, a wall-hung lavatory is the winner.

Drop-in lavatories need a countertop. It is not mandatory that a cabinet be installed under the counter, but it is customary. Drop-in lavatories are held in place with a metal ring that creates some cleaning problems. Dirt and grime collect around the ring and are difficult to remove. These lavatories are also a pain to install.

Self-rimming lavatories are also installed in a hole cut in a counter. However, there is no metal ring to contend with. The lavatory simply sits on top of the counter, with the bowl hanging below it. These units are easy to install and clean.

Pedestal lavatories lend a touch of elegance to a bathroom. Some people don't like them because there is no cabinet space beneath them for storage. Other people love them because they are sleek and attractive. The bowl of a pedestal lavatory hangs on a wall in the same way that a wall-hung lavatory does. You must install backing during the framing stage to attach the wall bracket when installing a pedestal lavatory. In addition to the wall bracket, the pedestal also supports the bowl. When pipes are roughed-in properly, they are concealed in the base of the pedestal.

Cultured marble lavatories are molded right into the countertop. The top is placed on a vanity cabinet, and that's all there is to it. These units are easy to clean, and most are equipped with a backsplash that helps to keep splatters off the bathroom wall. The cost of these tops is more than other lavatories, with the possible exception of upper-end pedestals. In addition to the added cost of the top, there is the need for a vanity, which won't be cheap.

FAUCETS

The price of a lavatory faucet can be less than $10 or more than $2,500. An average lavatory faucet will cost around $65. A lot of money can be spent on fancy faucets, but don't expect to the see the cost reflected on an appraisal. Basic, chrome faucets are the most logical type to install.

When you buy faucets for your bathtub or shower, you should spend a little extra money and get a faucet that is pressure-balanced. Anti-scald and pressure-balanced faucets are a good safety precaution, especially if children or elderly adults will be using them. I've been told in seminars that a young child or an elderly adult can receive serious burns in just seconds, since they are unable to react to scalding water quickly. You can get a good, name-brand, single-handle, pressure-balanced tub/shower faucet for less than $100.

Whether you want faucets with two handles or one is up to you. I prefer single-handle faucets, but a lot of people favor two-handle faucets. If you're looking for a cheap faucet, you can buy plastic ones for around $10. Kitchen faucets will be closer to $25. Name-brand faucets that are made of metal will run between $50 and $75.

SETTING PLUMBING FIXTURES

Setting plumbing fixtures is not hard work, but it can force you into some very uncomfortable positions. Curling up under a sink and trying to work in the confined space of a small cabinet may make you wish you had hired a plumber. About the only special tool needed for setting fixtures is a basin wrench. They can be purchased from hardware stores for less than $10. You will need this wrench to install faucets on sinks and lavatories.

The key to success in setting your own plumbing fixtures is taking your time. If you hurry, you will probably break something. Take toilets as an example. Toilets are very fragile. The fixtures must normally be bolted together and down to a flange. If any of these nuts and bolts are tightened to an extreme, the toilet will break. You should tighten the nuts until they are snug. Once the water is on, you can tighten them more, as needed, to stop any minor leaking. If you put a socket set on them and start cranking your ratchet, you are likely to be looking for a new toilet.

Plumbing fixtures are packed with installation instructions. The instructions are normally pretty easy to understand. If you follow directions well, you can install your own sinks, toilets, and faucets. Bathtubs and showers are installed before drywall is. The bathing units are put into place during the framing stage of a house.

With the use of plastic pipe for drains, vents, and water supplies, there is very little to prevent an average person from doing their own plumbing. The job takes some time, and novices will have to study some form of manual for directions on proper installation procedures, but the work itself is not very demanding. The tools needed are common hand tools. It is helpful to have a reciprocating saw during the rough-in stage. And a right-angle drill that is powerful enough to drill large holes for the drains and vents is a necessity. Both of these tools can be rented.

WATER HEATERS

When it comes to water heaters, you may not have a lot of choice in the type you buy. They are available in electric models, oil-fired models, and gas-fired models (both for natural gas and propane). A vast majority of homes are equipped with electric water heaters. These are the least expensive to buy, and probably the most expensive to operate. Oil-fired water heaters are expensive and fairly rare. Gas-fired water heaters are economical to operate, and they are not horribly expensive.

When you buy a water heater, you should look at more than the purchase price. Your water heater will be working every day to give you hot water, so you should be concerned about the cost of operating it. Water heaters are marked with efficiency ratings and estimated operating costs. Check these numbers out closely before you buy.

ODDS AND ENDS

There are many odds and ends that you may wind up with in your plumbing phase. For example, you may decide to install a garbage disposal or an ice-maker kit. There will be valves, supply tubes, and a lot of other miscellaneous needs. Most of these items are simple enough that you can shop around and find the best deals on your own. First-hand research is your best approach to saving money on your new home.

CHAPTER 21
THE ELECTRICAL INSTALLATION

The electrical installation in your new home doesn't take long to complete, and you may be able to do much of the work yourself. There are aspects of the electrical work that should be left to professionals, but there are many ways you can participate in the job and save yourself some cash. This chapter teaches you the basics of home wiring and when you should rely on professional help.

The electrical installation for your home is a phase where I feel anyone, except an electrician, should have professional help. If you make a mistake in plumbing, you might get wet, but a mistake made while working with electricity could be fatal. This is not to say that you can't do a lot of your own electrical work. You can. In fact, it is really quite a bit easier than plumbing or heating.

Until just recently, I had never wired a new house. Since I'm not a licensed electrician, I am not allowed, by code, to wire houses that I build for other people. As a homeowner, though, I am allowed to wire my own house, and I just did this not long ago.

I've known a lot about the basics of electrical wiring for a number of years, but until now, I had no real hands-on experience in a big job, such as wiring a new house.

Most of this book deals with work that I've done over and over again. I've done it so much that most of it is something I take for granted. Electrical work, however, is the one area where I can most relate to how you will feel when taking on the work at your own home.

It's hard for me to remember the first house I ever plumbed or built, but my first major electrical work is fresh in my mind, along with the mistakes that I made.

ACTING AS YOUR OWN ELECTRICIAN

Acting as your own electrician may be intimidating at first. It was to me. I've seen hundreds of houses being wired, but that only served to fuel my concern. In the past, I've looked at dozens of wires hanging by a circuit-breaker box and wondered how the electricians could ever figure out what the different wires were connected to. Now I know how they do it. The wires are labeled as they are pulled by writing on the sheathing with an indelible marker.

When I decided to be my own electrician, there were aspects of the job that concerned me. I also wasn't sure of what to do or how to do it. To solve this problem, I hired a master electrician as a consultant. I met with the electrician at the new house and talked with him for one hour. After that, I was on my own. The electrician would come back whenever I needed him, but the one-hour consultation was enough to get me started.

I ordered my electrical materials and got ready to work. There are different ways to wire a house, and I didn't do mine in the most cost-effective manner. I wanted to keep the house broken up into as many circuits as possible, to avoid overloads and circuit-breakers tripping. Basically, I put all the outlets for one room on a single circuit.

I grouped lights together on a circuit in a logical progression. For example, all the ceiling lights for all the downstairs bedrooms are on one circuit. I planned all of my circuits out in advance.

I ran #12 wire for all of my outlets and #14 wire for my lights. This made it easy, because there wasn't any complicated wire sizing to be done. The switch and outlet boxes I used were plastic. They had tabs on them that allowed them to be set with the proper protrusion for drywall. The boxes also had nails already inserted in them, so it was just a matter of placing them and nailing them.

For my ceiling lights, I used metal boxes that are mounted on an expandable support. The support is nailed between two ceiling joists, and the box can be moved along the support to give proper positioning. The support rods have ears on them that pre-set the depth of the box for drywall.

The exhaust fans in my bathrooms were just metal boxes that are nailed between the ceiling joists. In my case, they were fan/light combinations. All of the rough-in devices were very user-friendly.

The biggest problem I encountered in doing my own wiring was working alone. My wife was pregnant, and I had all of my other people working on other parts of the house. Therefore, I was left to pull all of the wire by myself. With the house being built over only a crawl space, the wire pulling was difficult at times. If I'd had a helper, the job would have gone more easily and much faster.

I had very few problems and didn't make many mistakes. On two occasions I caught myself running the wrong size wire, but this was caught early and caused very little disruption in my work. The biggest mistake I made was running too many circuits. This did cause me some grief.

My home is equipped with a 200-amp electrical service. The circuit-breaker box has 40 slots in it for circuits. When I had finished pulling all of my wires and counted up the circuits, I had over 50. Since the box is only big enough for 40 circuits, I had to revise my wiring scheme. I could have bought a breaker box with 42 slots, but these boxes cost quite a bit more, and it still wouldn't

have been enough to do the job the way I wanted it done.

When I discovered that I had too many circuits, I used junction boxes to combine circuits and to reduce the number of circuit-breakers needed. For example, I combined all of the ceiling lights for the upstairs onto one circuit. Lights don't pull much current, and there is no start-up surge with them, so this was an easy way to group circuits without the fear of overloading them. In all cases, I did my math to determine how many amps would be on each circuit. The light circuits are 15-amp breakers. This means that they can handle a load of 12 amps, 80 percent of the full rating. I kept all of my loads at 10 amps or less, just to be safe.

When I had completed my rough-in work, I had the master electrician come back out and look it over. The only mistake that I had made involved my smoke detectors. Code requires that all smoke detectors be wired in a way that if one goes off, they all go off. I didn't know that this meant I had to run 3-wire between the units, so I did have to change from my 2-wire Romex to 3-wire Romex. It wasn't a big deal, though.

Installing outlets, switches (except for 3-way switches), and light fixtures is pretty simple. Three-way switches get a bit complicated, so I asked the electrician to do those. I also paid the electrician to do the work where the main power would come in. He installed the weather head, the meter base, and the circuit-breakers. I didn't like the idea of putting my untrained fingers in a box that was supplied with lethal current. Even when the main breaker is turned off in a service panel, full power is still hot on the lugs, up near where wires have to be connected to gang blocks. It only cost me $100 to have the electrician do the hot work, and I thought that was very cheap insurance.

Would I wire another house if I was to build another one for myself? You bet. I learned a lot doing my own wiring, and I wouldn't hesitate for a moment to do it again. It took me several days to do the rough-in, and it will take a day or two for me to hang fixtures and install outlets and switches, but hey, I'm saving over $2,000 for less than 50 hours of my time, and that's after paying a licensed electrician to do the dangerous work.

WHAT CAN YOU DO?

What can you do to reduce the cost of your electrical work? If you have average physical abilities, you can do everything I did. There are a lot of holes to be drilled, and you can certainly do that. Nailing plastic boxes to wall studs is not hard work, and there are only a few measurements that you must keep in mind. Basically, wall outlets cannot be more than twelve feet apart. They are normally installed about eighteen inches above the floor. If you have a large room, you may want to put the outlets on two separate circuits, to avoid overloading a single circuit. I did this in some of my larger rooms.

If you are installing outlets for a kitchen, bathroom, garage, outside use, or other "wet" areas (where sinks are located, for example), they must be protected by ground-fault interrupters (GFI). You can use GFI outlets in each room, or you can protect the circuit with a GFI circuit-breaker. Kitchen outlets must be on two separate circuits. That's basically all the requirements on outlets. Don't get me wrong, there are some code requirements beyond this broad-brush description I've given you, but I found this information to be all that really affected my job.

Switches and lights are even easier than outlets. Most wall switches are mounted about four feet above the floor. A feed wire comes into the switch box and a load wire runs to the light location, where it is tucked into a light box, which is usually octagonal. That's all there is to it.

If you can drill holes, hammer nails, and pull wire, you can do all of your rough wiring. Setting in outlets and switches is just a matter of stripping wire, curling it, and installing it beneath the proper screw. Of course, you want the power turned off to the wires you are working with. Light fixtures are easy to install. They attach to the boxes you install during rough-in, and the fixture wires are mated to the load wires and secured with twist-on wire nuts.

I don't have the space to give you complete details on how to run your own wiring, but I think you can see that the job is not very difficult. In my opinion, it is the easiest of all the mechanical phases, and that's saying something since I'm a master plumber and find electrical work, even on my first job, to be easier than plumbing.

PRE-WIRE

If you do your own electrical work, remember to pre-wire for as many future needs as you can think of. You know you will need a certain amount of pre-wiring, such as for telephones, cable television, and the like. Think as far into the future as you can, and make provisions for expansion and future use while your house is still in its rough-framing stage. Doing this will save you a lot of trouble, aggravation, and expense later on.

COST SAVINGS

There are cost savings available to you in electrical work even in the role of a general contractor. You can save money on your fixtures, and you can drive a hard bargain with a hungry electrician. However, the opportunity for saving big money in the electrical phase is limited, unless you participate in the work. I'm sure you noticed that the last chapter, on plumbing, was full of fixtures, faucets, and other areas where money could be saved in the buying stage. Electrical work doesn't involve as much material as plumbing, in terms of cost-comparing savings. You should use copper wire, and copper wire costs about the same from any competitive supplier. The only big savings you can hope for in buying power comes from the light fixtures, and we will talk about them shortly. You can, however, save thousands of dollars by pulling your own wires, mounting your own boxes, and installing your own outlets, switches, and fixtures. I saved over $2,000 by wiring my home, and that was after paying a master electrician to do some of the work.

DEVICES

Electrical devices, such as outlets and switches, don't allow a lot of room for saving money. You can save a few pennies by shopping, but you might not save enough to make it worth your time. There are some super-cheap devices available, but I wouldn't use them. In my opinion, electrical work is too important to scrimp on material. I don't know that one brand of outlet or switch is better than another, but I would stick with name-brand devices, even if they do cost a little more.

Rough-in boxes come in a variety of styles, shapes, sizes, and prices. I recommend using plastic boxes for your outlets and switches. Get the type that have nails already inserted in the box, this makes installation a lot easier. Also, look for boxes that have rough-in tabs on them. With this type of box, you don't have to measure to make sure the box will stick out enough to allow for drywall; the tap will pre-set the location of the box. Boxes for outlets and switches are rectangular. They are available with different depths. It is normally best to buy the deepest boxes that will fit into your walls. This gives more room for wire and makes trimming out the job easier.

Boxes used to hold light fixtures will normally be octagonal. I favor metal boxes that can be moved along an expanding support rod. These boxes normally come with tabs that pre-set the boxes for drywall. For ceiling fans, I recommend a stronger octagonal box. There are box kits sold with the primary use being for ceiling fans. The support bars are much stronger than standard bars, and this is a real advantage when hanging heavy ceiling fans.

You will probably need some junction boxes. These are available in plastic and metal. Junction boxes are square and are meant to be attached with nails or screws directly to studs and joists. Selective use of junction boxes can reduce the amount of electrical wire needed in a house, and this saves you money. How can you do this? You can install junction boxes in convenient, accessible locations, such as a basement ceiling, crawl space or attic, and bring different wires together, allowing you to run only one wire to the service panel.

Assume that you are wiring your own home and that the house is fifty feet long. You are working in the end of the house that is farthest from the electrical panel. You have three bedrooms in this location, each of which has a ceiling light. You could run a wire from each of the three switches back to the panel box. This would require about 150 feet of wire. A less expensive procedure would be to install a junction box. You would run a wire from each of the switches to the junction box, where the wires would all tie in together. There would be three wires going into the box, but only one coming out. By using the junction box, you would probably cut your wire usage in half. This is a smart way to save money. You must, however, make sure that the wires that you are combining are compatible and that the feed wire will not be overloaded.

If you use plastic boxes for your outlets and switches, you will have to buy outlets and switches that are equipped with ground screws. Not all outlets and switches have these, so make sure you are pricing and buying the right ones.

WIRE

Wire is the most expensive part of your electrical work. You should use copper wire, and it must be rated for the usage you have planned. For instance, if you will be running a wire outside to a post lamp, you will need wire rated for outdoor use. If you're installing the wire below ground, it must be rated for such usage. It is easy to pick up the wrong wire by mistake, so pay attention to the ratings and use limitations.

Where should you buy your wire? An electrical supplier will probably be the least expensive place to buy wire. However, these suppliers normally sell only in full rolls. For example, if you only need thirty feet of range cable, you will be better off to buy it from a store where you are not required to buy a whole roll. Many hardware stores sell wire by the foot, and this is a good way to buy cable for your range and clothes dryer. The rest of the wire you need will be in quantities that justify buying complete rolls.

If you're installing a doorbell, you will probably do best to buy wire for it from some place other than an electrical supplier. When I went to an electrical wholesaler to buy my bell wire, it was only sold in 500-foot rolls. I went to an electronics store and bought it in 100-foot rolls. The same is true for thermostat wire.

THE SERVICE PANEL

The service panel is the heart of your electrical system. It provides you with power and it's your safety valve. Don't cut corners when buying your panel box and circuit breakers. Get name-brand equipment that is recommended by electricians in your area. You might get a great deal on a no-name box and save $50, but you might be buying a lot more trouble than you bargained for.

Unless you are building a very small house, you should install a 200-amp electrical service. A 100-amp service is adequate for some small homes, but with today's growing demand for electricity in the home, a 200-amp service is a good investment. Even real estate appraisers agree with this logic.

In my opinion, you should not attempt to make connections to and within your panel box. One wrong move can mean sudden death. Hire a licensed, insured electrician to install and trim out your panel box.

LIGHT FIXTURES

Light fixtures are one area of your electrical work where you can either save or spend a large sum of money. The spread between the prices of light fixtures can be tremendous. For example, you could pay $10 for an exterior wall lamp, or you could pay $250 for one. Your personal taste and budget will have a lot of influence in the selection of light fixtures.

It is not unusual for light fixtures to be marked up as much as 100 percent in retail stores. When in Virginia, I could walk through lighting showrooms with my customers and know that the prices on the fixtures were twice what they were going to cost me. This seems like a lot of profit for the retailer, and indeed it is. You must do some serious shopping to avoid overpaying for lights.

As a professional contractor, I normally give my customers a dollar allowance to work with in picking out their light fixtures. The allowance is a figure that I arrive at, based on average lighting. For example, if I had a customer who wanted me to build a starter home with three bedrooms and one and a half bathrooms, containing about 1,100 square feet, I'd offer a lighting allowance of about $500 to $600. This would be based on the bedrooms having switched outlets, rather than ceiling lights. On a larger home, say a two-story colonial, with about 1,800 square feet, the allowance might be $800 to $1,000.

I've used lighting allowances for the entire time that I've been building houses. Some people spend less on lights than what I expect, and they get a rebate on what they have saved. Many customers spend about the allocated amount on lights. Some of my customers, however, go way over their allowances. I remember one young couple I built a small starter home for. The wife picked out a chandelier for her dining room that cost almost as much as the entire lighting allowance. She didn't get it, but she wanted it.

It is difficult to predict what you will spend on lighting fixtures. Since light selection depends on house size and style, not to mention a customer's desire, it is hard to arrive at an accurate budget. While I can't tell you how much your lights will cost, I can show you some ways to save money when buying them.

SAVING MONEY ON LIGHTING

Saving money on lights is really very easy. You shop and shop and shop some more. Where will you get your best price? Probably from some large retailer who sells a variety of home-related products. You might get great pricing from electrical suppliers, but don't count on it. I've found that retail super stores are generally the most cost-effective place to shop for lights.

When you begin to look at lights, you will see a wide range in their prices. Ceiling lights with the old bug-catcher globes and shades can be bought for less than $15. Plastic fixtures have starting prices below $10. Fancy fixtures can cost hundreds of dollars. Before you can project your fixture allowance, you must know how many lights will be needed and what types of lights they will be.

Go over your blueprints and count all the lights you will need. Make a list as you go along, and note what type of lights are needed. Once you have a list, you can do some comparative shopping. Sending out a bid request for this type of purchase isn't very effective. If you can't see the lights being offered to you, it will be very difficult to know if you are getting a good deal. You're going to have to visit showrooms and put in some long hours of legwork, but the savings will be worth it.

I have bought dozens of light fixtures for less than twelve dollars that all looked good. You don't have to spend fifty dollars to get a decent fixture. But, you do have to shop around, a lot. If you are hiring an electrician to do all of your electrical work for you, don't get roped into having to pick all of your light fixtures from a single supplier. Some electricians try to get customers to do this, but it's not in your best interest. Reserve the right to buy your fixtures from any place you want.

Ceiling fans are a good example of how you can spend a little or a lot to get basically the same thing. If you watch advertising flyers and pay at-tention to sales, you can buy a decent ceiling fan for less than fifty dollars. If you walk into an electrical showroom at some high-dollar retailer, you could spend an extra two hundred dollars for a fan that is not a great deal more attractive. The choice is yours; it's your money. I believe you will do best to buy your fixtures from some super store that caters to homeowners and do-it-yourselfers.

GET YOUR HANDS DIRTY

If you're not afraid to get your hands dirty, you can save a considerable amount of money by doing your own rough electrical work. For those who are not mechanically inclined, the biggest savings opportunity lies in the selection of fixtures and subcontractors. If you harness all of your potential power and play both the administrative and physical ends of electrical work, you could save enough money to buy that spa you've always wanted. There is definitely money to be saved in the electrical phase of your job.

CHAPTER 22

INSULATING YOUR HOME

Insulating your home is a job you can do, but it may not be a cost-effective task to undertake. Many insulation companies will supply and install the insulation in your home for about what the material would cost you. Why get itchy for nothing? This chapter evaluates the pros and cons of doing your own insulation, shows recommended R-values, and much more.

Insulating your own home is not a complicated job, but it can be a very itchy one. I suppose that not everyone is affected by coming into contact with the glass fibers in some types of insulation, but I've never met anyone who didn't get at least some skin irritation from the stuff. Personally, all I have to do is look at fiberglass insulation to begin to feel uncomfortable. I've installed my share of it, but I've never enjoyed the work. As unpleasant as insulating your home can be, it is a job that most people can do themselves, so we will talk about it.

The geographical location of your home will have a lot to do with the amount of insulation you are required to install. Insulation falls under the authority of local building inspectors. Local code requirements set minimum R-values that must be adhered to.

R-VALUE

An R-value is a unit of measurement used to determine the effectiveness of a type of insulation. It doesn't matter if you are insulating with foam, fiberglass, or cellulose, they will all share an R-value rating. Some types of insulation have higher R-values per inch, than others. The type of insulation you choose for your home will be partially personal preference, and partially due to the space that you have. For example, if you have a vaulted ceiling to insulate and you want an R-value of more than R-19, you may have to use a combination of insulation types. You might stuff the bays between the ceiling joists and then apply boards of rigid insulation to the joists, prior to installing drywall. You might even insulate the outside of your roof; I did that once.

The first home I ever built was for myself. It was an A-frame home. Due to the design, there was a lot of roof area. The roof was made of tongue-and-groove planks that served dual duty. They were my inside finished walls and ceilings, and they were the roof sheathing for the outside. Since the boards were solid and there were no cavities to fill with insulation, I had a problem. To solve the problem as best I could, I had rigid foam boards of insulation installed on the roof before installing shingles. I forget what R-value I wound up with, but it satisfied the code officer and myself, and that was really all that mattered.

The requirements of R-values vary from location to location. For example, when I was building in Virginia, homes were required to have a minimum R-value of R-19 in the attic and crawl space. R-11 was required in the exterior walls. In Maine, R-19 is what goes into the walls and crawl space, and R-30 goes into the attic. The difference is due to the climates. You must check with your local building inspector to determine what your minimum requirements are. It may pay to install more insulation than you are required to, especially if you plan to live in the home for a number of years. In time, the extra insulation will pay for itself in energy savings.

When you compare R-value ratings, the ones with the highest numbers provide the best resistance. Resistance is what the letter *R* in R-value stands for. A rating of R-19 is better than R-11, and R-30 is better than R-19. This is just the opposite of what you look for in the insulating qualities of glass.

FIBERGLASS

Fiberglass insulation is probably more common in homes than any other type of insulation. This fuzzy stuff can get into your eyes, nose, throat, and on your skin. When it does, it can be very irritating, and I mean that in the literal sense. If you're going to install your own fiberglass insulation, you should wear a mask over your nose and mouth. A pair of goggles or safety glasses is good insurance for your eyes. Gloves are a given, and even if the temperature is warm, you should wear long pants and long sleeves. Button everything up tight. Some people even put rubber bands around the legs of their pants and the sleeves of their shirts to help block infiltrating insulation. You can pretty much plan on being miserable while you install fiberglass insulation.

Fiberglass insulation can be used in your floors, ceilings, and outside walls. It can even be installed in interior partitions for soundproofing. Other than its irritating effects on people, fiberglass insulation is simple to install. In attics, it normally just gets rolled out. Sometimes, such as in Maine, two layers are put in the attic, one on top of the other. When installed vertically, such as in exterior walls, fiberglass is usually stapled into place. Fiberglass that is pushed up into bays between joists, can be stapled, but it is normally held in place with flexible metal rods. The insulation is put in place and a rod is pushed up under it. This rod spans the distance between the two joists creating the bay, and it holds the insulation up. It's all very simple work.

You can buy fiberglass insulation in different ways. If you want to shake it or blow it into your attic, you can buy it as a loose-fill material. If you

prefer blankets or batts, you can buy it in large rolls, with or without facing. Facing is paper that acts as a moisture barrier. If faced insulation is used, the facing should be installed so that it is seen from the heated part of the home. Unfaced insulation is cheaper than faced insulation. It is routinely used in attics, where no moisture barrier is needed. However, when unfaced insulation is installed in exterior walls, it should have a moisture barrier. This doesn't mean it must be faced insulation. You can install unfaced insulation in the walls and cover the walls with plastic. This is the way most pros do it. If your home is built on a crawl space, faced insulation should be used in the joist bays of the floor with the facing up against the subfloor, and the unfaced side of the roll looking down into the crawl space.

When you insulate your house, you must remember to chink in the areas around the rough openings of windows and doors. Some people fail to do this, and they suffer from cold breezes blowing around their windows and doors. All you have to do is push the fiberglass into the gaps around the openings. You will need something to push it up into place with. A cedar shim works very well, but a screwdriver or putty knife will also work.

CELLULOSE

Cellulose insulation is often used in older homes by blowing the insulation into the walls with a machine. This insulation is also used as a loose-fill insulation in the attics of new homes. There are two ways to install cellulose. You can buy it in bags and shake it into your attic, or you can use a blower. Many stores that sell loose-fill insulation will loan you a blower if you are buying enough insulation, and the attic of a house is plenty to meet the requirements. If you can't get your hands on a free blower, you can rent one from a tool rental store.

I've insulated attics with and without blowers. When insulating attics that are hard to get to, a blower is very handy. If the attic is tall and accessible, I prefer to shake the loose-fill from the bag. This way, there is no lost time fighting the clogs that often occur in the hose of a blower.

FOUNDATION WALLS

Foundation walls for basements don't have to be insulated in most cases, but you can make your home more comfortable and more energy efficient by insulating these walls. There are two common ways of doing this. I believe the most effective way is to install thick foam boards of rigid insulation on the foundation walls before the foundation is backfilled. If you fail to do this, you will have to insulate the walls from inside the basement. Again, foam boards are the most common form of insulation used for this project, unless the basement is being finished off into living space. If there will be stud walls between the foundation walls and the living space, you can use fiberglass insulation, just as you would in the rest of your exterior walls.

OTHER TYPES

There are other types of insulation, such as spray-in foam. While many types of insulation are available, the ones we have discussed are the mainstay of residential building. I will provide you with a chart at the end of this chapter so that you can compare the R-values of various types of insulation, but I imagine you will use either all fiberglass or a combination of fiberglass and cellulose.

TO DO IT?

When you are trying to decide whether to do it yourself or to sub it out, you must weigh all the factors. Insulation is not difficult to install, but it can be a very unpleasant job. You might save some money doing the job yourself, but you probably won't save much. I don't know why, but it seems that insulation companies can provide and install insulation for about the same price as most of us pay for just the material. It's been this way for as long as I've been building.

I've built houses with the use of subcontractors, employees, and pretty much on my own. In all cases, I've never found it worthwhile to install my own insulation. If I were to do the work personally, I could save a few dollars, but if I pay even a low-paid employee to do the installation, it costs more than if I sub the work out. Again, I'm not sure why this is, but it has proved to be a fact every year and in every place I've built houses.

INSULATION INSTALLERS

Insulation companies are well prepared for what they do. Their crews can be very fast and affordable. I recommend that you strongly consider hiring a specialized insulation company to insulate your home. It's not that I think you can't do the job, it's just that I don't think you will save enough money doing it yourself to make the aggravation worthwhile.

When you solicit bids on your job, get several. It's always been my experience that major insulation companies are very competitive in their pricing. Unlike so many of the trades, where bids vary greatly, insulation prices tend to be very close. It still pays to get several quotes. I suspect that if you compare the bids with just the cost of materials you will have to buy to do the job yourself, you will find that the savings are minimal.

PROS AND CONS

The pros and cons of various types of insulation are not of much concern. For the most part, if you are getting the R-value you want, the type of insulation being used is not too important. Cellulose is probably the most user-friendly insulation in terms of installation and health issues. There were big problems several years ago with some foam spray-in insulation, because it created and gave off potentially harmful fumes. Fiberglass, as long as it is contained, is safe. It is only if fiberglass gets airborne and attacks your throat, eyes, nose, and other sensitive areas that it is undesirable. By far, the industry standard in new residential construction is fiberglass.

I suppose that if you conducted an exhaustive study, you could determine the longevity of various types of insulation. But, I would think these results would depend a lot on where and how the insulation was installed. In my opinion, fiberglass is the way to go.

CHAPTER 23

HANGING AND FINISHING DRYWALL

Hanging drywall is heavy work, and finishing drywall requires skilled hands. This chapter takes you on the job for a realistic look at the drywall phase of construction. You learn about the different types and sizes of drywall boards, but that's not all. You get some firsthand advice on how to hang and finish the walls of your new home.

Hanging and finishing drywall is a phase of construction where you can save some money by doing part of the work yourself. While you probably won't be able to finish the drywall to professional standards, it is very likely that you can hang it, especially if you have help from some friends or family. Drywall is heavy and awkward to work with, so you must keep this in mind when evaluating whether to do your own work or not. Another thing to keep in mind is whether or not you will have trouble finding finishers who are willing to finish drywall that they didn't hang. This can be a problem.

How difficult is it to hang drywall? Aside from the weight of the material, hanging drywall is not difficult. If you can cut straight lines and drive nails or screws, you can do the job. Ceilings are a bit of a challenge, but there are tricks of the trade that allow one person to hang most ceilings. Before we branch off into the many facets of drywall work, let me share a past experience with you.

MY FIRST HOUSE

When I built my first house, I did a lot of the work myself. My wife helped with a lot of the work, and between the two of us, we accomplished many work goals. One that we didn't do so well with was the drywall. We didn't have much trouble hanging it, but when it came time to finish it, we ran into some problems. The job wound up being pretty unique.

Our first home wasn't very large. The whole house contained less square footage than the upstairs of the home I'm building now. As I recall, it only had about 760 square feet in it. Most of the ceilings and a lot of the walls were exposed wood, so there wasn't too much drywall to worry with. But what there was of it gave us a fit.

At the time this house was built, I'd been working in construction for about seven years. I'd seen all of the trades work, but I didn't know a lot about some of them. Drywall was one trade I had never been taught. Even so, I figured Kimberley and I could get the job done to our satisfaction. Wrong.

Hanging the drywall went pretty well for us. It went so well, in fact, that I was growing quite confident in my newfound abilities. Then came the time to tape and first-coat the rock. I didn't have any trouble putting on the cornerbeads, and the tape was easy enough to work with. The taping started out fairly well. I actually had fun filling in nail holes and stuff.

After the first coat had dried, it was time for sanding. Aside from a lot of dust and some sore arm muscles, this part of the work seemed to be going pretty well. I did have some trouble gauging how deep to sand the compound. There were some spots that didn't seem great, but there were still two more coats to go, so I didn't worry.

When I put on the second coat of mud, the house was starting to look pretty good. Kimberley and I were impressed. After the second coat dried, it was time for more sanding. This time we took more pains with our work and tried to get a good job done. There was only one more coat left. Looking back, I know what we did wrong, but at the time, I had no idea we were creating problems for ourselves.

Finally it was time for our third and final coat of drywall compound. We spent hours trying to get it just right. However, even with our best efforts, the walls just weren't turning out too well. Some seams were humped up, and others had been sanded too much. We fought with the work until we decided to do another coat, to fix our mistakes. Try as we might, we never did get the seams to come out right. We tested our work by painting some of the walls with a light primer. The drywall seams showed far too badly to just paint over them. It was decision time.

We didn't possess the skills to finish the job properly. Our house was already way over our budget, so there wasn't much money available to bring in professionals. Not knowing what to do, we took a time-out and thought for a day or so. We had planned from the beginning to texture the ceilings. This inspired me to texture the walls. Surely that would hide the ugly seams. Well, that's what we did. Every piece of drywall in that house was textured.

We had a lot of trouble getting the texture compound to dry. We had put it on in coats that were far too thick. Again, we didn't know this at the time, but that was what was wrong. After many, many hours of work with putty knives and potato mashers, we called the job done. It wasn't a work of art, but it was passable. I was concerned that the unconventional walls would hurt our final appraisal, but they didn't. Some people thought the house was strange. We were satisfied with it, but I will admit, I was never impressed favorably by our texture job.

As it turned out, we didn't get to live in that house very long. Interest rates were around 12 percent when we started to build, and they soared to 18 percent before we could lock in our permanent financing. This made a huge difference in the monthly payment. Between a gigantic payment and an economy that was faltering, we had to sell the house. If you've never tried to sell a house when interest rates are higher than the legal voting age, you can't know how difficult we thought it would be to move the house.

Three prospective purchasers viewed the home. One left almost immediately. The other two were interested. Both people made us an offer. The lady who bought the house raved about two features that had sold her on the property. Both of the features she loved were ones that I thought would hurt our resale value. One was the drywall. She thought the textured walls and ceilings were fantastic. The other item was a sunken soaking tub. This tub was round and the lip of the tub was at floor level. The deep tub hung down under the house, into the cellar. This was the only tub we had. According to the purchaser, it was a key selling feature.

As much as we did wrong on our first house, it's a wonder we ever built another one, let alone sixty houses a year. Much of what I know I learned from experience. Some of the experience has been painful. A lot of it has been costly. All of it is invaluable. I've told you this story for several reasons. I want you to see that if you choose to do your own work, you won't be the first pioneer to tackle an unknown job. Should you mess up, there are ways to work it all out. It's also important for you to know that I'm far from perfect. The only advantage I may have over you is that I've done a lot and made a lot of mistakes. Your advantage is that you can learn from my mistakes, not yours. Now, let's dig into the basics of hanging drywall.

TYPES OF DRYWALL

You need to be aware of the different types of drywall before placing your order with a supplier. First there is regular drywall. Then there is moisture-resistant drywall—usually either green or blue—that is normally installed in bathrooms. A third type of drywall will be needed if your home will have an attached garage. Fire-resistant drywall will be installed in the garage at all points where the garage and finished living space share a common wall. In most localities this is ⅝" drywall. Some places may require double sheets of ½".

Not only must you know what types of drywall to purchase, you must know what sizes you want. Professional hangers order their boards of drywall in different sizes, to minimize waste. As a first-timer, you probably will have trouble doing a material take-off that is accurate enough to eliminate waste. Don't worry about it, you'll be saving a lot of money by hanging the boards.

If you're going to have help hanging your rock, you can order 12-foot sheets. These boards are four feet wide and twelve feet long. A person who is working alone will have better luck with smaller boards, like 4×8 sheets. There are other sizes available, but these two are all you really need to know about.

Professionals like to use 12-footers because it makes the job go faster and it reduces seams. This is all well and good if you are used to working with big boards and are in good enough shape to do it. For most do-it-yourselfers, 12-footers are just too hard to handle.

In addition to your drywall, you will need ready-mixed drywall compound. This stuff is normally sold in 5-gallon buckets, and they are heavy. Professionals put these buckets on little platforms that have four wheels. This allows them to roll the mud around, rather than having to lift and carry the bucket every time they move. Despite what the label says, drywall compound is not ready mixed. It will need to be transferred, a small amount at a time, and thinned very slightly with water to make it smooth and spreadable. There is an art to this. Finishers usually start off with a thinner mixture on the first coat and then use a thicker one towards the end of their work.

Some finishers use small, handheld troughs to carry their mud. These containers are easy to hold in one hand and even when full of compound, they are not very heavy.

The last things you need to order are drywall tape, nails or screws, and cornerbeads for all of your outside corners. The tape is used on inside corners. Once you have all these goodies, you are ready to work, and believe me, it will be work. If you're not willing to take on some sore muscles, lose a lot of sweat, and swear at yourself and the drywall, contract the job out to professionals.

HANGING DRYWALL

Hanging drywall is heavy work, and it can be an awkward job. If you hang your own drywall, it will be best to line up some strong, willing helpers. There are also a few tools you will need. Most professionals cut drywall with a razor knife. The razor is used to score the drywall. Once a line has been cut into the board, the drywall can be bent and broken. A chalk line is very helpful in marking lines on which to cut the drywall. Some type of straightedge is also needed. This can be a T-square or even a spare wall stud. As long as it is straight and long enough, it will work, but a special drywall square is well worth the money. No pro would go without one. You will need some miscellaneous items, such as a tape measure, some support to place the drywall on while it's being cut, a hammer, a ladder or two, and possibly an electric screw gun. The basic tools needed for hanging drywall don't cost too much.

GETTING STARTED

Getting started with your drywall will be easy. The first sheets are always the easy ones. Before you start, you must decide whether you will hang the board horizontally or vertically. Most inexperienced people use 8-footers and hang them vertically. Pros use 12-footers and hang them horizontally, to create fewer seams. The tapered edges aren't the big problem—it's the end edges that are tough to conceal. If you have eight-foot ceilings, you may want to hang your drywall vertically to keep from having to deal with the butt edges. Pros don't, but then they're pros.

Pick a room to start in. Are you going to hang the walls first or the ceilings? Most professionals agree that it is best to hang the ceilings first. There is a good reason for this. If you install the ceilings first, the drywall installed on the walls will support the edges of the ceilings. You don't have to start with ceilings, but I think you should.

If you happen to have two helpers, hanging a

ceiling is no big deal. When you only have one helper, the job gets a bit more interesting. Should you be working alone, the task can become quite an adventure and I don't recommend it unless you have a video camera running and hope to amuse your friends and family later on. I'm not going to cover every little detail of how to hang drywall. There are specialty books available on just about every trade that can give you step-by-step instructions. My goal is to educate you in the basic steps involved, so you can evaluate your ability to do the work and so that you can keep tabs on professionals you may decide to engage.

If you have two people helping you, they can hold sheets of drywall in place while you attach it to the ceiling joists. With only one helper, you can hold your end of the board with your head, and screw it to the joists with a screw gun. If you don't like the idea of wearing drywall as a hat, you can build a brace. A T-brace can be made out of scrap lumber. The vertical section of the "T" must be long enough so that the brace is a bit taller than the ceiling in the room where you are working. All you do is nail a couple of pieces of wood together to form a T-shaped brace. This brace can be wedged under the sheet of drywall being installed on the ceiling to hold it in place, while you attach it. This saves time and takes some wear and tear off of your head.

Should you be so unfortunate as to be hanging a ceiling by your lonesome, you will need two tall stepladders and two T-braces. Set the ladders up and place a board of drywall across the top of them. Then position the first T-brace to hold one end of the drywall up against the ceiling joist. Now set the second brace into place. Once the braces are secure, you can go about your business of securing the board to the joists.

After your ceilings are hung, you are ready for the walls. Compared to the ceilings you have just done, the walls will be like a relaxing vacation. If you are installing your boards horizontally, you will hang the lowest boards first. These are easy. When you get to the second level, you have to find a way to keep the boards in place. If you have any help, even just one other person, this is not a problem. Those of you working alone will

have to get creative. One way to do this is to nail some 16-penny nails into the studs, very near the top edge of the first piece of drywall you installed. The nails should be driven in at an angle, so that they will keep the second level of drywall from kicking out of place. With the nails installed, lift the second level of drywall into place and the nails should stabilize it. Now you can screw or nail the drywall to the studs.

Should you use nails or screws? Either one will work fine. Most professionals prefer screws, because they are less likely to work loose. Drywall nails, however, are made with ridges on the shank to help prevent the nails from pulling out. When nailing drywall you must double nail—wherever you put a nail, put another one about two inches away from it. Drywall tends to bounce as it is being hammered. The second nail ensures that the drywall and the studs are snug against each other. If you decide to use screws, you will need an electric screw gun. Installing drywall screws all day manually will wear you out. Whether you use nails or screws, you must make sure the heads sink into the drywall. There should be a dimple-like depression all the way around the heads of any nails or screws. This depression will be covered by drywall compound during the finishing stage.

As you cut and hang drywall, you should attempt to make all joints as straight and as smooth as possible. The better job you do hanging the drywall, the easier it will be to get a good finish. I recommend having factory ends butt together for the horizontal seams of a wall. The rough, cut end on the bottom sheet will be concealed by baseboard trim. The other rough end, where the top sheet meets the ceiling, can be hidden with drywall tape.

There really isn't much involved in the hanging of drywall. The tricky part is finishing it, and this is a job that you will probably want to hire professionals to do. It is possible for you to do your own finish work, but it is unlikely that you will be able to produce professional-looking results. I will, however, give you a quick breakdown on what is involved in the finishing stage.

FINISHING DRYWALL

Finishing drywall is not a very technical job. It is, however, a complicated process that requires a certain, special touch. You don't need many tools for finish work. A couple of putty knives are the only tools you must have. A four-inch putty knife, a six-inch putty knife, and a twelve-inch blade are the sizes that will do you the most good. You will need a hammer or a screw gun, to hang cornerbead. A sanding block is helpful, but not a necessity. The most important part of finishing drywall is the skill to do it.

You will probably be better off to hire professional contractors to do your finish work. This is not to say that you can't do it, but you probably can't do it within the standards set by professionals. I can tell you this, if you do your own finish work, you will need patience.

Assuming that you are not intimidated by being your own finisher, I will give you an outline of what you will be up against. The first coat during the finishing stage is perhaps the easiest. Filling in the depressions that surround the heads of nails or screws is the easy part. All you have to do is dip your putty knife into a bucket of pre-mixed joint compound and dab it into the depressions. By pulling the putty knife across the depressions, you can create a smooth surface. Be careful not to leave drywall compound in a hump that is higher than the plane of the wall. If you do, you will be facing a sanding and scraping nightmare. The compound will shrink when it dries. That is why it takes several coats to complete the job.

Taping joints is a bit more difficult than dabbing in depressions. Taping is not hard work, and it's not difficult in theory. Let's say you are ready to tape the horizontal seams of your walls. You will start with a four-inch putty knife. Dip it into your joint compound and pull your knife along the seam. You want to create a layer of compound all along the seam. Once this is done, you will lay drywall tape over the wet compound. Use the putty knife to press the tape into the mud. As you unroll the tape, press it into place with the putty knife. The tape, which contains no adhesive, will stay in place. Now you should go back over the tape with your putty knife to smooth it out and remove all air bubbles. When you're done, the tape will be embedded in the mud, with little to no mud on top of the tape.

A lot of first-time finishers, including myself at one time, make the mistake of putting joint compound on top of the drywall tape. I did it thinking that it was necessary to hold the tape in place. This is not the proper procedure. There should not be any significant amount of mud on top of the tape during the first coat.

Inside corners are covered with drywall tape. This is basically an easy task. A length of drywall tape is cut off and creased in the middle. Once the tape is creased, it can be placed in inside corners easily. Just as you would do with a horizontal seam, you spread joint compound on the surface of the drywall at the inside corners and push the creased tape into it. This is smoothed out with a putty knife and air bubbles are removed. It's really not a difficult task.

Outside corners are done differently than inside corners. Since outside corners often get bumped into and abused, metal cornerbead is used to finish them. Cornerbead is a thin, perforated metal strip that is formed to fit over outside corners. It is nailed or screwed into place. Cornerbead is installed directly against raw drywall. Joint compound is then spread out over the metal. A six-inch putty knife is used for this work.

After the first coat of finishing is complete, you have to wait for the joint compound to dry. This will normally take twenty-four hours, or less. However, if the weather is damp or the temperature is cool (below 70°), drying time can be much longer. If the joint compound gets too cold, it will shrink and crack. You should try to maintain an even temperature in the work area. Depending upon the time of year when you are doing your work, you may not have anything to worry about. Finishing drywall in the winter is a job that is almost sure to require some type of heat. There are many types and styles of portable heaters available from tool rental centers. You can rent what you need.

Once the first coat has dried, you are ready for the second coat. The second coat is normally applied right over the first coat, without any need for sanding. However, if, as you inspect your first coat you find major flaws in your work, you may have to do some sanding before installing the second coat. If sanding is needed, use a coarse-grit sandpaper. I've found the best way to handle the sanding work is with a plastic sanding block.

Sanding blocks are simple pieces of plastic that are designed to hold a sheet of sandpaper. Once the sandpaper is loaded on the block, you will be holding just the block. You will not have to handle the sandpaper until it is worn out. The block has grooves on it to make it easy to handle. These blocks are cheap, and they are easier and more comfortable to work with than just hanging onto a piece of sandpaper.

Don't use an electric sander. It is very difficult to control and monitor the results of sanding with an electric sander. When you sand manually, you are not as likely to cut too deeply into your tape and compound.

Some of your sanding work will involve ceilings and possibly some high walls, especially if you have vaulted ceilings. These areas can be done in a number of ways. You can work from a ladder or pipe staging. An overturned drywall compound bucket can provide a makeshift ladder that will allow most people to reach most ceilings. Admittedly, a bucket is not the safest way to reach high spots, but it is one of the tools many professionals use.

Professionals use special stilts for doing standard ceilings and walls. They normally use staging for doing work in higher locations. However, they also use sanding poles. These poles have long handles and a wide head that allows you to sand in high spots while keeping both feet on the floor.

Applying your second coat of joint compound will be done in about the same way that you did the first coat. There is one difference. You used a four-inch putty knife to apply your first coat along tape seams. On the second coat, you should use a six-inch knife. It is also helpful to have a drywall trowel. Your goal is to spread the second coat out more than the first coat. As you expand the area of your joint compound and feather it out to noth-

ing, you are making seams that will be harder to see when the house is painted.

After the second coat of compound dries, you will have a lot of sanding to do. You must smooth out all of your seams and spots. There is only one more coat after the second coat, so you want this stage of your work to be done as well as possible. When you're sanding, you want to avoid sanding too deeply. If you go too deep, you will rough up your tape and have to more or less start over again in those spots. What you should try to do is to get the compound as smooth and even as possible.

After sanding your second coat, you can apply your final coat of mud. Again, you want this application to spread out more than the second coat did. Remember, the wider your seam is as it feathers out, the harder it will be to see it after painting. The last coat will normally be a thin coat, and it should dry faster than the earlier applications. When it's dry, you should use a light-grit sandpaper to sand it. Don't get carried away with enthusiasm on the sanding. Sanding that dips into the seams at this stage will require an additional coat on the damaged areas. Take your time and strive for smooth, even seams.

CEILING FINISHES

Ceiling finishes in homes vary. Some people like smooth ceilings that are painted. A lot of people prefer some type of textured ceiling. The three main types of texturing are sprayed, stomped, and swirled. Of these, spray textures are generally the least expensive. I strongly recommend having your ceilings textured. Drywall seams on smooth ceilings almost always show at some point. Even if the seams are hidden when the house is first painted, they may appear as the house settles. A textured ceiling camouflages the seams.

SMOOTH CEILINGS

Smooth ceilings are done with the same finishing procedures that are used on walls. No matter which type of ceiling you are planning, the finish work on the drywall will be the same. Before the ceiling is painted, it should be covered with a coat of primer. If you're using a professional drywall contractor, the contractor may do the priming work for you. It is also very possible that you will do this work, to save some money. Then again, you might hire a painter to do it. We will talk about priming and painting a little later on.

SPRAYED CEILINGS

Sprayed ceilings are the least expensive route to a textured ceiling. This work can be done by drywall contractors or painters. You could do it yourself, but I doubt if this would be a good idea. Sprayed ceilings give a finished appearance that resembles, in my opinion, a lot of bumps on the ceiling. Sprayed ceilings are not the most ornate, but they do hide seams and are inexpensive.

There is an alternative to sprayed ceilings that you can do yourself. The finished result will be similar. You can buy textured paint that when it is rolled onto a ceiling will give a textured look. This texture will be lighter than that achieved with a sprayer, but it will hide many minor imperfections in the finish work of your drywall.

STOMPED CEILINGS

Stomped ceilings are done with a broom, a sponge, a potato masher, or anything else you want to use. When a ceiling is stomped, drywall compound is spread over the ceiling. While the compound is still wet, it is pulled. The pulling can be done with a number of different tools. I've used a potato masher with good results. Brooms and sponges are also common tools during the stomping of a ceiling.

You can stomp your own ceilings. Before you begin, decide on how thick you want your texture to be. If you spread compound on the ceiling in a thick coat, you will wind up with a ceiling that will take a long time to dry, and where the finished product resembles the roof of a cave. I made this mistake in my first house. On the other hand, if you start stomping a coat of mud that is too thin, you will wind up pulling the compound off the ceiling. You can experiment with a small section of ceiling to determine how thick your coat of compound should be.

There are no high-tech technical skills needed to stomp a ceiling. The process involves spreading joint compound over the ceiling. Once this is done, the stomping begins. If you use a broom, you can stomp the ceiling without ever leaving the floor. To stomp a ceiling with a broom or potato masher, all you do is press the stomping tool into the compound and pull it back. As the tool comes out of the compound, a texture will be created. This is not a difficult job, and you should be able to do it yourself.

SWIRLED CEILINGS

Swirled ceilings are much more difficult to create, depending upon their pattern, than stomped ceilings are. Sponges can be used to swirl a ceiling. Spread out compound on the ceiling and then use a sponge to create your pattern. If you are hoping for a beautiful, consistent pattern in your swirled ceiling, I recommend that you have a professional do the swirling. Simple swirls, such as arcs and sweeps are within the capabilities of average people, but more detailed ceilings can require the use of professionals.

PRODUCTION SCHEDULE

When you're planning your production schedule, allow plenty of time for drywall work. Even if professionals are doing the entire job, allow more time than what they estimate. I don't believe I have ever built a house that I didn't run into problems with the drywall phase. A small, starter home can normally be drywalled in one work week. Larger homes can take twice that long. Drying time plays a big part in the production time of drywall work.

IN REVIEW

You can almost certainly hang your own drywall, especially if you have some help. You will probably be better off to sub the finish work out to a professional contractor. Some types of textured ceilings will make seams in your ceilings less evident. The amount of money saved will depend on several factors. These factors include the size of your home, the prices you can negotiate with subcontractors, and so forth. You can expect the savings to run into the thousands of dollars.

INTO THE STRETCH

FROM HOUSE TO HOME

At this point, your house looks like a genuine home from the outside. Sure, the lawn is still mud or dirt. The drive and the trees, flower beds and shrubs are crude or nonexistent. But the structure looks nearly complete.

Meanwhile, on the inside, you are confronting an astounding square footage of wall, ceiling and floor that needs to be covered up. Very little of what you can see will be visible when the house is done. You will be covering up nearly everything with colors, textures and materials that *will* be visible to you and your guests for a long time. All of your work and your decisions from here on will be the result of trade-offs between your taste and your purse. While you can't satisfy the demands of each, you can get some great bargains through sweat and brain equity.

CHAPTER 24

INTERIOR PAINTING PROCEDURES

Anyone can paint an interior wall, right? Well, yes. Most anyone can paint an interior wall. But, there can be a big difference in the outcome of the painting jobs between professionals and amateurs. The odds are good that you can, with the help of this chapter, paint your own interior walls with professional results, but don't take the job lightly. This chapter addresses the various types of paints, primers, and installation methods for paint jobs with professional results.

Interior painting is a phase of home construction that a lot of people believe they can do themselves. As a general contractor, I've often allowed customers to do as much of the work as they were comfortable with. I can't recall a time when a home buyer who wanted to do some hands-on work didn't want to do interior painting. Can you do your own painting? I'm sure you probably can, but you may not want to. Painting is not as easy as it looks.

I want to take a little different approach at this point. Up to now, I've been doing most of the talking. It's your turn, now. I'm going to pretend that you are sitting with me in my office. You're meeting with me as a production consultant for the construction of your new home. During our discussion, you are asking me what phases of your job you can do. The one thing you are confident that you can handle is the interior painting. As a part of my evaluation, I have to ask you some technical questions.

Have you ever painted a home before? You admit that you've never done it before, but that you're sure you can do it.

Are you going to use an oil-based paint or a latex paint? You scratch your head and think. It's obvious to me that you don't know the pros and cons of the two types of paints.

How many coats of paint will you apply? You answer very quickly that two coats will be ap-

plied. This tells me something. Most professionals install one coat of primer and one coat of paint, not two coats of paint.

Will you paint your house with a brush, a roller, or a sprayer? You tell me that you are going to use a roller and some brushes. This is a good answer, and it tells me you have some potential.

What type of finish are you looking for in your paint? Do you want gloss, semi-gloss, or flat? This question causes you to wrinkle your nose in confusion. As you are contemplating an answer, I'm drawing a conclusion that you are going to need a lot of consultation before embarking on your own painting job.

The questions and scenarios I've just given you aren't far from the truth of many actual interviews with customers and clients. Most people start off feeling very good about their ability to paint their own home, but when they are put to the test, their confidence usually evaporates. There is some good news; this chapter is going to help you face the facts and rise above any deficiencies you may have.

INSPECT YOUR DRYWALL

Before you begin to paint, you should inspect your drywall. Look over all of the seams and finish work. If any of it is cracked, humped, or otherwise unacceptable, keep your paint in its can. Don't spread any paint until the surfaces of your walls and ceilings are ready to receive it. Once you are satisfied with your finished drywall, you can get ready to paint.

SELECTING THE PROPER PAINT

Selecting the proper paint can be confusing. Professional paint stores are usually the best places to look for expert advice. You can buy paint from any number of suppliers, but a store that specializes in paint is normally the best place to start your trek.

THE PRIMER

The primer or sealer you select is going to set the stage for the quality of your paint job. If the primer is of a poor quality, even a high quality paint isn't going to do its best. When you buy your primer, invest in the best. The primer is what will seal the drywall and hide the taping seams. If this isn't done effectively, the remainder of your job will suffer.

THE PAINT

The paint you use in your home should be one of high quality. Cheap paint produces cheap-looking results. I've used paint in some of my rental properties that was so wimpy that even after two coats, I could still see through the paint. Another problem I've encountered with bargain-basement paint is that when I clean it, it comes off on my cleaning rag. It's embarrassing to wash fingerprints off a wall and find that the paint came off with them. Don't skimp on your paint budget; buy the best.

FLAT PAINT

Most walls and ceilings are painted with flat-finish paint. This is standard procedure, although there is no rule that stipulates that you must use a flat paint. One room in a house where I stray from flat paint is the kitchen. I prefer a semi-gloss paint in kitchens. This type of paint makes cleaning easier.

SEMI-GLOSS

Semi-gloss paint is often used on wood trim. With the walls painted with a flat paint and the trim painted with a semi-gloss paint, there is enough difference to see it. This enhances the home in the eyes of most people. As I've just said, I prefer semi-gloss paint in kitchens, where grease and grime must be cleaned regularly, and in bathrooms, where moisture and mildew can become a problem.

OIL OR LATEX?

Will you use oil or latex paint? Either type of paint can be used. Most painters prefer latex paint for interior work. There are three key advantages to using latex paint. One is its lack of odor. Oil-based paint produces a strong odor. When used inside, without proper ventilation, the smell can be quite unpleasant. You can eliminate this problem simply by painting with latex. Another advantage to using latex paint is the ease with which it can be cleaned up. Soap and water is all that is needed to remove latex paint, compared to paint thinner or mineral spirits needed to clean up oil-based paint. A third and important advantage is that latex dries more quickly than oil paint.

The drying time of a paint is very important to professional painters. A paint that dries quickly allows painters to apply a second coat during the same day that the first coat is applied. This reduces travel time to and from the job, and increases a painter's profit. For the do-it-yourselfer, it can mean getting a lot more painting done in one weekend.

Will oil-based paint last longer than latex paint? It is the opinion of most professionals that a quality interior paint will hold up just as well whether it is latex or oil. Quality is a big factor in the durability of paint, and you often get what you pay for. When you are trimming the fat from your building budget, don't cut too deeply into the paint allowance.

ONE COAT OR TWO?

Will your walls and ceilings require one coat of paint, or two? Some paints say they will cover with just one coat. While this may be true in cases where walls and ceilings that have been painted before are being repainted, it doesn't generally apply to new construction. When you are starting with unpainted drywall, you should plan on two coats, one of primer/sealer and one of paint. There are people who skip the primer/sealer and apply two coats of regular paint. This can work out okay, but it is more professional to apply a first coat of primer/sealer and to follow it with finish paint.

When you will be using one coat of primer and one coat of paint, you should buy both products at the same time. By doing this, you can have the paint store tint the primer to a color that will work well with your finish paint. This isn't mandatory, but it will produce professional results.

THE TOOLS

The tools required to paint a house are not numerous or difficult to use. Brushes, rollers, power rollers, and paint sprayers can all be used to paint your home. For most amateurs, an old-fashioned roller and some common brushes will be the best choice in tools. Sprayers are a lot harder to use competently, and power rollers can make a mess when used by inexperienced hands.

In addition to your basic tools, you will need some other items. A ladder is certainly helpful when painting a house. Extension poles for your roller will make hitting the high spots easier. A paint mixer might be needed, and you will probably need paint pans, buckets, and a few other miscellaneous items.

HOW MUCH?

How much primer and paint will you need? If you are hiring a professional painter, you will not have to concern yourself with a material take-off. When you act as your own painter, however, the responsibility for ordering paint will be yours. Don't worry. Paint take-offs are pretty easy to do; they're much easier than a framing take-off.

Paint is sold with labels that indicate the expected coverage of the paint in terms of square feet. For example, if you read a label on a paint can, you might see that a gallon of paint is rated to cover 400 square feet. This recommendation is a good starting point, but don't take it too seriously. How you paint and the type of surface being painted will affect the coverage. While you

shouldn't expect the true coverage to mirror that of the label rating, you can use the rate coverage to create a decent take-off.

MEASURING A ROOM

Measuring a room for paint is quite easy. All you have to do is measure all of the surface area to be painted and convert the measurements into square footage. To determine square footage, you multiply width times length. For example, if you have a ceiling that measures twelve feet by ten feet, you multiply 12×10 to arrive at 120 square feet. If you will be applying two coats of paint, you will need 240 square feet of coverage. A wall that is eight feet tall and twelve feet long is 96 square feet. Two coats of paint will consume about 200 square feet of coverage, or in many cases, half a gallon of paint.

Professional painters often work with some rule-of-thumb to come up with quick take-offs. These estimates are sometimes off the mark by a little, but they are often close enough to keep the job on track. I suggest that you measure all painting surfaces and do a complete and accurate take-off. However, I will give you a hint of how you can arrive at a quick guesstimate of your paint needs.

If you figure one gallon of paint for each coat of paint applied to the four walls of an average room, you won't be too far off the mark. By an average room, I'm talking about a room that contains between 150 and 175 square feet. For this same room, figure one gallon of paint for two coats, or one-half a gallon for one coat. To paint the trim in our hypothetical average room, you should plan on buying one quart of paint for each coat. This type of estimating makes it possible for you to count up the number of rooms to be painted and prepare a take-off in a matter of minutes. There is, however, even a faster way to do the job. You can convert your estimating technique to a square-footage basis.

We know that for an average room, of say 150 square feet, you will need three gallons of paint for two coats on the walls and ceiling and one quart of trim paint for each coat applied to the trim. If we assume your new house will have 1,500 square feet in it, you can take your rule-of-thumb figures and multiply them by ten. You would need 30 gallons of wall and ceiling paint, and 20 quarts of trim paint. Once you have the total square footage, you can use this formula with any house. You know that three gallons of wall and ceiling paint and two quarts of trim paint will be needed for every 150 square feet the house contains. Simply divide the home's total square footage by 150 and use the resulting number to multiply your total paint needs.

As convenient as quick estimating is, it is not always accurate. If you want your paint take-off to be as accurate as possible, you are going to have to take some measurements and do some math. This isn't complicated, it just takes a little more time. When you measure a room, you might wonder how to deal with windows and doors; pretend they don't exist. Measure your walls as if the whole area will be painted, even if windows and doors consume some of the wall space. By leaving the windows and doors in your estimate, as painted surfaces, you are building in a margin of error. Some paint will be spilled, some will stick in the can, and the way you apply the paint will affect its coverage. By leaving in the area eaten up by windows and doors, you will be more likely to arrive at a solid working number for your estimate.

HOW LONG WILL IT TAKE?

How long will it take to paint your own home? This question could have a lot of impact on your decision of whether to paint the house yourself or to hire the work out. The time needed to paint a house varies with a myriad of possibilities. Your physical condition is one factor in the time required to paint a house. Experience can influence the speed with which a house is painted. Weather conditions might play a part in the time requirements for painting. Cold, damp weather can alter the drying time of paint, pushing your production schedule back. There are, to be sure, many factors to consider when estimating the time you will need to be your own painter.

It is impossible for me to predict how long it will take you to paint your house. I don't know enough about you, your house, and your region's climate to make a decent estimate. I can, however, cite you some examples from my past experience.

The style of your house can have a lot to do with how long the paint work will take. For example, my new house has many vaulted ceilings. The ceilings reach to a height of nearly thirty feet above the floor. Obviously, a ceiling that is thirty feet high will take longer to paint than one that is only eight feet off the floor. Since many of my ceilings are vaulted, they present more painting surface than a flat ceiling. This is another slowdown in the painting process. Just as my ceilings are high, so are the walls that support them. All of this high work brings the pace of painting to a crawl. I can't stand on a bucket and spray the ceiling or roll it out with a roller and extension pole. I've got to get up on an elevated platform to work, and this means crawling up and down the staging to relocate it. The going is slow. For this reason, my house is not the best example to use, so I will refer to some of the more traditional houses I have built for other people. None of my personal houses have ever been traditional.

I have built houses that contained between 1,200 and 1,400 square feet that professional painters painted in less than two days. Keep in mind, these were professionals, with professional equipment and years of experience. Houses of this same size have been painted by the customers who contracted me to build them. The homeowner paint jobs took considerably longer, some running into two weeks. Some professionals figure one day of labor, per coat, to paint the walls, ceiling, and trim of an average room. If you take this approach, a typical starter home would require about two weeks to paint. I think this is too much time, but it is an estimate that comes up when talking with the pros. I can see this type of estimate being used to repaint an existing house, where there are many obstacles to work around, but in new construction, there is nothing to get in the way, so the work should go faster.

When I build an average starter home, I allow one week for the painters. This allowance has usually proved to be adequate. If you will be doing the work yourself, you should allow extra time.

How much extra time will depend on your skills, circumstances, and available help. If you're doing the job alone, allow twice as long as you would for a professional. With a helper or two, you and your crew should be able to match the pace of a single professional painter.

I've always preferred to paint or stain trim before it is installed. This allows the work to be done much faster. The trim can be laid out across sawhorses and painted or stained in a fraction of the time that would be required if the trim were installed in the home. Once the trim is installed, some touch-up work will be needed, but the end result will be a considerable savings in time.

When doing production work, such as spec houses in track subdivisions, I usually have my painters use sprayers. This is the fastest way to get the job done, and the results are acceptable, not always great, but acceptable. When I'm building a custom home, I have the painters use rollers and brushes. The finished job, when done with rollers and brushes, is noticeably better than when it is sprayed. If you want fast and acceptable, spray your paint. When you want high quality, opt for rollers and brushes.

YOUR TRIM

The paint used on your trim wood should be different than the paint used on walls and ceilings; so should the primer. When painting wood, you should use an undercoater, rather than a primer/sealer. An undercoater prepares the wood surface better and creates a better bond between the painting surface and the finish paint. This leads to less cracking and maintenance. Undercoaters are available in both oil and latex forms.

Once your trim has been painted with an undercoater, you are ready for an enamel finish coat. This can be either oil-based or latex. Latex enamels retain all of the advantages mentioned previously, but some people feel that an oil-based product is better when painting trim. The reason for this is the fluid application of an oil-based paint. Oil paints tend to flow better than latex in certain weather conditions, leaving less chance of streaking. Since your trim is a big part of your home's appearance, the paint job is important. La-tex will give good results under most conditions, and it is a lot easier to work with. Talk with your local paint dealer when the time comes to do your painting, and ask for professional advice. You will probably find that it will be okay to use latex, but there may be enough circumstantial evidence to point you in the direction of an oil-based paint.

INTERIOR STAINING

The interior staining of wood trim and interior doors is very popular. Just like paint, the quality of the stain is very important in the finished results of the job. It doesn't take a lot of stain to dress up a new house, so don't buy the cheapest stain you can find. Go with a name brand that will give your home a look of elegance. Keep in mind that composite-type doors cannot be stained. They must be painted. Luan doors and wood doors can be stained. Also remember that fingerjoint trim should not be stained; it should only be painted. If you want stained trim, install clear, stain-grade trim.

TEXTURED CEILINGS

Many homes being built today are finished with textured ceilings. This work is normally done by the drywall contractor, unless the homeowner does it personally. When a textured ceiling is done, the paint can often be mixed in with the texturing compound. This eliminates the need for painting ceilings when the walls are ready for paint. If you can eliminate the need to paint your ceilings, the walls and trim work will be done more quickly than the estimated timetables I've given you. This is well worth considering.

SAVING MONEY

Saving money is usually important to most people. As you probably noticed by the title, the purpose of this book is to show you how to save money. Well, painting your own home's interior is a very viable way for you to cut the cost of construction. A little effort on your part can go a long way in reducing your monthly mortgage payment. Even if you don't want to get your hands dirty, you can save money on your paint job. Let's take some time now to discuss the use of professional painters and how you can control their costs.

LESS THAN HALF THE COST

When taking bids for the paint work on my new house, I found a way to get the job done by professionals for less than half the cost of most of the bids I received. The lowest bid price received for my house was $4,330. This included interior work only. The price was for two coats on everything, and the contractor would supply all materials. If I were building this house for someone else, I probably would have accepted this bid. However, since the bid was for my personal home, I had some thinking to do.

I'm not a professional painter, by any means, but I've spread my share of paint around. Knowing that I possessed the skills to paint my own home, it was difficult to decide whether or not to sub the work out. My plan called for me to do all of the mechanical work in the home and some other miscellaneous work. If I did the interior painting myself, there were thousands of dollars to be saved. I didn't want to throw away my money, but on the other hand, I wanted to get the house finished in a reasonable amount of time, and I had professional obligations in my day-to-day duties that had to be met. Confusion set in.

I'm not fond of painting, and I'm not very fast at it. Climbing around on shaky staging some twenty-five feet off the floor is not one of my favorite ways to spend a day either. On the other hand, I couldn't justify throwing away thousands of dollars to avoid a few minor activities that didn't suit my fancy. Being the way that I am, I set out to find an alternative, some middle ground.

My initial bid search had been done in the normal way. I went through the phone book, called contractors I knew, and asked around for referrals. The best price I got came from one of the painters I had a working relationship with, but the price was too high. Now I needed to find some way to beat the $4,330 price. This started my second search.

In the second stage of my bid taking, I could have gone to part-timers. The classified advertising section in newspapers are always choked with ads from part-timers seeking off-hours work. Many of these moonlighters are insured and do good work, and they can be a real bargain. They can also be your worst nightmare. No, I wanted to deal with known quantities. After calling around and asking friends for possible sources, I remembered two guys who used to do painting on a professional level. Neither of them were presently doing full-time painting, but they were still set up in business. I called them and negotiated a deal. It saved me more than half of what the lowest bid was in my first attempt at finding painters.

I offered to supply all of the material for the job. The painters would have no risk of not being paid for materials they supplied, because I was supplying it, at their specifications. They did their own take-offs and provided their own staging and ladders. I told them that I didn't care when they painted the house, whether it be by day or night, so long as they could meet my production schedule. This allowed them to do their routine work and to work my paint job in on the side. I agreed to provide heat, since it was already there for the drywall contractor anyway. The result of my second search and negotiations was a cash savings of over $1,600, and I didn't have to lift a paintbrush. You can use a similar strategy to save money on your paint job.

While it is unlikely that you have the contacts within the trades that I do, you can still dig up some hungry, but good, workers at discounted prices. Painting is a trade where some excellent talent can be rented for very low prices. If you supply the material and agree to quick payment for services rendered, you can probably save a lot of money when contracting out your work. This ploy will work with other trades too, but it works better with some than others.

Painters don't require a lot of equipment. This means it is pretty easy for them to set up to do business. Carpenters, plumbers, and other trades can require a significant amount of equipment to do their work. The cost of this equipment keeps a lot of wanna-be contractors out of business. Not so with painters. Check the ads for part-timers and ask around. Make sure anyone you use is insured properly, and licensed if a license is required. If you're afraid of the quality you will get, make your deal based on performance. Tell the contractor that the whole deal hinges on the outcome of the first room to be painted. Let the painter paint the first room and inspect the work. If it's good, keep going. If it's not, get a new painter. I've already told you, but I'm going to tell you again, don't try to save money on your primer and paint. Buy the best paint and stain you can find. If you want to save money on your painting, save it by doing the work yourself or by searching out qualified talent at discounted prices.

CHAPTER 25

INSTALLING INTERIOR TRIM

If you have an abundance of patience and can cut angles, you could save a lot of money by installing your own interior trim work. Interior trim is light work, but it is not a job for just anyone to tackle. This chapter discusses the requirements for installing interior trim, as well as the types of trim available.

Installing interior trim can be a fun and rewarding job. When I say rewarding, I mean in two ways. Hanging your own interior doors and installing the interior trim for your home can give you a great deal of self-satisfaction. Not only that, you can save a lot of money. The exact amount varies with the cost of professional labor in your area, but we're talking thousands, not hundreds.

The installation of interior trim is not hard or heavy work. It is, however, a job that demands attention to detail and patience. If you have these two qualities, you can save yourself some serious money. Even if you are building a very small home, installing your own trim should save you enough money to pay for your kitchen appliances. The larger your house is, the more you can save.

Professional trim carpenters usually charge for their services per square foot. In the old days, I used to pay less than a dollar a square foot. In my local market today, the rate is considerably higher. The exact amount varies with different subcontractors. With the smallest house you are likely to build, you should be able to save more than a thousand dollars. Since the labor rate is tied to the size of your home, larger homes can increase the savings substantially. I don't want to give you a specific number, since labor prices fluctuate a great deal in various locations.

WHAT IS INTERIOR TRIM?

What is interior trim? This phase of work can involve many parts of your home. It will definitely cover the inside trim for windows. There will be baseboard trim, and probably some shoe molding. Interior doors and their trim are lumped into this category. Kitchen cabinets may, or may not, be installed by a trim carpenter. You may find that it is more cost effective to have the supplier of your cabinets install them. If you buy custom cabinets, this will probably be the case. However, if you buy stock cabinets from a general supplier, your trim contractor will probably install them and their countertops.

WHAT SKILLS ARE NEEDED?

What skills are needed to install interior trim? Basic carpentry skills are needed. You must be able to use tape measures, saws, hammers, and so forth. The principles of this work are fairly simple. The on-site work is not so simple. Some of the task is done easily, but other parts of it get complicated. You must have patience to install interior trim. In addition to patience, you must possess an ability to work within tight parameters.

Interior trim is a major part of your finished home. The quality of workmanship put into the trim phase will set the tone for your whole home. If the trim is not installed properly, the job will suffer until the work is corrected. Therefore, you should not attempt to do your own trim work if you don't have the ability to do it properly.

What exactly must you do to install your own trim? Well, the basic carpentry skills are needed, but there is more. You must be able to cut intricate angles to install your trim properly. Many of the cuts will be simple, but where trim must be joined in the middle of a room, you will have to cut angles that will allow baseboard trim to meet without an obvious seam. Corners around windows and doors will require angled cuts. You can reduce some of this cutting by purchasing trim kits and pre-hung doors. I recommend that you do this. You will pay more for your materials, but you will save time, and saving time usually relates to saving money. Not only will you save time, you will cut back on the amount of skill you need to get the job done.

TOOLS

The tools required for trim work are not extensive or exotic. Basic hand tools, like hammers, screwdrivers, and such are required. The only special piece of equipment needed is something to cut uniform angles with. You can use a miter box and a backsaw to do the work manually. This will work fine, but it's slow going. A power miter saw is the best tool for the job. These saws can cost hundreds of dollars, so you may not want to buy one just to cut the trim for your house. But you can rent one. A nail set will be needed to countersink the nails used to support the trim. If you're into air tools, you can rent a pneumatic nail gun to install your trim work. This is not a necessity, however.

SET YOUR NAILS

When you install interior trim, you must set your nails. This is done with a power nailer or a nail set. Since you will probably be working with a hammer, you will need a nail set. I also suggest that you use a hammer with a smooth face. Framing hammers that have waffle-type faces are not good trim hammers. Use a light hammer with a smooth face to drive your trim nails in. Tap the nails in until the heads are close to the trim. At this point, use a nail set to push the heads of the nails up into the trim. You want to countersink the nails so that there will be a hole that can be filled with putty to hide the nail.

ROLL UP YOUR SLEEVES

When you are ready to roll up your sleeves and go to work, there are a few things that you should be aware of. The installation of interior trim is not one of the more complicated phases of building a house, but it is one of the more important ones, aesthetically. For novices, it can be difficult to determine where to start and what to do. Let's clear up this confusion.

DOORS OR WINDOWS

When you are ready to install your trim, you can start with the doors or windows. There is no impact on your progress one way or the other by doing windows or doors first. However, you should not start with baseboard trim. Let's assume you are going to start with windows and that you will be working with pre-cut trim kits.

TRIM KITS AND PRE-HUNG DOORS

Trim kits for windows and pre-hung doors are frequently used by professionals. They should, in my opinion, always be used by amateurs. What is a window kit? A window kit is a package of trim material that is factory cut to fit around a window. The kit includes all wood parts needed to trim a window. Buying the kits requires you to know the size of each window you will be trimming. Once you have the kits, they are easy to install. Since the wood is pre-cut, all you have to do is follow the instructions packed in the kits and nail the pieces into place.

Pre-hung doors are doors that are sold with their finish trim provided. The trim will pull off of the door frame so that it is out of the way while the jamb is being installed. Once the jamb is in place, the trim slides back into its groove and is nailed into place. These doors cost more than slab doors, which are not pre-hung, but almost all professionals use these easy-to-install units.

Open your trim kit and read the instructions. If you are good at following instructions, this is all you will have to know. You will start with the stool, sill, and other bottom parts of the window trim. Once this is installed, you can install the casing. If you're trying to estimate your time for this work, allow about thirty minutes for each window. A seasoned professional will do the job in half that time, but first-timers will need some extra time.

When you move onto doors, you will need some shim material. Cedar shims work very well for interior trim work. You will also need a long level. A four-foot level can be used, but a six-foot level will allow you to install your doors more accurately. It is critical that you install the door frames level and plumb. If you don't, the doors will not swing properly. Assuming that you are installing pre-hung doors, you must remove the trim. This is done by simply pulling the trim off. There will be two sections of trim, one on each side of the door. These sections will pull out of the frame easily.

With the trim and doors removed, door jambs are set into their rough opening. A level is used to level and plumb the frames. Shims are nailed between the jambs and the rough openings to allow the jambs to be installed properly. Once the jamb is in, the door is hung back on the hinges. The last step is sliding the trim sections back into place and nailing them to wall studs.

The door hardware is also a part of interior trim. Bathroom doors are normally fitted with privacy locksets. These door handles don't require a key for locking and unlocking, but they do lock. Other interior doors may, or may not, be equipped with privacy latches. Closets and other rooms where privacy is not a concern are fitted with passage sets. These are just door knobs that open and close the door, but that don't lock. Installing door handles is very simple. The door handles are packed with instructions, and if you are working with pre-hung doors, you should be able to install the hardware in less than fifteen minutes.

Bifold doors for closets are a bit more troublesome to install than pre-hung, swinging doors. It's not that bifolds are difficult to install, but their many parts and the installation of their tracks, make it a time-consuming job. If you can follow instructions, you can hang bifold doors.

WHAT KIND OF TRIM?
STAIN-GRADE TRIM

Stain-grade trim is a very clear wood. If you plan to paint your trim, stain-grade material is not needed, but if you prefer a stained trim, you will want to install stain-grade trim. If you don't, imperfections in the trim will show through the stain. People who want stained trim often make a mistake when ordering their materials. This can affect you as a general contractor or as the installer of your own trim. A lot of builders, novices and professionals alike, sometimes order clear trim and pre-hung doors that are fitted with fingerjoint trim. Most experienced trim people recognize their mistake immediately and correct their mistake. Less-informed individuals don't notice the problem until their trim is stained and no longer returnable.

I don't know if you've ever seen a fingerjoint casing that has been stained, but if you have, you know that it looks silly. When fingerjoint trim is stained, all of the joints in the trim show up in a very unpleasant way. Believe me, you don't want to stain fingerjoint trim. And I should add, even if you order your trim properly, there is no guarantee that the supplier will ship it as ordered. I've ordered doors with stain-grain trim and have been given doors with fingerjoint trim. In most cases I've caught the mistakes. There has been, however, a door, from time to time, that slipped past my watchful eye and got installed with the wrong type of trim.

FINGERJOINT TRIM

Fingerjoint trim is less expensive than stain-grade trim. If you will be painting the trim, there is no problem with fingerjoint trim. In fact, it would be foolish to use stain-grade trim if your plan is to paint it. Use stain-grade trim if you are going to stain it, and fingerjoint trim if you are going to paint it.

COLONIAL TRIM

Colonial trim is one of the most popular types of trim available. It is available in fingerjoint style and in stain-grade. I would recommend this trim for your house. It is not excessively expensive, but it does make a good impression on real estate appraisers, friends, family, and potential buyers.

CLAMSHELL TRIM

Clamshell trim is the cheapest trim you can buy. It's not an ugly trim, but it is plain and inexpensive. When you consider the total savings of using clamshell trim instead of colonial trim, you may feel the way I do. I don't see any justification in using a cheap-looking trim in a house. The money saved by installing a cheap trim is lost in perceived value, in my opinion. If you want to cut corners, install particleboard instead of plywood in the framing stages. Both of them will do the job, and once the job is done, no one will know what type of wall sheathing, roof sheathing, or subflooring was used. They will, however, know exactly what type of trim was used. Think about that.

ROUGH TRIM

Rough trim is an option for people who are building rustic homes. By rough trim, I'm talking about unplaned lumber, lumber with a rough texture and square ends. This type of trim is not normally mitered. It is usually not installed with a lot of angles. This makes installation easier. Also, the wood can be cheaper. If you're building a country-style home, you might want to consider butt-joint, rough trim. This trim should not, however, be used in formal homes.

TYPES OF TRIM
BASEBOARD TRIM

Baseboard trim is easy to install. The wood is lightweight, easy to handle, and not at all difficult to install. It is held in place by small nails that are nailed into wall studs. Finding the studs is one of the more complicated parts of the job for some people. However, a lot of drywall contractors don't cover the lowest nails in a wall. They know these nails will be covered by trim, so they don't waste joint compound on them. This is to your advantage. If you can see the nails, you know where your wall studs are. This makes attaching your baseboard trim easy.

Most wall studs in homes are set on sixteen-inch centers. Once you find one stud, you can find the rest of them. If you are installing your trim before your floor coverings are installed, and this is not uncommon, you can use a marker to mark where wall stubs intersect with your subfloor. So, if your finish flooring is in, you hit the first stud and then measure to hit others. If you are hanging the baseboard over a rough floor, you can simply make marks along the subflooring that you can line up with wall studs. In either case, hitting the studs should not be a problem.

Many of the cuts made for baseboard will be simple, straight cuts. You will have to cut angles for outside corners and splices in long runs of baseboard. Your miter box or miter saw will make this goal obtainable. By this stage of your job, you have your doors trimmed out. Your baseboard will just butt up against the door casing.

How you install your baseboard will depend on the type of look you are after. A rustic house with rough trim boards will normally have all butted joints. If you're using a colonial baseboard, the joints will be mitered. The exact method used for installing interior trim is up to you.

CASED OPENINGS

Cased openings are doorways that are trimmed out with wood, but that don't contain doors. These are common in most houses. Some openings are just wrapped with drywall, finished, and painted. This is fine, but for a more detailed trim job, a lot of people want the openings cased with wood. This is not a big deal, but trim-grade lumber must be used. Basically, three boards are used to cover the inside of the opening. The boards are installed on each of the vertical sides and along the horizontal section of the opening. After this is done, casing is used on both sides of the opening, just as it is with windows and doors.

SHOE MOLDING

Shoe molding is a small, thin, beveled piece of trim. It is installed after baseboard trim and vinyl flooring is installed. Shoe molding's primary function is to hold the edges of sheet vinyl down, so it won't curl up. This molding is not mandatory, and you can save a few bucks by not installing it. If you don't want to pay for shoe, install your vinyl flooring before you install your baseboard trim. If you don't have some type of trim holding down the edges of your vinyl, you are almost certain to face curled-up edges at some time in the not so distant future.

CHAIR RAIL

Chair rail is an expensive type of trim. It is normally installed in rooms such as formal dining rooms. The purpose of the molding, back when it had a real purpose, was to prevent chairs from being pushed into walls. Nowadays, chair rail is more decorative than functional, but it still works. If you have a formal dining room, chair rail will dress it up. Even though this is mostly a cosmetic improvement, it does impress appraisers. Chair rail is normally installed about four feet above a finished floor, and surrounds a room completely.

CROWN MOLDING

Crown molding is used where walls meet ceilings. This is an excellent way to hide bad drywall seams in these locations. It is, however, an expensive way to do it. Crown molding is normally found, when it is installed, in formal dining rooms and formal living rooms. It is not common practice to install it in other locations, although you can.

Do you have a feel now for what is involved in the installation of interior doors and trim? Well, you should. You've been given a broad-brush description of what you will have to deal with. Of course, some people will have no interest in doing their own trim work. So, let's spend some time on issues that are geared more to a general contractor.

TRIM CONTRACTORS

Trim contractors can be an independent bunch. You might say that some of them are eccentric. Don't be surprised if your trim contractor has a very different attitude than the rest of your carpenters. I've found this to be true, and I compare it to professional football players. If you are a football fan, you know that kickers don't fit into the team in the same way that other players do. Kickers are often loners, people who don't want too much association with other players before a big

kicking opportunity. I think it is fair to put trim carpenters into this same type of category. If you're not into football, perhaps you can compare trim carpenters to artists.

Trim installers often act as though they are special, and maybe they are. Someone who can do an outstanding trim job deserves respect. I don't know why participants in this trade are so different from plumbers, electricians, and other types of carpenters, but they often are. Don't get me wrong, trim carpenters are not weird, they're just different. The same can be said about painters and some other trades.

Trim carpenters with sales abilities will attempt to impress you with technical terms and their unique abilities. Their presentations might be very true, but the only way to cut through any smoke they are blowing is to visit some jobs that they've done. Real professionals let their work speak for them. I don't care if it's a trim contractor, a drywall contractor, a roofer, or a foundation contractor, if the contractor is good, past jobs will prove it. Listen to what contractors have to say as they toot their own horns, but the proof is in the pudding, so inspect their work.

MAKING THE CHOICE

Let's go over the basics of what you will need and want to trim out your home. I, of course, don't know your preferences, so I'm going to show you three ways to arrange the trim work in your house. We will start with the least expensive materials and work our way up. This information will be applicable whether you install the materials yourself or hire experts to do the work for you.

THE LEAST AMOUNT OF MONEY

If you want to trim your house with the least amount of money, this section is for you. The first consideration is the type of trim to use. Clamshell trim will be the most inexpensive commercial trim material available. Don't order window kits or pre-hung doors. Cut your own casing out of clamshell stock. Buy paint-grade trim. The least expensive interior doors you can buy are flat, hollow-core, luan doors. These doors can be stained or painted. If you're pinching every penny, don't use shoe molding. Have your vinyl floors installed before any baseboard is put in. Then, when you install the baseboard, it will help to hold the vinyl in place. Shop carefully for your passage and privacy sets. The type of door handles you choose can make a difference in your material cost.

THE MIDDLE OF THE ROAD

If you prefer to go down the middle of the road, this section is for you. The suggestions you are about to be given are the ones I would recommend that you follow. If I were building a spec house, this is the way I would do it. It is also the way I would outfit my own home.

I would buy window kits of colonial trim for my windows. Interior doors would be six-panel, composite doors with pre-hung colonial trim. I should add that composite doors cannot be stained. If you want a six-panel door that can be stained, you must buy solid wood doors. When painting the doors is your intention, composite doors will look as good as wood doors, and they will cost considerably less. If I were going to paint my trim, I'd use fingerjoint material. Should you want to stain your trim, which I personally prefer, you will need stain-grade material.

Colonial baseboard and casing would surround my walls, windows, and doors. I might add chair rail in the dining room, but this wouldn't be high on my list of priorities. For most homes, I wouldn't bother with crown molding. This mid-range strategy of trim work will cost more than the cheap route, but it will dress a house up very nicely.

THE FULL EFFECT

If you want the full effect, you're going to have to part with some serious cash. Colonial trim will probably be your choice of styles. The wood will be clear, stain-grade material. Most expensive homes have stained trim. Interior doors will be six-panel, solid wood units, which will also be stained. Chair rail will be installed in the formal dining room. Crown molding will be installed in the dining room and formal living room. The family room will be dressed up with wainscoting. What is wainscoting? It is when wood paneling is installed on the lower half of a wall and is topped off with a chair rail. The trim would be complimented with accent pieces, such as oak switch plates on electrical devices, oak bathroom accessories, and so forth. Expect to spend a pretty penny for all this trim, but you may decide it's worth it.

Trim is an expensive part of your house, but it is also a very important element in the home. Your trim will say a lot about you and your house. Skimping on trim can detract from the rest of your house. I know money can be tight, and I know that sometimes we can't do what we want to do, but if you can spring for a middle-of-the-road job, I think you will be happier in the long haul.

CHAPTER 26
FINISHED FLOOR COVERINGS

Finished floor coverings are an area of home construction that can burst a budget. When you consider that carpet can cost anywhere from less than $5 to over $30 per square yard, it is easy to see how you could skew your numbers. This chapter gives you the hard-core facts about finish floor coverings and their installation procedures.

Finished floor coverings are an area of home construction that can bust your budget. Outside of light fixtures, finished floors probably rank highest in cost overruns for my customers. Carpet can cost less than five dollars a square yard or more than thirty dollars a yard. With such a spread in price, it is easy to see how the cost of your finish flooring could get out of hand.

When you are planning the finish floors for your home, you will have a lot to choose from. Most floors are normally covered with carpet. Vinyl flooring is normally installed in bathrooms and kitchens. Hardwood flooring is a sought-after choice for formal dining and living rooms. Tile floors are used in bathrooms, sun rooms, and foyers. This boils down to the fact that you will have a lot of decisions to make when it comes to deciding what type of flooring will be used in your rooms.

We've hardly begun this chapter, and you can already see that there are going to be a lot of choices facing you when it comes to the flooring in your home. Just as there are numerous types of products to choose from, there will be a wide range in prices. All of this combines to give you a lot of control in the cost of your finish flooring.

THE STANDARD METHOD

The standard method for finish flooring in most modern homes is to install carpet in all areas ex-cept bathrooms and kitchens. Vinyl flooring is normally installed in wet areas, such as kitchens and baths. If you follow this procedure, you won't go astray in your general plan to build a conforming house with an average value. However, you may want to do more than just average flooring in some rooms, or perhaps in the entire house. You must be careful, however, not to overinvest in your flooring, unless you are not concerned about how much of your investment will be returned on an appraisal report.

Real estate appraisers don't generally give a lot of extra value to a home just because it has expensive carpet in it. Some upgrades will be reflected on an appraisal, but if you go too far over standard procedures, you are not likely to recover your money in the appraisal. Depending upon the size of your house, the amount of money involved could be staggering. Let me give you an example.

Carpeting and vinyl flooring is measured in square yards. To obtain the number of square yards needed for a house, you take the total square footage of an area to be covered and divide it by nine. In other words, if you had a house with 900 square feet of floor space in it, you would need 100 yards of flooring. With this in mind, let's say that you are building a home that contains 1,800 square feet of carpeting, not counting vinyl flooring. This means you will be buying about 200 yards of carpet and pad.

Now, let's set up some hypothetical numbers for the cost of carpeting and padding. We'll say that the cost of average carpeting including pad is $15 a yard. A better grade of carpeting, but one that is still in the ballpark of average carpeting, is $18 a yard. You, however, have fallen in love with a very special carpeting. It costs $30 a yard. Okay, let's see how these numbers play out when you buy 200 yards of carpet.

With a standard builder's grade of carpeting (the $15 stuff), you will pay $3,000 for the flooring, not counting installation. If you step up to the next level of quality, your cost will be $3,600. But, if you buy the flooring you have your heart set on, the bill will be $6,000. Wow, twice as much! Now, what's going to happen when an appraiser is called in to establish the value of your home? In many cases, the appraiser is not going to allow $6,000 for carpeting on an appraisal report. With the expensive carpeting installed, you will certainly get at least $3,600 for it on an allowance, but this leaves you $2,400 away from your actual investment. A liberal appraiser might allow something more, say about $20 a yard. This would give you a value of $4,000 for your $6,000 carpet, still a far cry from what you paid for it. Unless you are building a super house in a neighborhood where other homes have $30-a-yard carpet, you're going to lose out on your investment.

Hardwood floors are another good example of how you can spend a lot of money that you will have trouble recovering. While it may be safe to put hardwood flooring in your dining room or formal living room, it would probably be a financial flop to put it throughout your home. It may seem that you are helpless in making these decisions, but you are not. You can call licensed appraisers and consult with them before you make a buying decision. For a reasonable hourly fee, most appraisers will be happy to advise you on the values of various types of flooring.

SHOULD YOU INSTALL CARPETING?

Should you install your own carpeting? Probably not. Carpet installation is a job that is hard to do with the best tools, and very frustrating without the right tools. You can rent the tools, but you probably don't possess the skills to make the job go to your liking. This is not to say that you can't install your own carpet, but you should research what is involved carefully before you commit to doing so.

CARPET OPTIONS

If you sit down and make a list of all the possible carpet options available to you, your list will be very long. Most people shop for their carpeting by going to showrooms and browsing until they see a carpet that strikes their fancy. There is nothing wrong with this approach if it makes the buyer happy, but there are more business-like ways to get the job done. Preliminary research into various types and styles of carpeting can reduce the amount of time spent in showrooms. If time is money, saving time is saving money, so don't overlook the value of conserving your time.

Before you buy any carpet, you should educate yourself in the various types of carpeting that are available. If you understand the mechanics of carpeting, you will be better able to match your needs to specific types of materials. We can start your education right here.

OLEFIN

Olefin is a very popular material for carpeting. It will stand up to a lot of abuse, and Olefin enjoys a long life. Being moisture-resistant and non-absorbent makes it popular with families of all types. Couples with children appreciate the fact that Olefin is not easily stained by accidental spills. If there is a bad side of Olefin, it is that low-priced versions of it may crush after use. This gives the carpet a worn look earlier than would be expected of a new carpet. Prices for this material run the gamut from very affordable to rather high.

POLYESTER

Polyester carpet can be installed in practically any location. It is resistant to moisture and mildew, but susceptible to oil-based stains. If you like vibrant colors, you'll like the selections available with polyester products. The cost for this type of floor covering is mid-range.

NYLON

Nylon carpet is tough. If you need a carpet that can take a constant beating without giving up the battle, nylon is it. In addition to its excellent durability, nylon carpet is resistant to mildew and abrasions. It can even stand up to moths. Another advantage to a nylon product is its ability to conceal dirt. One drawback to nylon is its tendency to create static electricity. If you don't enjoy getting zapped by static electricity, you should plan on having this type of carpet treated before walking on it. You will find nylon carpet comes in a wide range of prices.

ACRYLIC

Acrylic carpet is priced in the middle of the spectrum. It stands up to mildew and abrasions, while repelling dirt. Moths and insects do not affect acrylic carpets. Crushing is not a problem, and the material is offered in a host of colors. There is, however, a likelihood of the floor covering shedding its fibers. These little tumbleweed-like balls can be a nuisance.

WOOL

Not many people install wool carpeting these days. This product is at the upper end of the pricing structure, and moths can ruin it. Aside from these two potential problems, wool is a good choice in that it is long-lasting and resistant to abrasions. Wool is not the easiest type of carpet to clean, but it can be cleaned.

CUT-PILE AND LOOP-PILE CARPET

There are two styles of carpet that are normally used in homes, cut-pile carpeting and loop-pile carpeting. What is the difference between cut-pile and loop-pile carpeting? Most modern carpet is made by attaching fibers to a mesh backing. If the fibers are attached in loops and left uncut, the result is loop-pile carpet. When the fibers are cut after being looped, the carpet is cut-pile. Both cut-pile and loop-pile carpets are excellent choices, and they come in a wide range of prices.

A CUSHIONED PAD

When a cut-pile or loop-pile carpet is used, it should be installed on top of a cushioned pad. A pad might have an egg-shape design or a closed-cell design. The design of the pad is not as important as the quality of it. Padding is very important to carpet. In fact, it is better to invest big bucks in your pad and less money in your carpet when you are on a tight budget. A good carpet on a great pad will last longer than an excellent carpet on a poor pad.

I was taught years ago how to determine the quality of a pad when shopping in a showroom. Looking at pads can be deceiving. Just because one piece of foam is thicker than another doesn't mean that it will perform better. Let me share with you the information I was given a long time ago.

When you go into a carpet showroom, you will find many samples of carpeting and padding to look at. The padding will vary in price, depending upon quality. However, you cannot use price alone to determine the worth of a pad. You must do some on-site testing.

Select a carpet sample from one of the many racks in the store. It's best if the sample is representative of the carpet you plan to buy, but this is not mandatory. Now lay out samples of all the various padding. You will probably have at least four samples of different types and grades of pads. With the pad samples lying on the floor of the showroom, place the carpet sample on one of them. Step up onto the carpet while it is on the pad. Stand on it for a few moments and then step off. Watch to see how long it takes for your footprints to disappear. Continue this process until you have tested all the pads. The pad that makes your footprints disappear first is the best pad.

CUSHION-BACK CARPET

If you're buying a cushion-back (or foam-back as it is sometimes called) carpet, you will not be shopping for an independent pad. The backing on this carpet is its pad. Cushion-back carpet is made with the intent of being glued directly to a floor. It can be used in any part of a home, and it is inexpensive when compared to the cost of a pile carpet and independent pad. This type of carpet is used more in commercial buildings than in residential homes, but it does have its place in houses.

There are some drawbacks to direct-glue, cushion-back carpet. Due to how it is installed, this type of carpet is not easy to remove, and it is not reusable. The flooring must be ripped out, and much of the foam backing will remain glued to the subfloor. This requires aggressive scraping to remove. In addition to this negative factor, cushion-back carpet is not nearly as comfortable to walk on as a pile carpet with a lush pad under it. A third problem can occur if moisture is found under the carpet. This can destroy the pad backing and render the carpet nearly useless.

MY ADVICE

My advice to you is to buy the highest quality pad you can afford and cover it with a good quality pile carpet. Shop seriously for the carpet and read all the fine print. Look for products with good warranties and from reputable manufacturers. Avoid foam-back carpet unless you have special circumstances that make it desirable. Let me give you an example of when you might find that it makes sense to install a low-end, foam-backed carpet.

My new house contains just under 3,000 square feet of living space, most of which will be covered with a pile carpet and a quality pad. Quarry tile and sheet vinyl flooring will cover some of the wet areas, like the foyer, kitchen, bathrooms, and sun room. I'm having a commercial-grade, foam-backed carpet installed in the upstairs of my home. Why? Well, there are several reasons. My office is upstairs, and it gets a fair amount of foot traffic, plus my dog, Travis, will be spending a lot of time up there with me. The combination of heavy furniture cutting into the carpet, a dog lying on it, and my boots tromping across it will cause the flooring to suffer an early demise. I can see no reason to pay top-dollar for a carpet that I know will have to be replaced in a few years.

Another place where the cheap carpet will be installed is in the upstairs play room. There is a large room and a long hall leading to it that will be the domain of our kids. This will be their space,

to do with what they please. I can see grape juice being spilled, modeling clay becoming embedded in the carpet, all types of paint being knocked over, and a dozen other carpet disasters. This is why I've chosen to go the inexpensive route on the flooring in this area.

A third room to be covered with foam-backed carpet is the exercise room. With a weight machine, treadmill, and other assorted heavy objects grinding into the carpet, you can bet that the flooring will have to be replaced if the room is ever used for more civilized purposes. Why spend big bucks on a fancy flooring that is going to be crushed quickly?

You've just seen three examples of when you might want to invest in less than the best. There are plenty of other examples that could be given. For example, if you have a basement that you want to install carpeting in for casual use, a direct-glue carpet would make sense. You will have to shop products carefully and plan your purchases around your budget and needs.

VINYL FLOORING

Vinyl flooring is the king of kitchens and bathrooms. This flooring is inexpensive to buy and install, it cleans and shines well, and it is well accepted in the construction community. All of this, of course, doesn't mean it is the type of flooring you will want in your home. However, it is the most logical choice for the flooring in wet areas.

Sheet vinyl is by far the most popular type of flooring for kitchens, bathrooms, laundry rooms, breakfast rooms, and other areas where water and spills are likely to come into contact with the finish floor. Available in many qualities, the price of sheet vinyl runs from the very affordable to the quite expensive. There are plenty of colors and designs to choose from in all grades.

A builder's grade vinyl, something in the midrange of prices, will give years of good service. The flooring will have a no-wax finish, and it will look good for a long time. Lower priced vinyl may lose its luster through time, and it is more likely to wear badly. High-end vinyl will be softer to walk on than low-end products, and it should last much longer. A trip to your local flooring showroom will allow you to do a hands-on comparison of the various types and qualities of vinyl.

INSTALLATION

The installation of vinyl flooring is not complicated, but the actual work can become quite complex, especially if the flooring must be cut to fit around obstacles, such as island cabinets. Vinyl flooring is normally installed before cabinets and fixtures. This makes laying the floor covering much easier. Assuming that you have a room with a standard width and no obstacles, you can certainly install your own vinyl, but I'd advise you not to. One mistake on your part could ruin the flooring, which would wind up costing as much, if not more, than what paying a professional to install it would cost. It has been my experience that carpet and vinyl should be installed by professionals, and that the cost of having this work done is not extreme.

TILE FLOORS

Tile floors are often installed in place of vinyl floors. While the per-foot cost of tile is expensive, the amount of money needed to upgrade a small floor from vinyl to tile is not unmanageable, especially if you do the work yourself, and you can. If you are looking at a large floor area, such as a kitchen and breakfast area, the cost can be prohibitive. A small bathroom, however, is going to have minimal floor space, so the cost of tile will not break the bank.

Tile floors are definitely a step above vinyl. Appraisers will normally make upward adjustments in value when they see tile on a floor. Too much tile, however, can get very expensive and present less of an effect on a house. You have to weigh all considerations. For example, it makes a lot of sense to install quarry tile in an entrance foyer. This is the first floor someone sees, the space is small, and the tile tells anyone entering the house to expect quality construction.

If your house has a powder room for guests, the floor area will be small. This is another good place to upgrade with tile. Family bathrooms can be floored with vinyl without guests seeing them. Kitchens come in all sizes and shapes. Putting tile

on the floor of a kitchen will enhance its appearance and value, but you may be getting into a considerably higher expense than what is absolutely necessary. You must make the decision on what you can afford.

YOU CAN DO IT

When it comes to installing tile, you can probably do it yourself. By providing your own labor, you might get a tile floor for just a little more than what you pay for vinyl installed by a professional. This is a good deal, and you will be building equity in your home. Many stores that sell tile will loan out the tools needed to install it. When this isn't the case, tools can be rented. With today's simplified installation methods, almost anyone can install tile in a room that has a standard, simple floor layout.

THE DRAWBACKS

The drawbacks to tile are few, but they do exist. Overall, tile is very durable, but it can be broken if a hard object is dropped on it. Most tile will become very slippery when it's wet. This can pose real danger in kitchens and bathrooms, or any other place where liquid might be spilled on the floor. Some tile is available with a textured surface that reduces the risk of falling due to a slippery surface. Breakage can be a problem associated with tile. Dropping a drinking glass on a vinyl floor may result in broken glass being strewn about, but dropping the same glass on a tile floor will almost certainly result in sharp pieces of glass flying about. Initial cost is a detriment to tile when it is compared to vinyl, but the long-lasting quality of tile may turn out to make the investment pay for itself over the years. The grout that fills the seams between tiles can become difficult to clean. It may also have to be replaced from time to time. This is something you don't have to worry about with a vinyl floor. All in all, tile is pretty, tough, and more elegant than vinyl. If the drawbacks don't sway you towards vinyl, tile is an excellent choice for flooring in your wet areas.

HARDWOOD FLOORS

Hardwood floors are not as common as they once were. Expense is one factor that keeps people from having hardwood floors installed. Upkeep is another reason. When hardwood floors are installed in modern homes, they are usually reserved for special rooms, such as formal dining and living rooms. It is very rare to find a new house that has hardwood flooring throughout.

If you want wood flooring in your home, you will have to evaluate where to put it and how much money you can afford to spend on it. I've had customers who wanted hardwood floors in their kitchens. To me, this isn't very sound judgment, but then, it's not my house. Putting hardwood floors in a kitchen, in my opinion, is asking for trouble. If the flooring gets wet, it can turn black. Should pots and pans be dropped on the floor, the wood can indent from the impact. The constant maintenance of having hardwood flooring in a kitchen is enough to make me look at other options. Now, a nice, wide-plank flooring that is soft and meant to look used, such as might be installed in a rustic country kitchen, is fine, but narrow, high-gloss oak floors just don't make much sense to me.

From a cost point of view, I would not recommend installing hardwood flooring in any of your rooms, unless the house is designed to be extremely elegant and is in a neighborhood that can support its value. Appraisers will normally give extra value for wood floors, but this type of flooring is not necessary, and carpet is just as well accepted.

WHAT YOU WANT

If hardwood flooring is what you want, then do your homework. There are different grades of wood available, and the grading has a lot to do with the price and appearance of a floor. Wood flooring also comes in many sizes. You will find that strip flooring normally will have a thickness of three-quarters of an inch. Widths will usually be available in one-and-a-half-inch, two-inch, two-and-a-quarter-inch, and three-and-a-quarter-inch versions. The length of your flooring will generally be available ranging from about nine

inches to as much as eight and a half feet.

As you begin to investigate the grading system for wood flooring, you are likely to become confused. The system doesn't always make a lot of sense. To avoid making a mistake in understanding the grading, you should ask your supplier to show you samples of all the various grades available. Don't settle for looking at just a single strip of wood from each grade. You may not see the whole picture. Ask to have several strips from each grade laid out, side by side, for a better comparison.

When most people think of hardwood flooring, they envision strips of wood that are tongue-and-grooved. This is the most traditional style of hardwood flooring, but it is not the only option. Hardwood flooring is available in squares that resemble tile. These squares of various sizes gained some popularity, but never took the industry by storm. If I were going to invest in wood floors, I would go for the tongue-and-groove strips of flooring.

Wide-plank flooring is often used in rooms with specialized motifs, such as country kitchens. Plank floors aren't suitable for all houses or all rooms, but they can do a lot for a country kitchen or a rustic family room. This option may be worth looking into.

Most wood flooring is made of oak, but it can be made from many other types of wood. Hard maple, birch, and beech can all be used for flooring. You may even find some flooring made from pecan wood. In addition to a variety of wood types, you can purchase the flooring in an unfinished condition or a prefinished state.

In addition to hardwood flooring, there is softwood flooring. This type of flooring is used less frequently than hardwood, and it is not nearly as durable, but it does have a certain charm when used under the right decorating conditions. Pine is the standard material for this type of flooring.

INSTALL IT

If you are going to use wood flooring, should you install it? Probably not. Tongue-and-groove strip flooring can be installed by homeowners, but the job can become overwhelming. If you decide to install it yourself, you should rent a special nailer to work with. The nailer allows you to nail the floor from an angle, so no nails are seen in the finished floor. If you have plenty of patience and are willing to pay attention to what you are doing, you can manage the installation of a strip floor, but don't expect the work to go quickly.

The installation of wood squares is done with an adhesive. The squares are glued into place. If you are able to lay out the pattern of the floor and work to your plan, this work isn't hard, but getting on track with the layout can be more than some people can handle. In my opinion, most homeowners should leave the installation of wood flooring to professionals.

OTHER TYPES OF FLOOR COVERINGS

We've covered all the most common types of floors for modern homes, but there are some other types of floor coverings available. The types of flooring we are about to discuss are not normally used, but they do have their places under special circumstances, so we will review them briefly.

VINYL TILES

Vinyl tiles are sometimes used in place of sheet vinyl. I've used this type of flooring in some of the rental properties I've owned. The tiles often come with a built-in adhesive on their backs. You simply peel away a protective paper coating to reveal the sticky back and press the tile into place. Other types require an adhesive to be troweled out on the subflooring for the tiles to be set into. This type of flooring is easy for do-it-yourselfers to work with, but designing a pattern and keeping the tiles in proper alignment as the job progresses can get tricky. Overall, vinyl tiles are not consid-

ered to be a good flooring in new houses. The tiles can come loose and pull up. Dirt can accumulate in the seams between the tiles. In general, this type of flooring is considered to be on the cheap side, in terms of market value.

BRICKS

You may not have thought of using bricks to create a finished floor, but they can be used, and they can build quite an atmosphere when installed in an appropriate room. Most homeowners can install their own brick floors, and the bricks give a very durable walking surface. While this type of floor wouldn't be used in a bedroom or a dining room, it might fit right into some kitchens and other specialty rooms.

INDOOR-OUTDOOR CARPET

Indoor-outdoor carpet is not a material many people would want in their living room, but the flooring can be quite fitting for a screened porch or sun room. The tough qualities offered by indoor-outdoor carpet make it ideal for some locations.

SLATE

Slate is often used in entry foyers. This material can be installed by amateurs with good results. Slate, however, becomes very slippery when wet, and for this reason, I don't favor it as a flooring material. There are many types of stone that can be used in the same locations that are suitable for slate, but most of them also become slippery.

As you browse through flooring options, you will find a great many of them. Choosing the ones that are right for you can take a lot of time, so don't wait until the last minute to make your flooring decisions. With enough research, you can find the perfect flooring for your home.

CHAPTER 27

CABINETS, COUNTERTOPS, AND APPLIANCES

> *Kitchen cabinets for a modest home can range in cost from about $1,100 to over $10,000. How could one phase of work have such a wide range in cost? Why do some refrigerators cost half what others do? For the answers to these questions, you must read this chapter. The chapter deals with all aspects of cabinets, countertops, and appliances.*

Cabinets, countertops, and appliances are all important to the completion of your new home. They can all be very expensive, too. Of the three, cabinets are the ones that give a majority of people the most trouble. Picking out the right cabinets requires more than just a casual look around a showroom. Controlling the cost of cabinets can be paramount to staying within your building budget. Countertops are not going to cost nearly as much as cabinets, but you will find that the cost of a countertop can double very quickly, depending upon the style you pick. Appliances for a modern kitchen can cost thousands of dollars. A lot of people overlook this expense when establishing the estimated cost of their home. You can't afford to do this. A kitchen without appliances is not much fun to cook in.

CABINETS

Since cabinets are a subject that gives many consumers problems, let's start with them.

MATERIALS USED

The materials used to make cabinets have a direct reflection on the price of the unit. For example, steel cabinets are usually cheap, but they also are not very desirable. They can rust, are usually noisy, and not many people like the looks of them.

Particleboard

Cabinets made of particleboard are generally at the low end of the pricing picture, but they are a step above steel cabinets. Better grades of this type of cabinet have a veneer that gives them the appearance of real wood.

Hardboard

Hardboard cabinets are okay, and they fall somewhere near the middle of the price range for cabinets. Don't confuse hardboard cabinets with hardwood cabinets. Hardwood cabinets are usually expensive and always sturdy. Hardboard cabinets are usually made with plywood that is then covered with a quality veneer.

Hardwood

Hardwood cabinets are best, and steel cabinets are usually the worst choice you could make. There is a lot of middle ground to shop around in. Most manufacturers combine various materials to come up with good, durable cabinets at affordable prices. Don't run away just because a cabinet contains some particleboard or isn't made of solid hardwood. You have to look at each cabinet on its own merit.

THE CONSTRUCTION

The construction of cabinets should be an important element in making your buying decision. A well-made cabinet that contains particleboard is a better buy than a plywood cabinet that is not made to quality standards. Even though you are not a professional builder, you can look for, and identify, many of the practices that indicate good cabinet construction.

When you are seeking cabinets that will stand the test of time, look for units that are made of particleboard or plywood. Ideally, the entire cabinet box should be enclosed. This is not always the case. Some cabinets don't have backs in them. This can be a cost-saving approach in buying cabinets, but you may lose some strength and stability in your cabinets.

Look at the joints of the wood making up the cabinets. If the joints are just butted together, you are looking at a lower-quality cabinet. Better cabinets will have mortise or dovetail joints that will hold up better than butt joints.

If the cabinets you are inspecting have shelves in them, make sure that the shelf placement is adjustable. A series of holes running up the inside walls of the cabinet will indicate that shelves can be moved to various heights. Metal or wooden pins that support the shelves can be relocated to different holes as needed. Higher quality cabinets will have metal brackets along the inside walls of the cabinets. These brackets will accept metal supports that hold shelves in place. This rack system is more enduring than drilled holes and movable pins. However, either type of shelf support is acceptable.

For cabinets with drawers, you must pull the drawers out and inspect the glide system. If the drawer simply slides on wood, you're looking at a low-end cabinet. If there is a plastic track for the drawer to slide in, you're one step up from the bottom of the line. Ideally, you should see a glide system that uses ball-bearing slides in a track. This type of glide works best and lasts the longest.

Open the cabinet doors and notice the latch. If the latch depends on spring tension to operate, you can expect problems down the road as the latch becomes worn. A magnetic latch with a strong magnetic seal is best. Weak magnets will result in difficult door closures.

Is the inside of the cabinet finished off with stain or lacquer? If it's not finished at all, you're looking at a cabinet that isn't top-notch. High quality cabinets will have finished interiors. The fact that a cabinet isn't finished on the inside may not be reason enough to discount it from your list of potential purchases, but you will know that it should cost less than units that are finished.

Operate the doors and drawers of cabinets. See if they open and close easily. Do they fit well? Put your hands on the two front corners of a cabinet and try to twist it. If there is a lot of movement in the cabinet, you're looking at a lower grade of cabinet. Check the interior construction. Do the base cabinets have small triangles of wood in each corner? They should. Are the doors and drawer fronts made of wood or plastic? How difficult would it be to replace a drawer front or door if it were damaged? These are the kinds of things you should look for in determining which cabinets to buy.

CUSTOM CABINETS

Custom cabinets are ones that are made to your specifications. Choosing this type of cabinet allows you to get exactly what you want, but the price you pay for this luxury may be much more than you are prepared for. A set of custom cabinets can easily cost over $10,000. To put this price into perspective, a store-bought set of good cabinets should cost less than half the price of custom cabinets. Inexpensive, but serviceable cabinets, might cost as little as $1,500. As you can see, you will be paying a premium to have your cabinets made to order.

Just going to a cabinet shop and ordering custom cabinets doesn't mean that you will receive quality cabinets. People who make them on a custom basis can turn out junk just as easily as manufacturers who make stock cabinets from thousands of miles away. You are going to have to educate yourself in what to look for in a good cabinet.

Choosing a Cabinetmaker

Choosing a cabinetmaker is best done with on-site visits to various shops. It's important for you to see samples of cabinets produced by the shop.

Only then can you begin to decide which cabinet-maker turns out work to your satisfaction. I might add, you should begin this process almost as soon as you know you will be building a house. Having custom cabinets made can take quite a long time; several months is not unusual. Since your house cannot be finished until the cabinets are installed, you need to order them early. Many houses are built in less than four months, and it could take nearly this long to have your cabinets made. Don't wait.

I don't want to scare you away from custom cabinets, but I do feel obligated to share some of my past experience on this issue with you. Many of the houses that I've built were built on specula-tion. I used stock, store-bought cabinets in these homes and never had a problem with availability. Some of the custom homes I've built presented me with more than a passing problem when it came to cabinets.

It has been my habit to order custom cabinets very early in the building process, sometimes be-fore the house is even started. Even so, I've had occasions when the cabinets were not ready. I can tell you how frustrating it is, for homeowners and contractors alike, to be at a dead standstill, wait-ing for cabinets.

There is a big problem when a promised deliv-ery date for custom cabinets rolls around with no cabinets delivered. The worst case I can remember was a new, fancy home where the cabinets were very extravagant. The cabinet shop had promised delivery in eight weeks. When the delivery day came, the house was ready for the cabinets, but the cabinets were not ready for the house. The homeowner was disappointed, but not yet upset.

My wife, and partner in the building business, pursued the cabinet company. We found out, to our great distress, that the cabinets were still three weeks away from completion. Now what would we do? If we told the cabinetmaker to eat his cabi-nets and ordered from another shop, we would have to wait six to eight weeks. Trusting the cabi-netmaker who was behind schedule was a risky proposition, but if we were being told the truth, the cabinets that were in the process of being made would be delivered in three weeks. Either

way, we were going to have a disgruntled cus-tomer, angry subs, excessive interest on our con-struction loan, and other problems. We gambled on the existing order, but we hedged our bets.

I went to the cabinet shop and inspected the work that had already been done. Then, I visited the shop every other day until the project was complete. My presence in the shop for so many days may have had no effect on the delivery of the cabinets, but at least I felt better seeing that the work was being done.

At the time of this incident, I was building about sixty homes a year and had a lot of clout with people in the trades. If this type of problem could happen to me, you can imagine the run-around a one-time amateur home builder might get. Unfortunately, there is no good way to ensure such a problem won't occur. You can write strong contracts and fierce penalty clauses, like I did, and still wind up waiting for your cabinets. Please, if you're going to order custom cabinets, do it as soon as possible.

STOCK CABINETS

Stock cabinets are a cost-effective alternative to custom cabinets. Since stock units are manufac-tured in mass numbers, they are much less expen-sive than custom cabinets. You can expect to save around 50 percent of your money when buying stock cabinets. What are you sacrificing? Not much. You won't get cabinets that are uniquely yours, but the quality of the cabinets can rival that of handmade units.

Stock cabinets come in a wide range of quality and price. Options seem endless, and features compete nicely with any custom cabinets. An-other advantage of buying stock cabinets is the short delivery time. The cabinets you pick may have to be ordered, but most production cabinets can be delivered in two weeks, or less. This is a big advantage over handcrafted cabinets.

Would I use stock cabinets in my home? You bet I would, and I am. I'm a big believer in produc-tion cabinets and have been for years. Previous homes that I have built for myself have been fitted with both custom cabinets and stock cabinets. Personally, I never felt the custom cabinets were any better than the production cabinets.

What should you look for when buying over-the-counter cabinets? The same features we discussed for custom cabinets apply to production cabinets. When you begin shopping showrooms for stock cabinets, you will find many different styles, colors, and qualities. Like anything else in life, some production cabinets are great and some aren't. Pay close attention to the bottoms, the backs and the drawer slides. These are the areas where manufacturers try to cut corners while making the fronts look good enough to sell you. Plan on spending a fair amount of time shopping. Visit several showrooms and examine many different brands of cabinets. You'll find something you like.

UNFINISHED CABINETS

The lure of low prices often leads people to unfinished cabinets. It's true that unfinished cabinets cost less than finished units, but I don't think the savings are worth the trouble involved with buying unfinished cabinets. The work required to finish the cabinets is extensive, and a certain amount of skill is needed. Mistakes in the finishing process can be costly, so much so that the savings evaporate.

Many super-supply stores that cater to retail buyers advertise unfinished cabinets in their sales flyers. For the uninitiated, the prices look great and the illustrations that depict the cabinets are also pleasing to the eye. If you intend to purchase unfinished cabinets, go into the process with your eyes wide open. I think you will regret buying unfinished cabinets, but some people may enjoy doing their own finish work.

CABINET ACCESSORIES

Cabinet accessories are so numerous that you may want to buy more cabinets just to get additional accessories. You can buy cabinets with recycling bins built right into them. Pull-out cutting boards and knife racks are also available. Potato bins can be found in cabinets, along with drop-down ironing boards. Most major cabinet manufacturers offer an extensive line of accessories. Before you buy

cabinets, you should spend some time checking out the accessories that you will want to incorporate into them.

RESALE VALUE

Resale value should be a consideration in every home buyer's mind. Even if you believe you will never sell your new home, you should consider the return on your investment. Appraisers are willing to increase a home's value based on the quality of the cabinets installed to a certain point. Beyond that point, the rate of return is not too good. As an example, steel cabinets could crush your home's appraisal. Stock cabinets from a quality manufacturer will bring a higher value than some glorified cardboard cabinets. Custom cabinets will almost never return their value. What does all of this mean? It means that mid-range to good quality stock cabinets provide the best return on your investment. This may not always hold true, but it usually will.

IN TERMS OF USE

In terms of use, some cabinets will do better than others. Cabinets with flimsy bottoms may warp, discolor, or even rot right through. A cabinet that has a plywood base is much better than one that has a low-quality base. If you check your cabinets for all of the qualities discussed in the section on custom cabinets, and they pass the test, you shouldn't have any problems for a long time to come.

Cabinet construction can be important to durability and dependability. Cheap latches may lose their ability to keep doors closed. Drawer bases with cheap, or no, glides will wear faster than good drawer bases. Cabinets that are made of soft, flimsy materials may suffer from having the door hinges pull out. Construction features definitely play an important role in the long-term use of cabinets. While it is not necessary to insist on the best, you should stick with name-brand cabinets that will give you years of solid service.

Are custom cabinets worth their extra cost? I don't think so, but this is just my personal opinion. There are many name-brand cabinets available as stock units that, in my opinion, are every bit as good as custom cabinets. I can see little reason to spend twice as much for a set of cabinets that are only better in terms of cosmetic appeal, but you may feel different. If you want unique cabinets and can afford to pay for them, custom cabinets are the way to go. Otherwise, you will be better off to stick to production cabinets from recognized manufacturers.

COUNTERTOPS

The counters you put on your cabinets can be simple or complex and inexpensive or expensive. The most common type of counter is pre-formed and covered with a smooth, nonabsorbent surface—usually a plastic laminate. The colors and patterns available for this type of counter are abundant. These basic counters are very affordable, good looking, durable, easy to clean, and they appraise well. When you step beyond the basics, prices go up and appraised value can go down, in terms of percentage of investment. If you want a perfectly acceptable counter that will give you the most return on your investment, a pre-formed counter is the way to go. If you have special circumstances or want something a little different, you must be willing to pay more and to recover less of your investment in the appraised value.

LESSONS FROM MY PAST

To illustrate the many possibilities with counters, I like to pull from some lessons from my past. We'll start with the first home I ever built for myself. The house was an A-frame home, and it was not a traditional home by any stretch of the imagination. As a part of our plans, Kimberley and I wanted a kitchen counter that was covered with ceramic tile. We chose a nice earth-tone base color with a wheat pattern on it. Kimberley installed all of the tile, and the counter turned out great. By doing the work ourselves, we got a tile counter and backsplash for about the same amount of money that a stock countertop would have cost us. The appraised value of a tile countertop will almost always be more than that of an average counter, so we made out just fine.

The next two houses we built for ourselves were equipped with store-bought, standard countertops. These counters were affordable, appraised well, and provided good looks and quality service. We had no regrets.

In the most recent home we are building for ourselves, we were planning to install a pre-formed, standard countertop. There was a glitch in our plans, however. Our new kitchen is going to have a corner sink. Pre-formed counters of standard quality would require a seam under the sink, where the turn for the corner is made. This seam would void the warranty of the counter, so we didn't want to go this route.

The standard top for our new kitchen was going to cost about $300. When we learned of the problem with the seam and looked for an alternative, we found one, but it cost over $600, twice as much. The $600 counter would look just like the $300 counter, except it would not have a seam and it would cost twice as much. We didn't want this, so I began to look for an alternative method. We've decided to build our own counter and to cover it with the same material that the store-bought models would have had. I don't want to do this work myself, so I've arranged for my carpenters to take care of it. After paying for labor and material to build the counter on site, the cost of a no-seam top will be about $300, the same price as the first counter we planned to use, but decided against. By building the top on site, we are shaving $300 off the cost of our counter.

If your kitchen is one that has many angles or some special requirements, it may very well pay for you to look into building your top on the job. Whether you do it yourself or sub it out, the finished cost could be considerably less than that of a store-bought unit.

A BASIC ROUNDUP

A basic roundup of countertops will result in several possible material choices. Tile is a good choice, but there are many more available. Some counters are made from material that is so tough that stains, even cigarette burns, can be sanded right out of the material, without any damage to the finish. Standard laminate tops are very common and popular, not to mention inexpensive. To some extent, your imagination is the only limit to your countertop options. You can use wood, brick, tile, marble, composition materials, and a lot more.

WHAT SHOULD I USE?

What should I use for a countertop? For most homes and most people, a good laminate top will be the best choice. It is the least expensive option, it wears well, appraises well, and gives a good impression. Tile is my favorite, but tile is expensive. Not only is tile expensive, its hard surface can break glass easily, and the grout joints can be difficult to clean. Unless you are building some type of specialty house, laminate tops are the most likely to give you all the best qualities that any one countertop can offer.

APPLIANCES

Appliances are a big part of a working kitchen. Can you imagine a kitchen without a range or refrigerator? Depending upon the region where you live, appliances in a kitchen can be numerous, and consequently, a substantial part of your home investment. Most appliances are not considered to be a part of the home. They are, in real estate terms, chattel, also known as personal property. Built-in appliances, like dishwashers, garbage disposals, trash compactors, and the like are considered to be part of the house. This little difference can be important in terms of your appraisal and home loan. Most lenders will allow you to finance the cost of a range and refrigerator, but when these items are used to boost a home's value or loan amount, they are not allowed to be removed when the home is sold.

If you specify appliances as a part of your home package when applying for a home loan, you must be prepared to leave the appliances in place when the home is sold. You may not have to do this in reality, but the theory is that if the appliances are used to create appraised value, they are part of the home. As long as you sell the home for enough to satisfy your mortgage, the lender will not care if the appliances are there or not. In a foreclosure, however, the removal of appliances that were used to secure a loan is a big no-no.

You don't have to include appliances like ranges and refrigerators in the specifications for your loan package. A lot of people don't want to be paying for their kitchen appliances over a 30-year term on a mortgage. On the other hand, many people don't have a lot of money to spend on appliances, so it is better for them to finance the items. This choice is up to you.

Some kitchen appliances are built-in units and should be included on the spec sheet used by an appraiser to value your home. Items like dishwashers, trash compactors, garbage disposals, and built-in microwave ovens can be considered real property, as opposed to chattel. This will increase your home's value and give you more borrowing power.

SHOPPING FOR APPLIANCES

When it comes to shopping for appliances, most anyone can read specifications and determine what appliances they like the looks of. If you don't know anything about appliances, it will pay for you to read books on what to look for. I could give you some suggestions here, but there are resources available to you that can do a better job than I can, in this limited space, in advising you on appliance purchases.

Different types of appliances require different types of investigation. For example, garbage disposals are available with motors of different sizes. A ⅓-horsepower disposal is not as powerful as a ½-horsepower disposal. One-half-horsepower disposals are not as powerful as ¾-horsepower disposals. Some garbage disposals will not operate until an electrical switch is turned on. Other models come on automatically as material is pushed into the disposal; this type is called a batch-feed disposal.

The intricacies of appliances can be sorted out by reading specifications and asking appliance dealers questions. Few people need detailed instructions on how to tell the advantages of a side-by-side refrigerator-freezer from an over-and-under refrigerator-freezer. This kind of decision is a personal one, and one that doesn't require extensive technical knowledge. Since I am relatively sure of your ability to know what appliances you want, I will not attempt to lecture you on your personal desires. However, you might like to know a little about what appliances pull their own weight in terms of resale value, so let's talk more on this subject.

RANGES

Ranges are a necessary part of a kitchen. Both electric and gas ranges are fine, but you will need some type of range to cook on. Common practice calls for buying a range that is coupled with an oven, but this is not always the case. Some homes are equipped with range tops that sit in cabinets. A range top doesn't have to have an oven. The oven is a separate appliance. This is okay, but you will normally be better off, financially speaking, if you buy a combination range and oven.

REFRIGERATOR-FREEZER COMBINATIONS

Refrigerator-freezer combinations are standard equipment in modern homes. The two types are side-by-side units and over-and-under units. Side-by-side units are generally considered to be better and of a higher value. Either type is acceptable. A refrigerator should have at least 18 cubic feet of storage space. Ice makers are nice, but they are not a necessity.

DISHWASHERS

An automatic dishwasher should be considered a necessity in the scheme of your kitchen. I can't imagine building or trying to sell a new house that did not have a dishwasher. The appliance doesn't have to have all the bells and whistles on it, but it should be a name-brand unit.

GARBAGE DISPOSALS

Garbage disposals are not one of your have-to-have appliances. In fact, if your home has a private sewage disposal system, some local code requirements prohibit the installation of a garbage disposal. Assuming that you decide to install a disposal, buy a good one. There are cheap disposals available, but they are often noisy, underpow-

ered, and prone to failures. A ½-horsepower disposal with a good insulating case should be considered the starting point in size and quality.

TRASH COMPACTORS

Trash compactors were very popular for awhile, but the demand for them seems to have dwindled. I wouldn't worry about installing a compactor unless it is something you particularly want for your own use.

MICROWAVE OVENS

Microwave ovens are one appliance that most people have grown to rely on. With today's hectic schedules, microwaves give working couples a chance to do more than just cook dinner when they get home. I feel every new kitchen should be equipped with a good microwave, preferably one that is built into the cabinets or that hangs under the cabinets.

INDOOR GRILLS

Indoor grills, that are vented to the outside to allow the use of charcoal inside the home, are very popular. They are also very expensive. These luxury cook tops work well in island cabinets and other locations. While it is difficult to justify the expense, these appliances make cooking out in the home possible.

WASHERS AND DRYERS

Clothes washers and dryers are mandatory in a new home. A house without laundry facilities is not much of a home. I mention these appliances because many people fail to include them in their housing budget. While washers and dryers are not the most expensive appliances in a home, their combined cost can put a big dent in your building budget if they are not allowed for.

Now that we have covered the basics of finalizing the interior of your home, let's move to the outside and look at final site work and landscaping. Just turn the page, and we'll jump right in.

CHAPTER 28

FINAL SITE WORK AND LANDSCAPING

The final site work and landscaping of your new home is a glorious time. You are almost ready to move in, but one wrong move from the dozer or loader could result in a cracked foundation. Planting shrubs too close to your home could cause moisture problems. The wrong grading might create an unwanted pond of rainwater or a flooded basement. This phase of the job requires close inspection and attention to detail. The advice in this chapter guides you to a safe conclusion of your exterior construction work.

By the time you reach the phase of final site work and landscaping, you are likely to want to sit back, relax, and soak in the fruits of your labor. Don't do it. You're almost done, but there is still plenty to do and even more that could go wrong. As a dozer or loader is putting the finishing touches on your final grading, the equipment could bump into your home and damage the foundation. That beautiful tree you've worked hard to preserve could become marred for life with one wrong swing of a bucket on a backhoe. Oh, there is a lot that can go wrong as you near the completion of your job.

Final grading and landscaping are very important to the finished product known as your home. If the grading is not done properly, you can suffer with moisture problems for as long as you live in your new home. The same could be true if you plant shrubs too close to your foundation. Just as the interior trim work is a cornerstone to the finished look of your home's interior, the final grading and landscaping will be one of the first things people approaching your home will see. So, you'd better do them right.

FINAL GRADING

Final grading is not the type of work you can do yourself. This work requires big, expensive equipment that should only be operated by trained peo-

ple. You can't just go down to the local rental center and come back with a bulldozer and dump truck. Even if you could, you probably wouldn't have a clue as to how to operate the equipment. With this being the case, you are going to have to rely on others to do the work for you. Your role will be purely that of a general contractor.

The contractor who did your rough grading will most likely be the one to do your final grading. The stages involved with final grading vary to some extent, but they are basically consistent with any home. Loam or top soil is hauled in and spread around the house to create a base for a lawn. The dirt should be graded out to provide good drainage around the home. Once the dirt is in place and raked out, it is seeded with grass and covered with straw.

The rough driveway that has been used during construction is also finished off at this stage. It may be topped off with a finish coat of stone, or it may be paved. When the finish grading is done, the grounds around your home should be neat and ready for landscaping. Now landscaping is something you should be able to do yourself, and it is a phase of work that can have a lot to do with your home's curb appeal and value.

BASIC LANDSCAPING

Basic landscaping doesn't require a lot of money or work. All that is really required are some shrubs around the foundation of the home. There are many types of plants to choose from, and many of them will be very affordable and easy to install. If you choose to keep your landscaping cost to a minimum, you can. However, if you would like to invest some extra money into the grounds around your home, you can do so safely. Landscaping is a very safe investment, so long as you don't get carried away. Every appraiser I've ever talked to has been willing to give extra value for nice landscaping. It is not until you start spending thousands of dollars on exotic landscaping that you may lose value on your appraisal, compared to the money spent on landscaping.

FOUNDATION SHRUBS

Foundation shrubs should be considered a necessity. Even if you have an attractive, brick foundation, shrubbery will break up the long lines of a house and enhance its appearance. The types of plants used for this purpose are numerous. You should, however, avoid plants that will grow extremely high or get too bushy. Tall, bushy plants provide something of a security risk, in that bad guys can hide behind them. Keep the plants low-growing and manageable in size.

When you plant foundation shrubs, keep in mind that they are going to grow. It is wise to plant the greenery at least a few feet out from the foundation, to reduce moisture problems. If you don't want weeds and grass growing up around your plants, you should lay down a layer of black plastic and cut holes in it to allow the planting of your shrubs. The plastic can then be covered with dirt, pine chips, or mulch. Having a plastic barrier will reduce the proliferation of unwanted weeds and grasses.

FLOWER BEDS

Flower beds always add to the appearance of a home. The ground for a flower bed can be prepared with a plastic barrier, just as we talked about for foundation shrubs. The bed itself can be surrounded by metal edging or landscaping timbers. I prefer landscaping timbers. Personally, I like pine-bark mulch in flower beds and around shrubs, but this is only a personal preference.

TREES

If you will be planting trees in your lawn, you may very well need professional help. Even small trees have large root balls and are very heavy and hard to maneuver. Landscaping companies have trucks with special equipment that allows them to set the trees with ease, but you won't have this advantage. If you think you are just going to pick up a small tree and set it in a little hole, you're mistaken. You can do this with a seedling, but even trees with minuscule diameters carry a lot of weight on their root balls. Don't attempt to plant your own trees.

TERRACED GARDENS

Depending upon the lay of your land, terraced gardens for your flowers and plants may be just the ticket. The use of landscape timbers and creative plant selection can create a fabulous garden that shows itself off well. This is also a great way to solve potential erosion problems on lawns with steep inclines.

WALKWAYS

A lot of people only think of flowers and plants when they think of landscaping, but walkways can be considered a part of your exterior decorating. Having a defined walkway to your entrance doors is nice, and many people expect them. The walkways can be made of concrete, stone, bricks, pebbles, or other materials.

Living in Maine, I don't see too many fancy walkways. People in my area are used to parking near their kitchen door and walking up the driveway to the door. Front doors are rarely used, and most of them have no formal walkway to them. This is quite a contrast to when I lived in Virginia. The homes in Virginia almost always had sidewalks to their entrance doors. Obviously, the importance of a walkway depends somewhat on where you live, but appraisers are usually kind when it comes to giving extra value for a walkway.

MORE EXOTIC OPTIONS

More exotic options for your exterior decorating might include a small pond filled with goldfish.

Fountains might be installed to spruce up the outside of your home. Park benches, gazebos, overhead flower arbors, and a host of other possibilities exist to make your grounds memorable. However, if you go too far into these expenditures, you may not recover your investment on an appraisal. While it is usually safe to spend a reasonable amount of money on landscaping, you shouldn't carry it to extremes.

EXTERIOR LIGHTING

Exterior lighting is a part of the electrical phase of work, but it can also be a part of your landscaping. Floodlights and spotlights are good for security and all-around use, but mood lighting can add a new dimension to your home's exterior appearance in the evening. Having low-voltage lights outlining your walkway can be quite impressive. The same can be said for lighting up your deck. A few in-ground floodlights aimed at the front of your house can give it a great look after dark. You might not recover much of your investment on exterior lighting, but you can bet that people will be impressed favorably by it.

HIRING LANDSCAPING CONTRACTORS

Hiring landscaping contractors is a good alternative for those people who do not have green thumbs or a desire to root around in fresh dirt. The expense of bringing in professional landscapers, however, might surprise you. Most contractors in this field of endeavor are not cheap. They can, however, still be a bargain.

If you are willing to put your money on the line, professional landscapers can work wonders around the outside of your home. They will start by drafting a plan of attack. The plan will be almost like a set of blueprints, except that instead of showing rafters, walls, and windows, this plan will show plant placement. With the use of a computer and a computer-aided drafting (CAD) program, a progressive landscaping company can give you a customized design for your home that is easy to visualize. This is important. If you are going to spend a few thousand dollars on plants, it is best if you can picture what the end result will look like. It's one thing for someone to stand in a nursery and tell you that you need this there and that here, but seeing a blueprint of your landscaping plans will put it all into perspective.

Shopping for a reputable landscaping contractor is not much different than hunting for any other type of subcontractor. There are, however, some advantages when seeking professional landscaping advice and assistance. When you are trying to find a quality plumber, you can look at other jobs the plumber has done, but you can't see the exact plumbing that will wind up in your house. Buying landscaping is a little different in that you can hand pick the plants you want in your lawn. You still have to gamble a little on the landscaping company's dependability and willingness to stand behind their work, but at least you can see a tangible item that you will be purchasing.

Before you hire a landscaping company, you should check them out the same as you would any other contractor. Confirm that the company is insured to protect you from any unexpected and unwanted expenses, such as an on-the-job accident. Check references provided by the company, and whenever possible, ride by some of the jobs they have done for other people. Just because a company has a greenhouse full of beautiful plants doesn't mean that the company is skilled in the installation of them. If you follow the basic rules of picking good subcontractors, you should come up with a landscaper who's work you will appreciate and enjoy for many years to come.

CHAPTER 29

PUNCH-OUT WORK

What is punch-out work? It is work that crops up at the end of a job that makes you want to punch out the contractor. No, not really. Punch-out work is the final adjustments made to doors, the correction of plumbing leaks, the touch-up of paint, and similar final touches. Every job has some type of punch-out work needed before the house should be moved into. This chapter prepares you for the types of punch-out work that routinely show up and tells you how you can ensure that your contractors will take care of the minor problems promptly.

What is punch-out work? It is the fixing of odds and ends at the end of a job. It might entail touching up some paint, oiling a squeaky door hinge, adjusting a window latch, or repairing a hole in a wall. Punch-out work is a combination of all the repairs and adjustments needed to finalize a job. Who's responsible for doing punch-out work? The contractor who installed the work that needs attention is responsible for the punch-out work. When I'm asked by people what punch-out work is, I have a standard reply: punch-out work is a combination of problems at the end of a job that makes you want to punch the contractor out.

Now that you know what punch-out work is, let's talk about what to expect to have happen near the end of your job. It will be your job to list all the deficiencies that need to be tended to. This list is called a punch-out list. If you did the work that needs attention, you will be the punch-out person. If the problems are associated with a phase of work that you contracted out, the sub-contractor will be responsible. You should never make final payments to contractors until you've done a punch-out inspection and made sure the final job is done to your satisfaction.

Punch-out work is normally associated with the end of a job, and this is when it is most often encountered. However, not all trades are involved

in work that turns up at the completion of a job. Some trades do jobs that must be inspected long before a house is finished. Take foundation contractors as an example. Foundations are built early in the construction of a house, and if they are in good shape when they are done, they should remain in good shape. There should be no need to inspect the foundation for a punch list at the completion of your home. This type of work should be inspected as soon as it is completed, and any problems should be corrected at that time. To help you with the requirements of quality control, inspections, repairs, adjustments, and regular punch-out work, let's go on a trade-by-trade basis through the construction of a typical house and see what you might encounter.

ROUGH SITE WORK

Rough site work will normally be the first stage of work in the construction of a house. This work should be inspected when it has been completed. If there are problems, they should be taken care of as soon after the work is completed as possible. What's likely to go wrong with rough site work? Trees that are supposed to be removed may be left standing. Worse yet, trees that were intended to be saved may be cut down by mistake. Culvert pipe may not be installed for a driveway. Tree stumps may be left on the job. Don't let the site contractor tell you that the stumps will be removed before final grading. Insist on having the contractor remove the stumps before you pay for services rendered. With site work, and all other work, you should compare the materials used with the specifications you provided to the contractor. If you specified a number-three stone for the base layer of your driveway, make sure that you get number-three stone. When you inspect the labor and material provided by subcontractors, you must pay very close attention to detail. It is extremely easy to overlook flaws, and you may get only one chance to find them and bring them to the attention of a contractor while you are still in control of the contractor's cash. Once you pay the bill, getting satisfaction for work that needs to be altered can be a lot more difficult.

FOUNDATION WORK

Problems with foundation work usually show up fast. When a framing crew moves in and begins to frame a house, the carpenters find flaws with foundations quickly. If you are inexperienced in building, it can be very difficult for you to pick up on problems with a foundation. Unless you own, and know how to use, a transit, you may have to wait for your framing crew to point out any problems with a foundation. If you are not going to have a framing crew move in on the foundation quickly, you should at least have a representative of the crew come in to check the foundation for you. Find any problems that exist early, before you pay the foundation contractor.

What kinds of problems crop up with foundations? There are two very common problems associated with new foundations. They may be out of square or out of level. Either of these problems can make the job of a framing crew much harder. Not only this, but if the foundation is out too far, the appearance of your home can be compromised. Another frequent problem is piers being left out or installed in the wrong locations. Due to the technical aspects of foundation work, you should have the leader of your framing crew inspect the foundation for you.

It is unusual for the condition of a foundation to change between the time it is finished and the time when a house is finished; although, there are times when foundations crack before a house is finished. In the case of homes with full basements, the basement walls may develop leaks during the construction of a home. While it is unlikely that there will be any tail-end problems with a foundation, you should check your foundation during the punch-list process at the completion of your home.

FRAMING

The framing phase of your job can provide you with a host of problems. Some of them will show up right away, and others won't surface until near the end of your job. Again, if you are not an experienced builder or carpenter, you will have trouble determining if the framing work is up to snuff. You should consider hiring a professional inspection service or consultant to help you. Doing this will cost some money, but the cost of a professional inspection can be a lot less than paying for problems that you are not trained to see. Need some examples? I'll give you some.

WRONG DOOR SIZES

If your framing crew builds walls that contain the wrong door sizes, you might not catch the problem until drywall is hung and painted. If this problem is detected before wall coverings are installed, it is relatively simple to correct. Once the walls are done, the job becomes much more difficult. You can go out to your new house and measure the rough openings for doors. This simple task can save you a boatload of trouble later on.

HITTING THE BEAM

What are you going to do if your new garage door is hitting the beam in your garage? You cannot move the beam very easily, and you may not be able to do anything about the height of your garage door. Can you imagine having a garage where the door cannot be opened properly? It can, and does, happen. This is something you may or may not have the ability to check yourself, but it is a potential problem that may not show up until long after the framing crew has been paid in full and moved on.

SQUEAKY FLOORS

Squeaky floors can result from subflooring that is not nailed properly. If your framing crew cuts corners in the nailing of your flooring, the job may look fine but wind up squeaking like crazy once you move in. What can you do then? You aren't going to pull up your carpet and vinyl to install extra nails in the subflooring. This is the type of problem you must catch early. If you don't know what should be done or what you're looking for, hire someone who does to inspect the work.

The list of potential problems arising out of the framing stage could more than fill this chapter. Since we have a lot of other phases to discuss, we must abbreviate our look at framing problems. The moral to this story, however, is that someone who has a keen eye for construction should inspect all framing work before any final payments are made. If you can't do this yourself, spend a little money to protect your investment. Property inspectors aren't cheap, but they are a bargain compared to the problems that could arise from a bad framing job.

THE EXTERIOR
ROOFING

Most problems with roofing work will be present as soon as the job is done. It's possible that the quality of a job could deteriorate as it goes along, but it's not likely. If the job is good, it's good. But, how many armchair contractors are going to climb up on a steep roof to inspect valleys, flashings, and roof caps? For that matter, how many amateur general contractors are going to know what to look for? Are you getting the idea that you should establish a good relationship with a reputable construction inspection service? Well, you probably should. You can gamble and hope that your subs are doing what they are supposed to. If you do this, expect to be on the losing end from time to time. Money paid to professional inspectors is usually money well spent.

SIDING

Siding is another phase of work that should be inspected immediately following its installation. Siding can be inspected by average people. If it looks good, it probably is good. As long as the job is pleasing to the eye and doesn't have big gaps, it should be okay. An experienced eye might pick up on some sections that are not even or some other minor mistakes, but all in all, you should be capable of inspecting your own siding. One thing to check long before the siding is finished, in fact it should be checked when the work is started, is the type of nails being used to install the siding. Don't let your subcontractor use nails that will bleed rust on your new siding. Stainless steel nails should be used with wood siding. These nails cost more than other types, but they are the best insurance you can buy against rust stains.

WINDOWS

Assuming that you are acting as your own general contractor, you will probably be buying and supplying your own windows. The first thing to check is that the supplier has shipped the proper windows in the right sizes. When this is the case, you can relax until your framing crew installs them. Once the windows are installed, you should check to see that they are installed plumb and level. You don't need a college degree or a trade license to check this work. All you need are a few good levels. Check the windows both vertically and horizontally. If the bubble is in the middle, you're all set. If the windows are installed sloppily, they won't operate properly. This is easy to fix before drywall goes up, but it's a real pain if you don't discover the problem until the house is finished.

EXTERIOR DOORS

Exterior doors are a lot like windows in terms of quality control. When these units are installed, you should inspect them to see that they were installed level and plumb. You should use a long level to check the vertical installation. A four-foot level is a minimum, and a six-foot level is better. Open and close the doors to see if they work smoothly. Once the door handles (locksets in trade terms) are installed, make sure the doors close securely and open easily. Just like windows, rough door installations are not difficult to correct, but once drywall is hung, fixing problems with exterior doors can result in a real mess.

Aside from doors that are not installed level or plumb, latch problems are the most common type of trouble. Strike plates may need to be moved. In the case of sliding glass doors, simple adjustments can smooth out the operation of the doors. The key is to catch the problems early, before you pay the framing crew. Both exterior doors and windows fall into the domain of framing crews.

THE MECHANICALS
THE HEATING INSTALLATION

The heating and air-conditioning installation usually follows the framing stage. This early heating and air-conditioning work is called the rough-in. This is when heat ducts, heating pipes, or in some cases, electric wiring goes into place. With mechanical trades, like heating, air-conditioning, plumbing, and electrical work, there are two stages that must be inspected. The first is the rough-in, this is done before drywall is hung. A second inspection is needed as the house is being finished and the trim-out work has been done. Let's talk first about the rough-in stage.

Air-conditioning rough-ins always involve the installation of ductwork. Many heating installations also involve ductwork, sometimes the same ductwork as that of the air-conditioning. Whenever ducts are installed, there is a good chance that some structural members may be cut and damaged. If this happens, you need to catch the problem early and have it corrected before walls, ceilings, and floors are installed. Typically, floor and ceiling joists should not be cut within two inches of their top or bottom edges. If a mechanic notches a joist to allow ductwork to sneak into place, you could be losing structural integrity in your home. This is certainly something that you can check for. However, you are unlikely to possess the skills to know if the ductwork is sized properly. You can trust your subcontractor and hope that the ducts are the right size, or you can call in an independent inspector to make sure they are. Code enforcement officers inspect this type of work, but they are looking only for code infrac-

tions. What meets minimum code standards may not coincide with the specifications in your plans and contract. I think it is a wise decision to hire an independent professional to verify that you are getting what you are paying for.

Not all heating work involves ductwork. If your home will be heated with a boiler, the heat distribution will be done with copper pipe and baseboard heaters. Electric baseboard and wall heaters rely on electrical wiring to fuel them. There is less likelihood with these types of heat that joists will be cut, but you cannot afford to assume that they won't. There is also more to look for than just hacked-out floor joists.

When copper pipe is installed for a forced hot-water heating system, the pipe should be insulated to prevent noises when the pipe is expanding and contracting. Plumbing pipes are generally installed differently than heating pipes, even though the pipe material may be exactly the same. If a heating pipe is secured too tightly in an uninsulated environment, the pipe will squeak or make other strange noises as it expands and contracts. Any reputable heating contractors won't install pipes in a fashion to allow problems down the road, but there are always some who are in a hurry or who don't know any better. You should confirm the type of supports used on heat pipes, and you should also make sure the system is tested for leaks before it is concealed with drywall.

Trim-out problems with heating and air-conditioning systems show up at the end of a job. The problems are usually minimal, but that doesn't make them any less important. Let's talk about punch-out items that you may come up with when installing a duct system. You may find that the air grilles and registers don't open and close smoothly. This may require minor adjustment or the replacement of a defective part. Other problems might involve equipment controls, thermostats, or other items related to the system. Most of the problems associated with these things will not be obvious to an untrained eye. However, if you find the system is not working properly, you don't have to troubleshoot it for your subcontractor. Describe the type of problem you're having, and leave the burden of responsibility on the shoulders of your subcontractor.

Forced hot-water heating systems don't generate many punch-out deficiencies that are easily detected by an average person. Problems that may exist will show up as system failures. Of course, you may have a baseboard cover that has been scratched or an end-cap missing, but most problems will involve the boiler or the devices installed close to it. Circulator pumps can go bad, controls may need adjusting, nozzles can become plugged up, and a lot of other things can go wrong. Of all the things that are likely to create problems, most of them will have to be sorted out by a skilled professional.

PLUMBING

The plumbing in your home can generate a lot of punch-out work. This can happen in both the rough-in stage of plumbing and the trim-out. The types of punch-out problems that arise during the rough-in stage can be difficult for an inexperienced general contractor to catch. For example, if a plumber neglects to install backing for a wall-hung lavatory, a first-time home builder may not even notice the mistake. Seasoned veterans will pick up on this problem right away. If this problem is not caught and corrected during the rough-in, there are going to be big problems when fixtures are set. Without backing to secure a wall bracket, hanging a wall-hung lavatory is a delicate situation, to say the least. This example is just the tip of the plumbing iceberg.

Plumbers sometime butcher floor joists, studs, and other wood members. If this happens on your job, you should make sure the damaged structural members are repaired before the house is closed up with drywall. It can take an experienced eye to see problems with cutting and notching.

Nail plates are metal strips that are used to protect pipes from nails. If a pipe is installed in a location where a drywall nail or screw might hit it by accident, plumbers are supposed to install nail plates to protect the pipes. This is something a plumbing inspector should catch, but some local code officers might be pressed for time and miss a few code violations. It's bad when an inspector misses a code violation, but it can be a lot worse when a nail pierces your new plumbing. To ensure that this doesn't happen, you must do your own inspections.

Pipes that are installed in the wrong places can be a real headache as a job progresses. It may be difficult for you to confirm that all pipes are where they are supposed to be, but this is something you should definitely do. If you don't, the price you pay could be costly. Let me tell you quickly about a horror show from my past that involved misplaced pipes.

Seventeen years ago I was a project superintendent for a 360-unit townhouse complex. Each block of townhouses contained six housing units. One big foundation and a few party walls made up the basis for six townhouses. In a lot of ways this layout made plumbing easy, but it also created some complications. When underground plumbing was installed, it was installed for all six townhouses at once. Pipe placement was critical on this job. One wrong move and a pipe was covered with concrete and left outside of a wall.

My job as the superintendent was to make sure that everything went well. It was not unusual for a pipe to be installed so that a small portion of it was bulging past a wall. However, there was one occasion when I was fortunate enough to head off a full-scale disaster. I went out on the site to inspect the work of the plumbing crew. I'd done so many of these cookie-cutter townhouses that I knew them inside out. Something seemed wrong with the location of the plumbing stacks. I got my assistant superintendent to help me pull some lines to represent walls in the six townhouses. It's a good thing we did. The plumbing contractor had made a big mistake in the layout of the building. Each party wall location, as determined by the plumbing contractor, was about two inches off the mark of where the actual walls would go. This meant that the interior partition locations were also wrong. So was most of the plumbing. If I hadn't checked the plumbing very carefully, the plumbing contractor would have been breaking up a lot of concrete and relocating a lot of pipes. You can't afford to let this type of problem happen to you, so you must make sure the plumbing rough-in locations are correct. You may be able to do this yourself, or you may find it prudent to have a professional inspect the rough plumbing.

Final plumbing tends to cause a number of punch-out problems. The list can range from faucets that are installed crooked, hot and cold water being piped to the wrong sides of fixtures, pop-up plugs that don't work, leaks around cut-off valves, and a lot more. While you may not be qualified to find all of the problems associated with rough plumbing, you do, most likely, possess the ability to check out final plumbing.

When your plumber has finished your job, you should do some poking around to make sure the work is up to snuff. Most localities have plumbing inspectors who check out the work to see if it is in compliance with local code requirements. This doesn't mean that you shouldn't verify that the work has been done to your satisfaction. Plumbing inspectors look for code infractions, not contract compliance. To assure that you are getting what you're paying for, you will have to inspect the work yourself.

Final plumbing installations can be plagued with problems. There are also a host of troubles that can crop up within the first week or two of finishing a plumbing installation. Compression fittings are famous for developing after-installation leaks. Slip joints often present problems after final plumbing is installed. There is a long list of potential problems to look for.

It is unfortunate, but true, that not all plumbers test their work thoroughly. If this happens with your house, you may face a lot of challenges after your trim plumbing is installed. When you inspect your own plumbing fixtures, the first thing to look for is general appearance. Are the fixtures installed straight, or are they twisted and crooked? A tape measure will tell you. For example, you can measure from the wall behind a toilet to the holes in the toilet bowl where the seat attaches to see if the bowl has been installed with an equal distance from the back wall to the fixture. If the bowl is cocked to one side, your tape measure will expose the deficiency. If the distance from the seat holes to the back wall are not identical, the fixture was not installed properly.

After doing a visual inspection for general appearance, you should test the plumbing thoroughly to see if it functions properly. This should be done before the plumbing contractor is paid. How do you test your own plumbing? Well, it's really not hard, but you should follow certain guidelines during your test.

Kitchens

In the kitchen, you have to look for leaks in the sink, the drainage piping, and the water supplies. Buy a roll of paper towels. Spread the towels out in the bottom of your cabinet where the kitchen sink is installed. Look closely at the water pipes and cut-off valves. Try the valves to make sure they cut the water off to your fixture. While it is not common, it is possible to get a defective valve, so you should check to see that the cut-off works properly. The paper towels that you lay out under the sink will serve as a second safety measure when trying to detect leaks. Plumbing can leak so slowly that a casual inspection will not turn up the problem. Having the paper towels in place will tell you if there are any leaks. Even the smallest leaks can be ascertained when paper towels are used. If a leak is present, dampness will expose it.

A lot of experienced plumbers make mistakes when testing their work. I've seen master plumbers test a kitchen sink for drainage leaks by just running water from the faucet. If a big leak is present, this approach will turn it up. However, there are a lot of leaks that cannot be found by simply running water out of the faucet. The proper procedure for testing a sink is to fill it with water and then drain it. By releasing a full sink of water all at once, more pressure is put on the drainage system. If a leak is present, it will show up.

If your kitchen has a dishwasher or a garbage disposal, you have to check the connections to these appliances. The same can be said for ice makers. To find whatever problems may be present in your kitchen, you must check everything closely. In the case of a dishwasher, you should run the appliance through a complete cycle, while you watch the plumbing connections. If there's a leak, you should see it.

To test a garbage disposal, fill the sink bowl with water and then pull the plug. As water is rushing through the disposal, turn on the disposal and see if you find any leaks. If you have an ice maker, check the piping connections to see if any leaks are there. Paper towels can be a big help in finding these leaks.

As you check out your kitchen sink and appliances, be sure to look beneath the surface, such as in the base cabinet, where the sink is installed. Wipe all connections with a paper towel to see if any moisture is present. It is not uncommon for compression joints and slip joints to test fine for the plumber and then develop a small leak within the first few days of use. If these leaks go unnoticed, the result can be water-damaged cabinets, walls, and floors.

Bathrooms

Bathing units, tubs and showers, are installed during the rough-in stage. These fixtures can be very delicate, and they can become damaged easily. It is also possible that the units will not be installed plumb and level. Use a long level, say a four-footer, to check the installation of your bathing units. As soon as the tubs and showers are installed, check them over carefully. Look for scratches, cracks, and other defects. You need to find these problems before drywall is installed. Once drywall goes up, getting most tubs and showers out of their holes is going to be difficult and damaging.

In the bathrooms, you have several things to check out. Start with the bathtub or shower. Turn the valve on and see if the hot water is on the left and the cold water is on the right. They should be. If your bathtub is equipped with a shower head, test it.

Check the lavatory the same way you checked the kitchen sink. While you are running the water in the lavatory, close the drain and fill the bowl. Once it's full, let the water out all at once and look for leaks in the drainage system under the lavatory.

Flush your toilet a few times and see that the fixture cycles properly. Look closely around the base of the toilet to make sure that water is not seeping out.

Other Fixtures

Other plumbing fixtures should be tested in about the same way described for the kitchen and bathroom. Turn on your washing machine and make sure it works properly. If you have a laundry tub, test it the same as you would a kitchen sink. Go to each and every fixture in your home and make sure the hot water is on the left and the cold water is on the right. You'd be surprised how often professional plumbers mix up the hot and cold water lines.

Outside faucets should also be checked. Are they secured to the walls? Have they been caulked at their mounting flanges? Are backflow preventers installed on the hose bibbs? Basically, you should use all of your plumbing fixtures and confirm that they work well.

ELECTRICAL

Rough-in electrical is hard for an average person to check out. To an untrained eye, rough wiring tends to look like a mangled maze of endless wiring. You pretty much have to depend on either your local electrical inspector or an independent inspector to check your electrical rough-in.

Final electrical punch-out is pretty simple. Go through your home and test all outlets by plugging a light into them and turning it on. Use all of your switches to see that they work the right lights. If you want to get picky, you can go around with a torpedo level and check cover plates to see that they are installed perfectly. As long as everything looks good and works right, you should be all set.

INSULATION

Insulation is easy enough for most people to inspect. If the material is the right type and size, and if it is installed so that it separates heated areas from unheated areas, the job should be fine. One common problem to look out for, however, is when insulators forget to stuff insulation around window and door frames. If the gaps around these frames are not chinked, cold air will blow through the openings.

THE INTERIOR
DRYWALL

Drywall is a phase of your job that will be difficult for you to inspect. I've known people who thought that the first coat of drywall finishing was the final coat, even though there were two more coats needed. It is very difficult for an untrained person to pick out problems with the finish work of drywall. You should hire an independent inspector to check this work for you.

PAINT WORK

Paint work is something you can depend on your own inspection skills for. If a primer/sealer is applied first and followed with a coat of high-quality paint, the remainder of what you have to be concerned about is the appearance of the job. If you like the way the paint looks, that's all you have to worry about.

TRIM

Trim work is not structural, but it is of key importance in the construction of your home. Fortunately, you can tell if the trim in your home is installed satisfactorily. If the work looks good, you should be happy.

FLOORING

Flooring installations involve some technical work, but the finished job depends mostly on appearance. If the flooring looks good, you will probably be satisfied. Check seams to make sure they are tight and nearly invisible. Look the job over carefully, and if it suits you, that's fantastic.

CABINETS

Cabinets are pretty easy to check out. If they are installed properly, the doors and drawers will open and close easily. Everything will fit nicely. As long as there are no gaps between the units, the doors latch properly, and the drawers don't stick, you've got a good cabinet job.

COUNTERS

When you are inspecting your counters, look at the seams. Check the overhang. See if the counter is attached securely to the cabinets it is sitting on. Look for scratches on the counter. Pay particular attention to the corners of the counter; they often get beaten up during installation.

MISCELLANEOUS WORK

There will be plenty of miscellaneous work to give your attention to, for example, the installation of shower doors or garage doors. This work will require just as much of your interest as any other type of work. Every time anything is done as part of the construction of your new house, you should check it out carefully. Paying for work that has not been done properly is a poor practice. Never, and I mean never, pay anyone for any work that you are not completely satisfied with.

FINAL GRADING

Final grading must be done right, or your house will not look its best. This means grading the ground away from your home's foundation, raking the top soil, seeding the ground, and applying cover over the seeding. Most of your final grading will be easy to inspect. If it looks good, it is good. Should you have any questions or concerns, you should consult a professional inspector.

WATCH OUT FOR FRIENDS

Watch out for work done by your friends, even if they are professional tradespeople. Friendships can end abruptly during a construction job. I know this from experience. If you have a friend who is a plumber or a carpenter, don't cut corners on your business procedures. Stick closely to detailed contracts and firm business principles. If you assume that your friends won't do you wrong, you may find yourself shocked and surprised, not to mention out a lot of money. The punch-out process is a very important one, so don't take it lightly.

CHAPTER 30

CLEANING UP AND MOVING IN

When all the subcontractors are gone, it is time for cleaning up and moving in. This is work you can do yourself, but there are some basic rules that you should follow to avoid damaging your new home. This chapter shows you everything from how to remove the big, black letters from your new vinyl flooring to how to get your king-size mattress up the stairs without marring the paint on the walls.

Cleaning up and moving in is not the most technical or the most difficult part of seeing your dream home come to life, but it is a part of the job. Cleaning a new house requires some physical effort, but you don't need a trade license to do it. Almost anyone can prepare their new home for the move in. However, there are occasions when your best efforts create more problems than they solve.

Moving furniture into a home can require some heavy work, but it also demands some brain power. If the moving process is not executed properly, your new house can be marred and damaged. Whether you move yourself or have professional movers do the job for you, there are risks involved. Let me tell you about a house that I built where the moving-in process caused a lot of trouble.

I built a contemporary-style home many years ago that didn't have a class-A design. The stairs leading to the upstairs had low head clearance. The stairs met code requirements, but the headroom for moving large furniture up the stairs was very limited.

The people who bought this house had a king-size bed. When they attempted to get the mattress up the stairs, it wouldn't fit. Try as they might, the mattress just wouldn't go up the stairs. You can imagine their frustration at building a house that couldn't accommodate their furniture. Unfor-

tunately, the dilemma extended over to me, since I had been the general contractor. I had built the house in compliance with the plans and specifications, so I wasn't really responsible for their problem. However, I felt compelled to help the young couple. I put my crew back into the house and—at no charge—cut an angle into the problem spot. This allowed the furniture to fit through the space with ease. The changes cost me a few hundred dollars but the customers were ecstatic and proved to be fabulous references. My point in telling you this story is to make you aware that you are not out of the woods until the job is finished, cleaned up and moved into.

CLEANING

A lot of the cleaning you will face in your new home will not be unusual to you. Your carpets must be vacuumed. Your vinyl floors must be mopped. The vinyl is likely to have large, black letters running across it. A concentrated floor cleaner available at your local grocery store will take the black letters off of the flooring with little effort. As you vacuum the carpet, you will likely see a lot of shedding. This is normal.

WALLS

Your walls shouldn't need any cleaning. There may be a few fingerprints here and there, but there shouldn't be many. Windows, on the other hand, will require some time to clean. Stickers will have to be scraped off with a straight-edge razor blade and the glass cleaned with a standard window cleaner.

PLUMBING FIXTURES

Plumbing fixtures are often spotted with labels and stickers. Some stickers can be pulled off with minimal effort. Others will tear leaving adhesive and paper behind. The combination of a sponge and hot, soapy water is usually all that is needed to remove labels from the fixtures. If you run into one spot that is particularly stubborn, you may have to resort to a razor blade. Take your time, and work the razor blade slowly, taking care not to scratch the fixture.

COUNTERS

Counters sometimes have letters printed across them. A standard, concentrated cleaner will remove them. You should not use an abrasive cleaner, scouring pad, or other cleaning device. A liquid cleaner and a sponge will normally remove any lettering found on counters.

LIGHT FIXTURES

Light fixtures don't usually need any special cleaning. You may have to wipe dust from the fixtures, but there should be no need for specialized materials or techniques to get your fixtures up and running. You will, however, need light bulbs. Professional electricians don't normally include light bulbs in their pricing and work. This surprises many new homeowners. Unless you have contracted specifically for your electrician to supply and install light bulbs, you should plan on doing it yourself.

APPLIANCES

New appliances often contain packing materials that must be removed before they can be put into service. These materials may be cardboard, foam, or plain packing paper. In any case, be sure to remove the packing before using your appliances.

THE REMAINDER

The remainder of your cleaning chores should not be any different than those required for an existing home. Cleaning a home that has just been built is not much different from routine cleaning. There are only a few things—like the black letters on the vinyl flooring and the labels on plumbing fixtures—that require special consideration.

MOVING IN

Moving into your new home is very exciting. As wonderful as this time is, it can quickly turn into disappointment. A piece of furniture gouges a new wall. Sliding your new refrigerator into place cuts through your new kitchen vinyl flooring. The principles behind moving furniture into your home are simple, but the actual procedure can get complicated.

I'm not a professional mover or moving contractor. While I would never consider giving you expert advice on exactly how to get your belongings safely into your home, I'm sure you can learn from some of my mistakes and experiences.

FLOORS

I've seen a lot of new, vinyl floors ripped, torn, and cut by appliances. Anytime an appliance is pulled out or pushed in, the flooring needs to be protected. Cardboard can be an effective protection for the new flooring.

DOORWAYS

Doorways have a high potential for damage when moving furniture into a home. The trim casing often gets damaged when pieces of furniture are jammed, slammed, and bumped into it. Before bringing your belongings in through a door, protect the casing by wrapping it with cardboard—available from appliance and furniture cartons or similar packaging. The cardboard will protect the door trim from most accidental bumps and scrapes and can be replaced as often as required.

CARPET

New carpet can be damaged by the wheels on moving equipment. Before rolling heavy objects over your new carpeting, take some precautionary steps. Laying down a path of cardboard will be sufficient for most items. Extremely heavy items should be rolled over sheets of plywood.

The plywood distributes the weight and prevents ruts from being crushed into the carpeting.

CEILINGS

Ceilings are probably the last place you would expect to have damage when moving into your home. Based on the number of new ceilings that I have seen get hit, banged, bumped and punched, this is a universal feeling. When bed frames and other large items are being taken into rooms, ceilings often become targets. Damage to ceilings can be avoided by paying careful attention to clearances.

LIGHT FIXTURES

Light fixtures can be broken when furniture is moved in. This is especially true of wall-hung fixtures. These are easily broken when moving bedding or other large pieces of furniture through the hall. Avoid these problems by looking ahead and paying strict attention to what you are doing.

SIT BACK AND RELAX

Once you are completely moved into your new home, sit back and relax. This is your time to relish the rewards of your time and effort. You can count up how much money you saved, admire the work you did yourself, and envision your next project. Maybe you will upgrade your bathroom from painted walls to wallpaper. Perhaps you will add skylights in your living room or an island cabinet in your kitchen.

The fact is, very few people ever build a house to suit their exact needs and desires on their first attempt. I've built several houses for my personal use, and I've never built one where I didn't wish something were different. There is a good chance you will have little odds and ends to tend to during your first year in a new home. This is to be expected.

Well, we've reached the end of the line. Your textbook house is built. You're all moved in and ready to reap the rewards of all your efforts. There is no doubt that you will feel fantastic when your *real* dream home is complete and occupied. With what you've learned from this book, you should be well prepared to seek the reality of your dream home. I wish you the best of luck.

Appendix

The contracts, clauses, and forms presented here are not to be used as ready-made documents. They are included as samples of the kind of documents that you might need. These samples are not complete, nor do they represent all of the documents you may need to execute as a developer, general contractor, homeowner, or contractor in the business of construction.

Before the creation or use of any legal instrument, you should consult legal counsel.

SAMPLE CONSTRUCTION CONTRACT

This agreement, made this _____ th day of _____ , 19--, shall set forth the whole agreement, in its entirety, between Contractor and Customer.

Contractor: _____ referred to herein as Contractor.

Customer: _____ , referred to herein as Customer.

Job name: _____

Job location: _____

The Customer and Contractor agree to the following:

SCOPE OF WORK Contractor shall perform all work as described below and provide all material to complete the work described below:

All work is to be completed by Contractor in accordance with the attached plans and specifications. All material is to be supplied by Contractor in accordance with attached plans and specifications. Said attached plans and specifications have been acknowledged and signed by Contractor and Customer.

A brief outline of the work is as follows, and all work referenced in the attached plans and specifications will be completed to the Customer's reasonable satisfaction. The following is only a basic outline of the overall work to be performed:

_____

_____

_____

_____

_____

_____

_____

_____

Page 1 of 3 initials _____

COMMENCEMENT AND COMPLETION SCHEDULE The work described above shall be started within three (3) days of verbal notice from Customer; the projected start date is _____. The Contractor shall complete the above work in a professional and expedient manner, by no later than twenty (20) days from the start date. Time is of the essence regarding this contract. No extension of time will be valid, without the Customer's written consent. If Contractor does not complete the work in the time allowed, and if the lack of completion is not caused by the Customer, the Contractor will be charged one hundred dollars ($100.00) per day for every day work is not finished beyond the completion date. This charge will be deducted from any payments due to the Contractor for work performed.

CONTRACT SUM The Customer shall pay the Contractor for the performance of completed work, subject to additions and deductions, as authorized by this agreement or attached addendum. The contract sum is _____ ($ _____).

PROGRESS PAYMENTS The Customer shall pay the Contractor installments as detailed below, once an acceptable insurance certificate has been filed by the Contractor, with the Customer:

Customer will pay Contractor a deposit of _____ ($_____) when work is started.

Customer will pay _____

($ _____) when all rough-in work is complete.

Customer will pay _____

($ _____) when work is _____ percent complete.

Customer will pay _____

($ _____) when all work is complete and accepted.

All payments are subject to a site inspection and approval of work by the Customer. Before final payment, the Contractor, if required, shall submit satisfactory evidence to the Customer that all expenses related to this work have been paid and no lien risk exists on the subject property.

WORKING CONDITIONS Working hours will be 8:00 A.M. to 4:30 P.M., Monday through Friday. Contractor is required to clean work debris from the job site on a daily basis and to leave the site in a clean and neat condition. Contractor shall be responsible for removal and disposal of all debris related to their job description.

CONTRACT ASSIGNMENT Contractor shall not assign this contract or further subcontract the whole of this subcontract without the written consent of the Customer.

LAWS, PERMITS, FEES, AND NOTICES Contractor is responsible for complying with all required laws, and obtaining permits and fees and posting notices required to perform the work stated herein.

WORK OF OTHERS Contractor shall be responsible for any damage caused to existing conditions. This shall include work performed on the project by other contractors. If the Contractor damages existing conditions or work performed by other contractors, said Contractor shall be responsible for the repair of said damages. These repairs may be made by the contractor responsible for the damages or another contractor, at the sole discretion of Customer.

The damaging contractor shall have the opportunity to quote a price for the repairs. The Customer is under no obligation to engage the damaging contractor to make the repairs. If a different contractor repairs the damage, the contractor causing the damage may be back-charged for the cost of the repairs. These charges may be deducted from any moneys owed to the damaging contractor.

If no money is owed to the damaging contractor, said contractor shall pay the invoiced amount within seven business days. If prompt payment is not made, the Customer may exercise all legal means to collect the requested moneys. The damaging contractor shall have no rights to lien the Customer's property for money retained to cover the repair of damages caused by the contractor. The Customer may have the repairs made to his or her satisfaction.

WARRANTY Contractor warrants to the Customer all work and materials for one year from the final day of work performed.

INDEMNIFICATION To the fullest extent allowed by law, the Contractor shall indemnify and hold harmless the Customer and all of their agents and employees from and against all claims, damages, losses and expenses.

This Agreement entered into on _____ , 19-- shall constitute the whole agreement between Customer and Contractor.

_____   _____

Customer   Date   Contractor   Date

_____

Customer   Date

SAMPLE COMPLETION SCHEDULE CLAUSE

COMMENCEMENT AND COMPLETION SCHEDULE The work described above shall be started within three (3) days of verbal notice from the customer; the projected start date is _____ . The subcontractor shall complete the above work in a professional and expedient manner by no later than twenty (20) days from the start date. Time is of the essence in this subcontract. No extension of time will be valid without the general contractor's written consent. If subcontractor does not complete the work in the time allowed and if the lack of completion is not caused by the general contractor, the subcontractor will be charged one hundred dollars ($100.00) for every day work is not finished after the completion date. This charge will be deducted from any payments due to the subcontractor for work performed.

SAMPLE DAMAGE CLAUSE FOR CONTRACT

SUBCONTRACTOR LIABILITY FOR DAMAGES Subcontractor shall be responsible for any damage caused to existing conditions. This shall include new work performed on the project by other contractors. If the subcontractor damages existing conditions or work performed by other contractors, said subcontractor shall be responsible for the repair of said damages. These repairs may be made by the subcontractor responsible for the damages or another contractor, at the discretion of the general contractor.

If a different contractor repairs the damage, the subcontractor causing the damage may be back-charged for the cost of the repairs. These charges may be deducted from any moneys owed to the damaging subcontractor, by the general contractor. The choice for a contractor to repair the damages shall be at the sole discretion of the general contractor.

If no money is owed to the damaging subcontractor, said contractor shall pay the invoiced amount, from the general contractor, within seven business days. If prompt payment is not made, the general contractor may exercise all legal means to collect the requested moneys.

The damaging subcontractor shall have no rights to lien the property where work is done for money retained to cover the repair of damages caused by the subcontractor. The general contractor may have the repairs made to his or her satisfaction.

The damaging subcontractor shall have the opportunity to quote a price for the repairs. The general contractor is under no obligation to engage the damaging subcontractor to make the repairs.

SAMPLE INDEPENDENT CONTRACTOR AGREEMENT

I understand that as an Independent Contractor, I am solely responsible for my health, actions, taxes, insurance, transportation, and any other responsibilities that may be involved with the work I will be doing as an Independent Contractor.

I will not hold anyone else responsible for any claims or liabilities that may arise from this work or from any cause related to this work. I waive any rights I have or may have to hold anyone liable for any reason as a result of this work.

_____

Independent Contractor

_____

Date

_____

Witness

_____

Date

SAMPLE SUBCONTRACTOR SCHEDULE

Type of Service	Vendor Name	Phone Number	Date Scheduled
Site Work			
Footings			
Concrete			
Foundation			
Waterproofing			
Masonry			
Framing			
Roofing			
Siding			
Exterior Trim			
Gutters			
Pest Control			
Plumbing/R-I			
HVAC/R-I			
Electrical/R-I			
Insulation			
Drywall			
Painter			
Wallpaper			
Tile			
Cabinets			
Countertops			
Interior Trim			
Floor Covering			
Plumbing/Final			
HVAC/Final			
Electrical/Final			
Cleaning			
Paving			
Landscaping			
NOTES/CHANGES			

SAMPLE ADDENDUM TO CONTRACT

This addendum is an integral part of the contract dated _____ , between the
    Contractor,_____,
    and the Customer(s), _____,
    for the work being done on real estate commonly known as _____ . The
    undersigned parties hereby agree to the following:

_____

_____

_____

_____

_____

_____

_____

_____

_____

_____

_____

The above constitutes the only addition to the above-mentioned contract. No verbal agreements or
    other changes shall be valid unless made in writing and signed by all parties.

_____   _____

Contractor   Date   Customer   Date

                                        _____

                                        Customer   Date

SAMPLE CHANGE ORDER

This change order is an integral part of the contract dated _____, between the
customer, _____,
and the contractor, _____ , for the work to be performed.
The job location is _____.
These changes shall now become a part of the original contract and may not be altered again without
written authorization from all parties.

Changes to be as follows:

_____

_____

_____

_____

_____

_____

_____

_____

_____

_____

_____

These changes will increase/decrease the original contract amount. Payment for these changes will
be made as follows: _____. The amount of change in
the contract price will be _____
($ _____). The new total contract price shall be _____
($ _____).

The undersigned parties hereby agree that these are the only changes to be made to the original contract.
No verbal agreements will be valid. No further alterations will be allowed without additional
written authorization, signed by all parties. This change order constitutes the entire agreement
between the parties to alter the original contract.

_____   _____
Customer   Date   Contractor   Date

_____
Customer   Date

SAMPLE REQUEST FOR SUBSTITUTIONS

_____   _____
Customer name   Job location

_____   _____
Customer address   Plans & specifications dated

_____   _____
Customer city/state/ZIP   Bid requested from

_____   _____
Customer phone number   Type of work

The following items are being substituted for the items specified in the attached plans and specifications:

_____

_____

_____

_____

_____

_____

_____

_____

_____

_____

_____

_____

_____

_____

Please indicate your acceptance of these substitutions by signing below.

_____   _____
Contractor   Date   Customer   Date

                                       _____
                                       Customer   Date

SAMPLE SHORT FORM LIEN WAIVER

Customer name _____   Customer address _____

Customer city/state/ZIP _____   Customer phone number _____

Job location _____   Date _____

Type of work: _____

Contractor: _____

Contractor address: _____

Subcontractor: _____

Subcontractor address: _____

Description of work completed to date: _____

_____

_____

_____

_____

_____

Payments received to date: _____

Payment received on this date: _____

Total amount paid, including this payment:_____

The contractor/subcontractor signing below acknowledges receipt of all payments stated above. These payments are in compliance with the written contract between the parties above. The contractor/subcontractor signing below hereby states payment for all work done to this date has been paid in full.

The contractor/subcontractor signing below releases and relinquishes any and all rights available to place a mechanic or materialman lien against the subject property for the above described work. All parties agree that all work performed to date has been paid for in full and in compliance with their written contract.

The undersigned contractor/subcontractor releases the general contractor/customer from any liability for non-payment of material or services extended through this date. The undersigned contractor / subcontractor has read this entire agreement and understands the agreement.

_____   _____

Contractor/Subcontractor   Date

SUBCONTRACT AGREEMENT

This agreement, made this _____ th day of _____ , 19--, shall set forth the whole agreement, in its entirety, between Contractor and Subcontractor.

Contractor: _____, referred to herein as Contractor.

Job location: _____

Subcontractor: _____, referred to herein as Subcontractor.

The Contractor and Subcontractor agree to the following:

SCOPE OF WORK Subcontractor shall perform all work as described below and provide all material to complete the work described below:

Subcontractor shall supply all labor and material to complete the work according to the attached plans and specifications. These attached plans and specifications have been initialed and signed by all parties. The work shall include, but is not limited to, the following:

_____

_____

_____

_____

_____

_____

_____

_____

_____

COMMENCEMENT AND COMPLETION SCHEDULE The work described above shall be started within three (3) days of verbal notice from Contractor; the projected start date is _____ . The Subcontractor shall complete the above work in a professional and expedient manner by no later than twenty (20) days from the start date. Time is of the essence in this contract. No extension of time will be valid without the Contractor's written consent. If Subcontractor does not complete the work in the time allowed, and if the lack of completion is not caused by the Contractor, the Subcontractor will be charged fifty dollars ($50.00) per day for every day work extends beyond the completion date. This charge will be deducted from any payments due to the Subcontractor for work performed.

CONTRACT SUM The Contractor shall pay the Subcontractor for the performance of completed work subject to additions and deductions as authorized by this agreement or attached addendum. The Contract Sum is _____ ($ _____).

PROGRESS PAYMENTS The Contractor shall pay the Subcontractor installments as detailed below, once an acceptable insurance certificate has been filed by the Subcontractor with the Contractor: Contractor shall pay the Subcontractor as described:

_____

_____

_____

_____

_____

All payments are subject to a site inspection and approval of work by the Contractor. Before final payment, the Subcontractor shall submit satisfactory evidence to the Contractor that no lien risk exists on the subject property.

WORKING CONDITIONS Working hours will be 8:00 A.M. to 4:30 P.M., Monday through Friday. Subcontractor is required to clean work debris from the job site on a daily basis and leave the site in a clean and neat condition. Subcontractor shall be responsible for removal and disposal of all debris related to his or her job description.

CONTRACT ASSIGNMENT Subcontractor shall not assign this contract or further subcontract the whole of this subcontract, without the written consent of the Contractor.

LAWS, PERMITS, FEES, AND NOTICES Subcontractor shall be responsible for complying with all required laws, and obtaining permits and fees, and posting notices, required to perform the work stated herein.

WORK OF OTHERS Subcontractor shall be responsible for any damage caused to existing conditions or other contractor's work. This damage will be repaired, and the Subcontractor charged for the expense and supervision of this work. The Subcontractor shall have the opportunity to quote a price for said repairs, but the Contractor is under no obligation to engage the Subcontractor to make said repairs. If a different subcontractor repairs the damage, the Subcontractor may be back-charged for the cost of the repairs. Any repair costs will be deducted from any payments due to the Subcontractor. If no payments are due the Subcontractor, the Subcontractor shall pay the invoiced amount within ten (10) days.

WARRANTY Subcontractor warrants to the Contractor all work and materials for one year from the final day of work performed.

INDEMNIFICATION To the fullest extent allowed by law, the Subcontractor shall indemnify and hold harmless the Owner, the Contractor, and all of their agents and employees from and against all claims, damages, losses and expenses.

This agreement, entered into on _____ , 19--, shall constitute the whole agreement between Contractor and Subcontractor.

Contractor	Date	Subcontractor	Date

Index

More Books
Packed With Great Ideas!

Build Your Own Kitchen Cabinets—Easy-to-follow, step-by-step instuctions to plan, construct and install custom kitchen cabinets, accessories and more. Superbly illustrated, this one-of-a-kind book makes kitchen cabinetmaking accessible to woodworkers of all skill levels. *#70376/$22.99/136 pages/170 b&w illus., 8 page color insert/paperback*

Build You Own Entertainment Centers—This exceptional project book offers numerous designs and styles for entertainment centers that fit every tpe of home—from contemporary to traditional. *#70354/$22.99/128 pages/229 b&w illus./paperback*

Home Color Harmony—This clear, accessible guide takes the guesswork out of choosing great color schemes for the home. Brilliant, full-color photographs of more than 50 rooms in an array of distinctive colors, moods and atmospheres offer plenty of inspiration for do-it-yourself decorators. *#70408/$18.99/128 pages/250 color illus./paperback*

The 30-Minute Decorator—More than 60 easy-to-accomplish decorating ideas for today's busy do-it-yourselfers. Each page of this beautifully illustrated book features unique and inspiration decorative tips for dressing up everything in your home from flowerpots and candles to curtains and picture frames. *#70407/$18.99/128 pages/250 color illus./paperback*

Mortgage Loans: What's Right for You?, Fourth Edition—Don't make a big-money mistake on the wrong mortgage. Find the facts on which mortgage is best suited to your financial situation. Plus information on caps, points, margins and more. *#70336/$14.99/144 pages/paperback*

Creative Paint Finishes for the Home—Dozens of full-color, step-by-step designs for decorating floors, walls and furniture with distinctive marbling, sponging, stencilling, gilding and woodgraining techniques. Includes how to use the tools, develop the ideas and master each technique. *#30426/$27.99/144 pages/212 color illus./hardcover*

Make Your House Do the Housework, Revised Edition—More than 150,000 copies sold! Now you can teach your house how to keep itself in order. Nationally acclaimed cleaning expert Don Aslett offers page after page of practical, environmentally friendly new ideas and methods for minimizing home cleaning and maintenance. *#70293/$14.99/208 pages/215 b&w illus./paperback*

Creative Bedroom Decorating—Add charm, color and character to any bedroom—from contemporary to country to whimsical—with this vast array of inexpensive and easy-to-do decorating ideas. *#70305/$16.99/128 pages/350 color illus./paperback*

The Single Person's Guide to Buying a Home: Why to Do It & How to Do It—This buying guide offers you worksheets and checklists that show you what to look for in buying a home on your own. *#70200/$14.95/144 pages/paperback*

Creative Kitchen Decorating—Beautify your kitchen—or create an all-new one—with this recipe book of fabulous design and decorating ideas. Vivid color photographs and clear explanations cover everything from lighting and layout to storage and work surfaces, plus much more! *#70322/$16.99/128 pages/250+ color illus.*

Creative Wall Decorating—Turn your walls—and your rooms—into masterpieces with this idea-filled book. You'll find exciting examples of innovative techniques including stenciling, sponge painting, rubber stamping and more. Plus, brilliant color photos and easy-to-follow instructions make your decorating as easy as 1-2-3. *#70317/$16.99/128 pages/250+ color illus.*

Creative Color Schemes for Your Home—Breathe fresh life into every room of your home with hundreds of creative color treatments. Photographs of successful interiors show you how to create just the right effect. *#70304/$16.99/128 pages/250 color illus./paperback*

The Complete Guide to Designing Your Own Home—Soon-to-be homeowners—create a place that's uniquely yours. Learn about every step in the home design process—from site selection to financing and decorating. *#70267/$17.99/144 pages/33 b&w illus./paperback*

The Art of the Stonemason—Let a fifth generation stonemason show you how to choose stone; build a wall on sloping ground; create circular walls, windowsills, fireplaces, stairs, arches and hunchbacked bridges. Materials needed and techniques to use are covered in detail. *#70005/$17.99/176 pages/133 illus./paperback*

The Complete Guide to Contracting Your Home, 3rd Edition—75,000 copies sold! Learn how your home will be built and where you can save money! This book covers it all, from financing and site selection to working with "subs" and building inspectors. You'll get all the information you need whether you watch from a distance or roll up your sleeves and manage the project! *#70378/$18.99/320 pages/paperback*

It's Here . . . Somewhere—More than 70,000 copies sold! Here is the solution to the perennial challenge of household clutter. Authors Fulton and Hatch take you step-by-step through every room, closet, drawer and corner, advising you on what to keep, where to keep it and how to get your home back into order. *#10214/$10.99/192 pages/50 b&w illus./paperback*

The Complete Guide to Log and Cedar Homes—Scores of illustrations lead you through all aspects of purchasing or building your log or cedar home—including all phases of construction. *#70190/$17.99/168 pages/18 illus., 56 photos/paperback*

Building and Restoring the Hewn Log House—If you yearn for the rustic life, this practical guide will help you build or restore the traditional log cabin. *#70228/$18.99/176 pages/220 b&w, 45 color illus./paperback*